THE WORLD SERIES
A Complete Pictorial History

THE WORLD SERIES
A Complete Pictorial History

By John Devaney and Burt Goldblatt
with Barbara Devaney

RAND McNALLY & COMPANY
Chicago • New York • San Francisco

Acknowledgments

The authors received a great deal of help from dozens of people in collecting the photographs, data, and information for this book. We would particularly like to thank Pete Sansone and Marty Stern of United Press International; Joe Reichler of the office of Baseball Commissioner Bowie Kuhn; Jack Redding at the Baseball Hall of Fame in Cooperstown, New York; Robert Fishel, Marty Appel, and Ann Mileo of the New York Yankee staff; *The Sporting News;* Burt Goldblatt's daughters Leslie and Heather; and the more than one hundred baseball players, past and present, who were good enough to take the time to share their memories with us.

Copyright © 1981, 1976, 1972 by **Rand McNally & Company**
All rights reserved
Printed in the United States of America
by Rand McNally & Company

Library of Congress Catalog Card Number: 80-54648
  Devaney, Barbara, & John Devaney
    The World Series.
  Chicago, Ill.: Rand McNally
  416 p.
  8104   801125

Designed by Burt Goldblatt and Barbara **Devaney**

For our fathers, who
loved baseball

Photo Credits

Preface

It is lodged like a pit in the memory—my first World Series.

I am swinging a heavy schoolbag home from St. Jerome's school on a windy, rain-swept day in the early fall of 1936. Stopping some 50 yards short of the corner of Willis Avenue and East 138th Street in the Bronx, I see three or four men listening to a radio perched on a chair outside what I remember was a shoe store. The radio announcer is describing a game at the Polo Grounds, only an hour's walk from where I am standing but a place I have never seen. He is talking in excited tones about a man named Carl Hubbell, who is pitching gallantly, the announcer tells us, in the rain and the mud at the Polo Grounds. I drop my schoolbag between my legs. I stand there for an hour or more in the gusty, dripping autumn wetness, sharing the discomfort of Hubbell, who has become—within the hour—a hero to me. Hubbell and the Giants beat the Yankees that day, 6-1—I have never forgotten the score—and after the game I walk with a 10-year-old's swagger along Willis Avenue, glowing inside, proud to be a Carl Hubbell fan and a Giant fan.

That afternoon's events had fated me to root for a Giant team that would cause me heart-sinking anguish during the next few decades, this team that usually lost more often than it won. But this would also be a team that would, on another autumn day in 1951, reward me for my anguish with one of the most exalted moments of my life.

When Burt Goldblatt asked me to work with him on this book, I recalled Hubbell and that day in 1936. "Now," I thought, "I will get the chance to talk to Hubbell and ask him what it was like for him that afternoon on the slippery mound at the Polo Grounds." Several months later I did interview Hubbell, and I told him how I had marveled at his performance. "Ah, well," he said in a shy and uncertain way, "you know, ah, it was as tough for their pitcher as it was for me."

True enough, of course, except that Hubbell had triumphed in the rain and mud while the Yankee pitcher had lost. I came away from the interview wishing I had heard more stirring words from Hubbell, words that perhaps he could not express. But later I realized I now knew something of the man, while before Carl Hubbell had been to me only a lanky, grim-faced, left-handed pitcher. As you read the World Series memories of the players I have talked to, I hope that you also will see at least a little bit of the man.

Most photographs for this book were chosen by Burt Goldblatt from hundreds of old pictures in private collections and newspaper files and picked frame by frame out of thousands of feet of motion picture film. The pictures show the way it was in 1903 and in 1980 and in all the years in between when it was World Series time—a time for America to slow down and turn to an electric scoreboard outside a newspaper office, to cock an ear toward a radio, to peer at a television set, and find the answer to a question asked a million or more times each October: "Who's winning?"

The World Series is a time for us to measure our heroes against the heroes of another league. "Without heroes," Bernard Malamud has written in *The Natural,* "we are all plain people and don't know how far we can go." I think that because of Carl Hubbell and people like him I am not as plain as I might have been. It changed me a little, standing on East 138th Street on that rainy day and imagining I was on the mound at the Polo Grounds.

J. D.
New York City

The World Series
Still No. 1

There are those who will tell you that the first World Series took place in 1868. There are others who will insist that the New York Mets were the first Series losers. There is something to be said for both arguments.

In 1868 there was so much interest in baseball in Detroit that a tournament was arranged. Invited were semiprofessional teams from Detroit, Chicago, Pittsburgh, Buffalo, Albany, Boston, New York, Brooklyn, Philadelphia, Cleveland, Montreal, Quebec, and Hamilton. The tournament winner—and first "world champion"—was the Hamilton team from Canada. Fortunately for United States national pride, no one was as yet calling baseball the national pastime.

Fourteen years went by without another series. By 1882 two professional leagues were operating, the National League and the American Association. The 1882 winners in each league, Chicago (National) and Cincinnati (American), met in a series that ended after two games, each team winning one before bickering canceled the rest of the games. Two years later Providence (National) played the New York Metropolitans (American), and Providence beat the original Mets three straight in a best-of-five series.

That series continued until 1890, when the American Association folded. In 1894 William Chase Temple, a Pittsburgh baseball enthusiast, donated the Temple Cup to the winner of a series between the first-place and second-place teams in the National League. There were four Temple Cup series, from 1894 to 1897. Interest in the games was never very high, although it was billed as a "world series"; the two teams had played each other often enough during the regular season to dispel any doubts about the superiority of one over the other.

In 1901 the American League began play as an eight-team league. The older National League, which reorganized in 1900 as an eight-team league, scorned the new league as "outlaw" and "minor." After three years of wrangling, peace was restored. And in the summer of 1903, with Pittsburgh well ahead in the National and Boston ahead in the American, the owners of the two teams challenged each other to what was first termed a "postseason series" in the newspapers and soon elevated in importance to a "World Series." The name distinguished this series for the world's baseball championship from other postseason series of the time: the city series between the St. Louis Browns and the St. Louis Cardinals, and several series between the champion teams of minor leagues.

The Pittsburgh and Boston owners agreed on a best-of-nine Series, splitting the box office receipts between them. The Pittsburgh players, although the losers, received more money than the winning Boston players because Pittsburgh owner Barney Dreyfuss gave his players his share; each of them took home $1,316. The winning Boston players got $1,182 each. The eight-game Series attracted around 100,000 spectators, who paid 50¢ for their tickets, a goodly sum above the 25¢ usually charged for general admission to games.

The next year, 1904, the New York Giants were winning in the National League while the New York Highlanders (now the Yankees) held a slight lead in the American. Giant manager John McGraw said he would not meet the winner of the American League pennant because the league was "minor." Actually he and Giant owner John T. Brush did not want to build up the stature of the Highlanders, their New York rivals, by meeting them in a series that could be embarrassing to the lordly Giants, then New York's favorites. McGraw's comment rattled National League owners, fearful of more costly legal battling. By 1905 an agreement had been reached: After each season there would be a postseason series matching the two pennant winners, to be played under the supervision of the three-man National Commission, which then governed baseball. The money was to be divided among the players, the owners of the two teams, and the National Commission.

Most of the games during the next decade drew crowds that packed the small ball parks of the

The Temple Cup. On the base is a list of the four winning teams. On the neck, in the uniform of his time, is an old-timey ballplayer.

9

Some of the participants in the 1884 Series between Providence and the New York Metropolitans of the American Association. Top to bottom (l.): "Truthful" Jim Mutrie, manager of the Mets, and Dave Orr, Met first baseman. Top to bottom (r.): Charley (Old Hoss) Radbourn, Providence pitcher who won all three games three days in a row, and Providence rightfielder Paul Radford. In the middle is Met pitcher Tim Keefe. Bottom (l. to r.): Providence first baseman Joe Start and Met rightfielder identified only as Brady. Opposite page: A scorecard for the first Temple Cup Series in 1894. One reason so many players wore moustaches: They thought hair above the lip improved their vision.

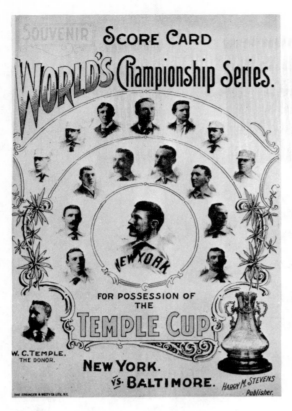

time. A quarter-million people watched the 1912 Series, paying almost a half-million dollars. But with the Series' growing popularity—throngs massed outside newspaper offices across the country to watch telegraphed play-by-play accounts—there were problems. Scalpers sold tickets at inflated prices and there were continual rumors that ball-club owners sold the tickets to the scalpers. There was heavy betting on the games, even by the players, and from 1905 there were published rumors of players being bribed to throw games.

By World War I baseball officials as highly placed as Garry Herrmann, a member of the National Commission, were asking for an end to the World Series. Writers in *The Sporting News* worried that the tail was wagging the dog: Would the World Series become so big that it would destroy interest in the pennant races, in the also-ran teams, and in the minor leagues? In 1916 John McGraw charged that some of his players had not tried hard enough in a pennant series with the Dodgers, permitting Brooklyn to walk into the rich World Series. The teams finishing in second, third, and fourth places began to demand a part of the World Series receipts. When they did get a share, the World Series players got less, and that precipitated a strike before the start of one Series game in 1918. When a Chicago grand jury in 1920 dis-

closed that White Sox players had been bribed by gamblers to lose the 1919 Series, there were confident predictions in the newspapers that fan disgust would wither interest in the Series.

The Series not only survived that scandal, it prospered in the Twenties and even in the gray days of the depression in the Thirties. It drew crowds despite the travel restrictions of World War II and it remained popular while some of the teams that had played in it became so unwanted that they had to move to other cities (the St. Louis Browns, the Boston-Milwaukee Braves, *et al.*). Now closing in on its 80th birthday—the 1980 Series was the 77th played between the two leagues—the Series is the grandfather of a family of post-season sports events—the Rose Bowl, the Super Bowl, the Stanley Cup playoffs, the National Basketball Association and National Collegiate Athletic Association basketball playoffs. And while more people watch pro football's Super Bowl than any single World Series game, the seventh game of a World Series seemingly can cause Americans to drop whatever else they are doing to find out "Who's winning?"

What follows on the succeeding pages, in pictures and in the words of the men who have played in them, are all the World Series since 1903.

11

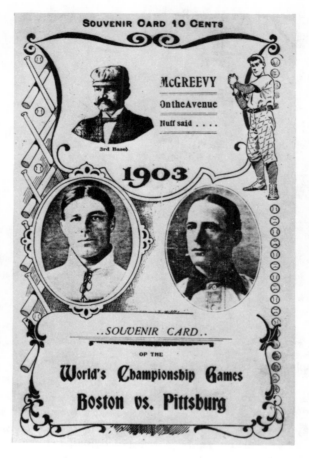

SOUVENIR CARD 10 CENTS

McGREEVY

On the Avenue

Nuff said . . . .

3rd Base

1903

..SOUVENIR CARD..

OF THE

World's Championship Games

Boston vs. Pittsburg

Deacon Phillippe

Freddie Parent

BOSTON RED SOX
PITTSBURGH PIRATES 1903

On the 13th Day, a Winner

The first modern World Series was arranged by the owners of the Boston and Pittsburgh teams during the summer when both clubs led by wide margins in the pennant races. The owners agreed on a best-of-nine Series. Because of traveling days and postponements, the Series lingered for 13 days. At the Vendome Hotel in Boston, the Series headquarters, as much as $10,000 was bet in the lobby during one morning. Pittsburgh won three of the first four games, but Boston won the next four to win the Series, five games to three. Pittsburgh's Deacon Phillippe pitched five complete games, Boston's Bill Dinneen four, and Cy Young, also for Boston, three. The Boston rooters, who paraded around the field behind a brass band, acclaimed Dinneen the Series hero after he won three games, two of them by shutouts, including the eighth and decisive game.

The total attendance for the eight games, a little more than 100,000, was huge for the tiny ball parks in Boston and Pittsburgh, neither of which held 20,000. For some games crowds sat on the outfield grass. In Pittsburgh fans climbed over the outfield fence to get into the park.

Jimmy Collins:
". . . a bit of prize money . . ."

Jimmy Collins, the Boston player-manager, was quoted in the October 17, 1903, issue of *Sporting Life* as saying: *I should not be surprised to see post-season games each fall as long as there are two big leagues. There is no reason, when the games are played out on their merits, as they were in this case, why they should not be successful. They give the public a high article of base ball and enable the championship teams to pick up a bit of prize money for the cold winter.*

Boston's shortstop, Freddie Parent, was the only player on either side to survive to the 1970s. Speaking from a nursing home in Sanford, Maine, he said: *My cut of the World Series [$1,182] wasn't bad when you consider what it bought in those days. Yes, I outhit [Honus] Wagner [the Pirate shortstop and Hall-of-Famer]. Wagner wasn't in very good shape. And I outfielded him, too. . . . But it's hard for me to remember now. You came to me too late to talk about those days, boy.*

Men and boys mill outside Huntington Avenue Grounds before the third game in Boston. Also shown are a souvenir card of the first World Series and portraits of two of the '03 heroes: Pittsburgh's Deacon Phillippe and Boston's Freddie Parent.

13

Right: Fans watch the fourth Series game at Pittsburgh's ball park on October 6. These extra seats were erected on the field in front of the grandstand. Bleachers (r.) are jammed. Note the scarcity of women, one reason being the earthiness of grandstand language. Below: Crowd spills from beyond ropes onto the field at the end of a game in Boston. Flyballs hit over the ropes into the crowd were usually ruled doubles.

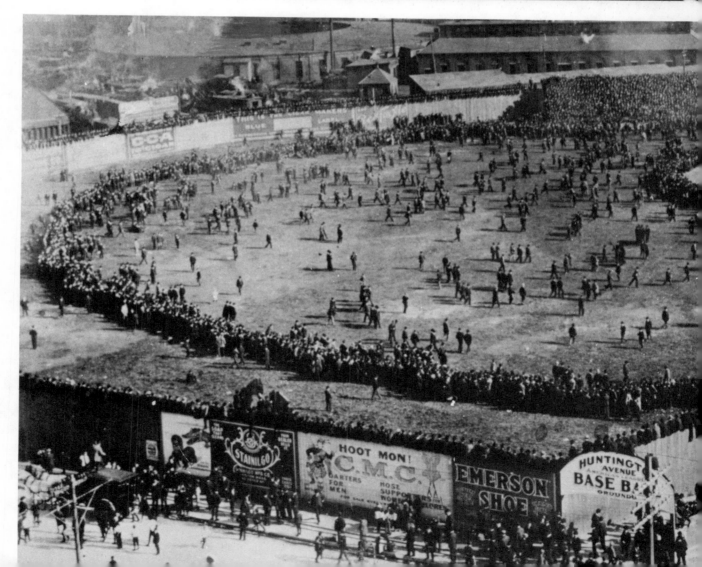

FIRST GAME (Oct. 1, at Boston)

PITTSBURGH................401 100 100   7 12 2
BOSTON....................000 000 201   3 6 4
Phillippe
Young

SECOND GAME (Oct. 2, at Boston)

PITTSBURGH................000 000 000   0 3 2
BOSTON....................200 001 00x   3 9 0
Leever, Veil (2d)
Dinneen

THIRD GAME (Oct. 3, at Boston)

PITTSBURGH................012 000 010   4 7 0
BOSTON....................000 100 010   2 4 2
Phillippe
Hughes, Young (3d)

FOURTH GAME (Oct. 6, at Pittsburgh)

BOSTON....................000 010 003   4 9 1
PITTSBURGH................100 010 30x   5 12 1
Dinneen
Phillippe

FIFTH GAME (Oct. 7, at Pittsburgh)

BOSTON....................000 006 410 11 14 2
PITTSBURGH................000 000 020   2 6 4
Young
Kennedy, Thompson (8th)

SIXTH GAME (Oct. 8, at Pittsburgh)

BOSTON....................003 020 100   6 10 1
PITTSBURGH................000 000 300   3 10 3
Dinneen
Leever

SEVENTH GAME (Oct. 10, at Pittsburgh)

BOSTON....................200 202 010   7 11 4
PITTSBURGH................000 101 001   3 10 3
Young
Phillippe

EIGHTH GAME (Oct. 13, at Boston)

PITTSBURGH................000 000 000   0 4 3
BOSTON....................000 201 00x   3 8 0
Phillippe
Dinneen

15

Fans help each other to scale the fence into the Boston park on October 3 for the third Series game. Right: The Vendome Hotel, the Series headquarters in Boston; it burned down in 1972. Opposite page, top: The Pirates in their dugout, guarded by a cop. Derbies were definitely in. Bottom: The Red Sox in their dugout, Cy Young standing and being admired by the knickered boy. Note the rakish caps on the players and the ankle-high shoes.

NEW YORK BASE BALL CLUB

NATIONAL LEAGUE

JOHN J. McGRAW, M'G'R.

CHAMPIONS 1905

McGINNITY, P.   AMES, P.   ELLIOT, P.   G. WILTSE, P.   MATTHEWSON, P.

L. TAYLOR, P.   DUNN, SUB.

BOWERMAN, C.   WARNER, C.

McGANN, 1ST B.   GILBERT, 2ND B.   DAHLEN, S.S.   DEVLIN, 3RD B.

MERTES, L.F.   BRESNEHAN, C & O.F.   DONLIN, C.F.   MARSHALL, C.   BROWNE, R.F.

Sporting Life
Phila.

NEW YORK GIANTS
PHILADELPHIA ATHLETICS
1905

Blank...Blank...Blank... Blank...Blank

There had been no Series in 1904. The National League champion Giants refused to play a "minor league" American League team for a number of reasons, one being a feud between American League president Ban Johnson and Giant manager John McGraw. But in 1905 Giant president John T. Brush drew up rules for World Series play and the division of the receipts among the players, owners, and the National Commission. These rules were approved by the National Commission, which supervised the games, assigning umpires and otherwise giving the Series an official stamp that the casually arranged '03 Series did not have. The commission also shortened the Series to a best-of-seven affair.

In this "shutout Series"—in which each of the five games was won by a shutout—the Giants' Christy Mathewson pitched what is still a record three shutouts. Baseball fans had looked forward to a duel between Matty, a 31-game winner, and Rube Waddell, who had won 24 games for Connie Mack's Philadelphia A's. But Waddell, his shoulder injured, did not play. Disappointed fans grumbled that Rube had been bribed by gamblers to feign the injury. The talk grew louder after the Giants won in five games, and newspapers published stories of a coup by gamblers. Although the charges were not substantiated, and it seemed evident that Waddell had hurt the shoulder wrestling with a teammate, there were gossips 30 years later still insisting that the first "official" Series had been fixed.

John McGraw:
Disgusted with his winners

Said John McGraw, writing of that 1905 Series in his autobiography, *My Thirty Years in Baseball:* *Of all the World's Series in which I have taken part, I think the picture of that one stands out most vividly in my memory.*

To begin with, we decided to do the thing right. We had special uniforms made for the Giants.

I will never forget the impression created in Philadelphia and the thrill that I got personally when the Giants suddenly trotted out from their dugout clad in uniforms of black flannel trimmed with white. The letters across the breast were in white.

I have heard army men say that the snappiest-looking outfit is usually made up of the best fighters. I can well understand that. The psychological effect of being togged out in snappy uniforms was immediately noticeable upon the players. The Athletics in their regular-season uniforms appeared dull alongside our champions. . . .

The only setback to that Series was the discovery of the fact that many of the Giants and Athletic players had paired off in arrangements to divide the receipts equally no matter which side won. I was disgusted at this—at their unwillingness to take a chance.

[Roger] Bresnahan, Matty and myself, however, refused to do any pairing. After getting the big share of the receipts we had the laugh on the others. Several of them, I understood afterwards, tried to run out on their agreement. . . .

A montage of the time shows the team that John McGraw later called his greatest. An opposing manager called the team "the fastest ever assembled." Note misspelling of names of Matty and Bresnahan.

19

Above: Derbied fans line Coogan's Bluff atop Polo Grounds to get a free view of the game. Right: John McGraw warms up with Matty watching (the two were almost like father and son). They are wearing the black uniforms of which Muggsy McGraw was so proud. Opposite page: The Giants' George Browne takes a pitch, the A's Ossee Schreckengost the catcher. The gap between catcher and batter was usual for the time. Opposite page, bottom: The Giants' Sam Mertes is out at first.

20

FIRST GAME (Oct. 9, at Philadelphia)

NEW YORK 000 020 001   3 10 1
PHILADELPHIA 000 000 000   0 4 0
Mathewson
Plank

SECOND GAME (Oct. 10, at New York)

PHILADELPHIA 001 000 020   3 6 2
NEW YORK 000 000 000   0 4 2
Bender
McGinnity, Ames (9th)

THIRD GAME (Oct. 12, at Philadelphia)

NEW YORK 200 050 002   9 9 1
PHILADELPHIA 000 000 000   0 4 5
Mathewson
Coakley

FOURTH GAME (Oct. 13, at New York)

PHILADELPHIA 000 000 000   0 5 2
NEW YORK 000 100 00x   1 4 1
Plank
McGinnity

FIFTH GAME (Oct. 14, at New York)

PHILADELPHIA 000 000 000   0 6 0
NEW YORK 000 010 01x   2 5 1
Bender
Mathewson

CHICAGO WHITE SOX
CHICAGO CUBS
1906

The First Trolley Series

The Cubs, with their famous Tinker-to-Evers-to-Chance double-plays, had won 116 games in a 154-game schedule, then and still a record. The weak-hitting White Sox had hit only .228 during the season, the lowest in the American League. But in a duel of fine pitching staffs, the White Sox's Big Ed Walsh, Frank Owen, Nick Altrock, and Doc White beat the Cubs' Mordecai Brown, Ed Reulbach, Orval Overall, and Jack Pfiester. Despite cold weather huge crowds came to the final games of this first crosstown Series. In the last game club-swinging cops had to push the crowd behind ropes that ringed the outfield. During that final game Cub rightfielder Frank (Wildfire) Schulte drifted back to the ropes for a long fly. As he set to catch the ball, he claimed later, a fan pushed him. The ball dropped into the crowd for a double. The Sox got three runs in the inning and won the game, 8-3, taking the Series, four games to two.

Ed Reulbach:
The wisdom of a manager

In an article several years later in *Baseball* magazine, Cub pitcher Ed Reulbach explained the upset this way: *In a 154-game season the best club is pretty certain to win, but there is no such certainty in a World's Series. . . . The Cubs in 1906 were in their prime. I think no person, however prejudiced, will claim the White Sox were their equal. . . . Much credit has been given the generalship of [Sox manager] Fielder Jones, upon this occasion, and it is doubtful if the wisdom of a manager's policy ever proved a stronger factor in the final result. . . . Miner Brown was going at a wonderful clip. It was certain that Chance [Frank Chance, the Cub manager] would pitch him in the opening contest. Fielder Jones attacked the problem somewhat in this light: 'If I pitch Walsh, who is my best pitcher, I will probably lose, for Walsh is certainly not as good as Brown. Then I will have opened the Series with a defeat and temporarily used up my best man. On the other hand, if I use another pitcher and he loses, I am no worse off and I can bring Walsh into the second (or third) contest and probably win.'*

So he chose Altrock to pitch the opening game feeling that if Altrock won [which he did] it would be a tremendous moral victory, while if he lost it would not be such a serious affair, since no one expected him to win. Jones felt that Altrock might as well lose a game by 15 to 1 as to let Walsh lose by a score of, say, 2 to 1. A defeat was a defeat. . . . It was by this adroit method of matching his weakest points against the enemies' strongest, and his own strongest against their weakness, that he hoped to make a relatively inferior pitching staff show up as effectively as possible against an admittedly stronger one. . . . That Jones was entirely successful . . . is now a matter of history.

A bunt situation in the third game, the Cubs' Jack Pfiester throwing to a White Sox batter. Blustery weather caused one *Sporting News* writer to suggest that the baseball season dragged on too long.

Warm-up time before the third game at West Side Park. Fans are jammed on the roofs beyond centerfield. The Cubs are taking hitting practice, the sweatered White Sox loosening their arms along the third-base line. Notice that the players of the time did not wear numbers. Wives of the players met their husbands after the game in carriages "to carry them from the madness," wrote one reporter. After the Series Sox manager Fielder Jones wrote in the *Saturday Evening Post:* "There are salaries of more than $6,000 per man paid under these [baseball] contracts, and that for a short season of 154 ball games is not a bad rate of compensation... From the ballplayers' standpoint [however], I am practically a slave. So is every ballplayer in the 31 [major and minor] leagues... We are 'commercial chattels' in the sense that we cannot sell our ability... in any market to which we may elect..." Sixty-odd years later Curt Flood was making much the same argument.

Cubs' Tinker (top)-to-Evers-to-Chance (r.) double-play combination. Below: The White Sox' Billy Sullivan waits for a pitch, Johnny Kling the Cub catcher. Opposite page: Kling reaches for a foul tip from the bat of Fielder Jones. And a cartoonist sums it all up: the Cubs' skin is tacked to the White Sox wall. The low-hit pitching in the second, third, and fourth games may be the best ever in three straight Series games.

FIRST GAME (Oct. 9, at West Side Park)

WHITE SOX 000 011 000   2 4 1
CUBS 000 001 000   1 4 2
Altrock
Brown

SECOND GAME (Oct. 10, at Comiskey Park)

CUBS .031 001 020   7 10 2
WHITE SOX 000 010 000   1 1 2
Reulbach
White, Owen (4th)

THIRD GAME (Oct. 11, at West Side Park)

WHITE SOX 000 003 000   3 4 1
CUBS 000 000 000   0 2 2
Walsh
Pfiester

FOURTH GAME (Oct. 12, at Comiskey Park)

CUBS .000 000 100   1 7 1
WHITE SOX 000 000 000   0 2 1
Brown
Altrock

FIFTH GAME (Oct. 13, at West Side Park)

WHITE SOX 102 401 000   8 12 6
CUBS 300 102 000   6 6 0
Walsh, White (7th)
Reulbach, Pfiester (3d), Overall (4th)

SIXTH GAME (Oct. 14, at Comiskey Park)

CUBS .100 010 001   3 7 0
WHITE SOX 340 000 01x   8 14 3
Brown, Overall (2d)
White

AT THE HOME OF THE WHITE SOX

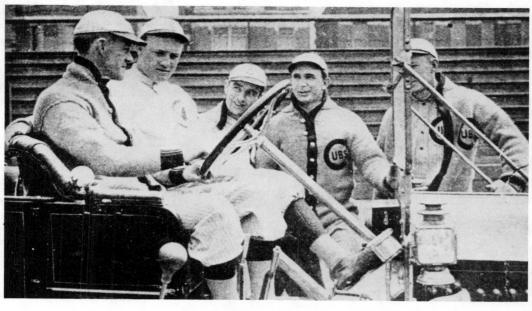

CHICAGO CUBS ——— 1907
DETROIT TIGERS

The Cubs Seek Revenge

Frank Chance's powerhouse Cubs again ran away in the National League, winning the pennant by some 17 games. In the American League the Detroit Tigers, led by a fiery young base-runner and superb hitter, Ty Cobb, edged out Connie Mack's Athletics in a close finish. This time the strong Cub pitching staff displayed its superiority, holding Cobb, the American League batting champion, to a .200 average. Cobb's hard-hitting teammate, Sam Crawford, hit only .238 in the Series.

Apart from the pitching, the key to the Series was the catching. For the Cubs, the shrewd Johnny Kling handled his pitchers so adroitly that one newspaperman remarked that "Chicago's twirlers pitched to Kling, not the batter." By contrast the Detroit catcher, Charlie Schmidt, seemed to disintegrate as the Series went on. In the first game he missed a third strike that cost Detroit a 3-2 victory, the tying run coming in from third. The game ended in a 3-3 tie, called in the 12th because of darkness. In the next four games the Cubs stole bases with such ease—18 altogether—that Schmidt heard only laughter and abuse. After the Series a writer said, "Schmidt went under a doctor's care to get his nerves back in condition." The Cubs won four games to none with one tie.

Johnny Evers:
". . . the boys were looking for trains that were not on the schedule."

The Cubs' tempestuous second baseman, Johnny Evers, returned home to Troy, N.Y., where he owned a shoe store. One of the Series heroes, he had batted .350 against the Tigers. He told an interviewer from the *Troy Times* about the final game. *Detroit was very gloomy and the only noise heard in all the streets were Chicago rooters. . . . Every where the general talk was that as our superiority was shown we would in all probability throw Saturday's game so as to get back to Chicago Sunday, thus getting the receipts of probably a 30,000 crowd. But such was not to be the case. . . .*

All that morning [pitcher Mordecai "Miner" or "Three Finger"] *Brown was consistently asking, and almost begging, Chance to let him pitch that afternoon. . . . But Frank wouldn't give him a decisive answer, simply telling him to wait and he would see.*

We arrived at the ball park at 1:15 p.m. and after the usual practice by both teams [umpire Hank] *O'Day announced the batteries as Brown and Kling for Chicago and Mullin and Archer for Detroit. Brown's name was cheered loudly and he thanked Chance for pitching him. . . .*

As the innings went by with no change in the [2-0] *score, the crowd, which was indeed very small, grew uneasy, and at the end, with the score just the same, one could see disappointment. . . . As the last man was retired, a little cheering was done, but everybody, with a few exceptions, was eager to get away.*

Many of our Chicago admirers crowded about our bench, offering congratulations, and every one of the players was almost tickled to death, as we had at last reached the highest point in a ball player's life. . . .

We returned to our hotels and were invited to drink a little toast by almost everybody we met, and by train time most of the boys were looking for trains that were not on the schedule.

A cartoonist depicts how the Cubs made mincemeat of Ty Cobb, Wahoo Sam Crawford, and the other Tigers. But Cobb got rich by being paid in stock for testimonials for Coca-Cola. Below: Johnny Evers shows off his new Hudson.

FIRST GAME (Oct. 8, at Chicago)

DETROIT	000 000 030 000	3	9	3
CHICAGO	000 100 002 000	3	10	5

Donovan
Overall, Reulbach (10th)

SECOND GAME (Oct. 9, at Chicago)

DETROIT	010 000 000	1	9	1
CHICAGO	010 200 00x	3	9	1

Mullin
Pfiester

THIRD GAME (Oct. 10, at Chicago)

DETROIT	000 001 000	1	6	1
CHICAGO	010 310 00x	5	10	1

Siever, Killian (5th)
Reulbach

FOURTH GAME (Oct. 11, at Detroit)

CHICAGO	000 020 301	6	7	2
DETROIT	000 100 000	1	5	2

Overall
Donovan

FIFTH GAME (Oct. 12, at Detroit)

CHICAGO	110 000 000	2	7	1
DETROIT	000 000 000	0	7	2

Brown
Mullin

SLAGLE   CF.
SHECKARD   LF.
CHANCE   1B.
STEINFELDT   3B.
EVERS   2B.
SCHULTE   RF.
BROWN   P
TINKER   SS.
KLING   C

Cub fans could. travel to Detroit for $5.50, or they could watch the progress of the game on one of the first electric scoreboards, mounted outside the *Tribune* office. Below: The second game at Chicago. Fans in the overflow crowd on the grass were asked to remove their hats; they shielded their heads from the sun with handkerchiefs.

CHICAGO CUBS
DETROIT TIGERS 1908

For the Tiger Bugs, the Same Sad Story

The Cubs and Tigers were again pennant winners, the Tigers winning on the last day of the season, the Cubs the day *after* the regular season by beating the Giants in a replay of the game ruled a 1-1 tie when the Giants' Fred Merkle didn't touch second base. For many Chicago and Detroit fans, often referred to as "bugs" by the players and press, the tumult of the pennant races had left them too wilted to get excited about the World Series. At one Sunday game in Chicago only 17,-760 people were in West Side Park, about 10,000 fewer than the attendance a week earlier during the frenzy of the pennant race. And when the Cub machine again rolled over the Tigers to lead the Series three games to one, only 6,210 Tiger fans dribbled into Bennett Park for the fifth and final game, the smallest crowd ever to witness a Series match. The Cubs outhit the Tigers, while Mordecai (Three Finger) Brown and Orval Overall pitched shutouts for the Cubs. But Detroit's Ty Cobb opened National League eyes as he hit .368. "He's not a lemon," wrote W. A. Phelon in *Sporting Life,* "but a peach." The Georgia Peach would win nine straight American League batting titles.

Ed Reulbach:
Conversations at the mound

In *Baseball* magazine Cub pitcher Ed Reulbach explained the importance of a catcher like Johnny Kling to a pitcher. *I well remember a little incident in a game against the Tigers* [in 1908]. *There was a man on first and second and Ty Cobb at bat.* [Mordecai] *Miner Brown was pitching. Kling strolled leisurely out to the box and said to Brown: 'Now Cobb will bunt. If the bunt goes to first base, all you can possibly do is get Cobb, and you will have to work hard to do that. . . . But if he bunts in the other direction there will be a fair chance of nailing the runner at third and in any case the third baseman can get Cobb. . . . Pitch one on the outside.' Brown did so. Cobb's bunt shot almost directly into Brown's hands, and he caught the runner easily at third. Crawford was now at second and Kling began to use the same kind of tactics to get him also. As a preliminary, he signed to* [Joe] *Tinker to go way off the bag to put Crawford off his guard. He then had another conversation with Brown in which he told him to pitch the next two wide, no matter what he might signal for. Brown did so, Kling got the ball and shot it down to second, catching Crawford off the sack by as neat a throw as I ever saw. Kling then signalled to Brown for another wide one, again shot it down to second and caught Cobb trying to steal. . . . Much of the brilliant work of the Cubs against the Tigers was owing to John Kling, one of the greatest catchers who ever wore a mask.*

Cartoon shows rival managers Hugh Jennings and Frank Chance whipping their charges into the Series, whose progress was shown on indoor electric boards—for a fee (and thus a predecessor to pay-TV). Bottom: Fans who prefer live action, despite the rain.

Far left: Cubs' Harry Steinfeldt punches a hit; Hugh Jennings debates with an umpire; Joe Tinker breaks for first base. Top left: Frank Chance slides home for the Cubs. Below: Ty Cobb scores for Detroit. The winners got only $1,317 each, the losers $870, mainly because of poor crowds in Detroit. Cub players grumbled that Cub owner, Charles Murphy, had sold tickets to speculators and pocketed the money. "The World Series," wrote a reporter in *Sporting Life*, "has caused another crisis in baseball."

FIRST GAME (Oct. 10, at Detroit)

| CHICAGO | 004 000 105 | 10 14 2 |
| DETROIT | 100 000 320 | 6 10 4 |

Reulbach, Overall (7th), Brown (8th)
Killian, Summers (3d)

SECOND GAME (Oct. 11, at Chicago)

| DETROIT | 000 000 001 | 1 4 1 |
| CHICAGO | 000 000 06x | 6 7 1 |

Donovan
Overall

THIRD GAME (Oct. 12, at Chicago)

| DETROIT | 100 005 020 | 8 11 4 |
| CHICAGO | 000 300 000 | 3 7 2 |

Mullin
Pfiester, Reulbach (9th)

FOURTH GAME (Oct. 13, at Detroit)

| CHICAGO | 002 000 001 | 3 10 0 |
| DETROIT | 000 000 000 | 0 4 1 |

Brown
Summers, Winter (9th)

FIFTH GAME (Oct. 14, at Detroit)

| CHICAGO | 100 010 000 | 2 10 0 |
| DETROIT | 000 000 000 | 0 3 0 |

Overall
Donovan

Dinner tendered to the
Officials, Past and Present of the National League
Visiting Officials of the American League
The National Commission, and
The Members of the Base Ball Writers' Assn. of America
by
The Pittsburg Base Ball Club
in honor of
Winning the National League Championship and the
World's Championship, 1909
Wednesday evening, December 15th 1909
The Waldorf-Astoria, New York

PITTSBURGH PIRATES
DETROIT TIGERS
1909

Now It's the Pirates
Who Twist the Tiger Tail

Shiny new Forbes Field was almost a bigger attraction than the Series itself as the Pirates faced the Tigers, who were playing in their third straight Series. For the third straight time the Tigers lost. The Pirates' Big Three—Howard Camnitz, Vic Willis, and Al Leifield—had won 66 games during the season, but the Pirate pitching hero for the Series was Charles (Babe) Adams, who had won only 12. Adams won three games in the Series, shutting out the Tigers in the seventh and final game. It was the first Series to go the full length of games, coming down to a seventh "no-tomorrow" game.

Adams started the first game because the Pirate pitching star, Camnitz, was in shaky condition. (He had been given a $1,200 bonus to stop drinking and hadn't earned it.) Adams, a Missouri farm boy who went to bed early and never drank, won that game and two others and became the idol of Pittsburgh. Women camped outside his hotel room and clamored for a kiss; but Adams said he didn't think that his wife, back home in Mount Morah, would allow it.

The attendance, nearly 120,000 for the seven games, was a record for a Series, as were the box office receipts. Prices had been set by the National Commission at $2 a box seat, $1.50 a reserved seat, and 50¢ for the bleachers.

Fans had looked forward to seeing the game's two greatest hitting stars, Ty Cobb and Honus Wagner, playing against each other on the same field. "You can't compare us," Cobb told writers. "He is a baseball veteran and I am only a youngster." But the writers and fans did compare them,

and in the Series, Cobb's last, he hit only .231 while Wagner, the hulking Flying Dutchman, led the Pirates with a .333 average.

Ty Cobb:
"... the way I had it doped out ..."

During the Tigers' second-game victory, Ty Cobb daringly stole home with two out and two runners in scoring position. Later he revealed the Cobb cunning that made him so bold and successful a base-stealer. *The minute I saw that Willis was going to relieve Camnitz on the mound, I decided to make the try to steal home. I calculated that Willis, coming in at such a time, would give no thought to me at third—that his mind would be centered entirely on the batsman and his own ability to get the ball over. So, when I saw him get on the rubber, ready to pose, I walked some distance off third base to see if he was paying any attention to me. I observed that he was looking at Gibson [the catcher]. I turned back toward third base in order to disarm Byrne [the third baseman] and Gibson, and then just as Willis raised his arm to go through the preliminary motions of pitching, I dashed for the plate. As there was a righthanded batter up, I had some protection and in sliding I threw my body away from the plate, giving Gibson only my foot to touch in case he got the ball on time. I ripped up the ground about 30 inches with my spikes before I touched the rubber, but I made it all right. If I had failed I suppose I would have been called a mutt. But the way I had it doped out left little chance for failure.*

Above: Detroit manager Hugh Jennings, coaching at third, flings out his "wee-a-ah" cry to encourage Tiger hitters. It infuriated Pirate fans. Below: Tiger wives bundle against the wet and cold in Detroit. And Ty Cobb (l.) meets Honus Wagner.

Crowd fills new Forbes Field in Pittsburgh. Ticket scalpers hired some 150 women to stand in line and buy tickets. After buying the limit of two tickets each, the women switched coats and hats, went back into the line, and bought more tickets. Some 40 Pinkertons were hurling known scalpers out of the line, but the Pinks shrugged when they saw the women and the scalpers had won again. Below: Four of the Pittsburgh stars. Seated (l. to r.) are Honus Wagner, Tommy Leach, and player-manager Fred Clarke. Hurling a pitch is Babe Adams, ''a cherub-cheeked farm boy'' who told reporters: ''When I was a boy on the farm Dad made a set of rules to be followed in work. One of them was any job started must be completed, and that everything must be done well. This has always been a rule of mine.'' For his Series work he got a $1,000 check from fans.

PRESS TICKET	PRESS TICKET	PRESS TICKET	PRESS TICKET	PRESS TICKET	PRESS TICKET
WORLD'S SERIES 1909	WORLD'S SERIES 1909	WORLD'S SERIES 1909	WORLD'S SERIES 1909	WORLD'S SERIES 1909	WORLD'S SERIES 1909
FORBES FIELD, PITTSBURGH	Forbes Field, Pittsburgh	Forbes Field, Pittsburgh	Forbes Field, Pittsburgh	Forbes Field, Pittsburgh	Forbes Field, Pittsburgh
SEAT NO. 11	GAME NO.	GAME NO.	GAME NO.	GAME NO.	GAME NO.
PRESS GATE Blanc B³ magazine	5	4	3	2	1
11	PRESENT AT PRESS GATE 11	PRESENT AT PRESS GATE 11	PRESENT AT PRESS GATE 11	PRESENT AT PRESS GATE 11	PRESENT AT PRESS GATE 11

FIRST GAME (Oct. 8, at Pittsburgh)

DETROIT....................100 000 000   1 6 4
PITTSBURGH................000 121 00x   4 5 0
Mullin
Adams

SECOND GAME (Oct. 9, at Pittsburgh)

DETROIT....................023 020 000   7 9 3
PITTSBURGH................200 000 000   2 5 1
Donovan
Camnitz, Willis (3d)

THIRD GAME (Oct. 11, at Detroit)

PITTSBURGH................510 000 002   8 10 3
DETROIT....................000 000 402   6 10 5
Maddox
Summers, Willett (1st), Works (8th)

FOURTH GAME (Oct. 12, at Detroit)

PITTSBURGH................000 000 000   0 5 6
DETROIT....................020 300 00x   5 8 0
Leifield, Phillippe (5th)
Mullin

FIFTH GAME (Oct. 13, at Pittsburgh)

DETROIT....................100 002 010   4 6 1
PITTSBURGH................111 000 41x   8 10 2
Summers, Willett (8th)
Adams

SIXTH GAME (Oct. 14, at Detroit)

PITTSBURGH................300 000 001   4 7 3
DETROIT....................100 211 00x   5 10 3
Willis, Camnitz (6th), Phillippe (7th)
Mullin

SEVENTH GAME (Oct. 16, at Detroit)

PITTSBURGH................020 203 010   8 7 0
DETROIT....................000 000 000   0 6 3
Adams
Donovan, Mullin (4th)

39

"Johnny" Evers and "Charlie" Williams

Invite their friends and fellow baseball fans to the

Opening of Their New Shoe Store

84 and 86 E. Monroe St.

Today, October 15th

They will both be glad to shake your hand and have you see their beautiful Shoe Store, where they will sell the FINEST LINE OF MEN'S SHOES SHOWN IN CHICAGO

ALL
STYLES
"EVERS-WEAR"

Evers & Williams Shoe Co.
84-86 MONROE ST. CHICAGO

1910
PENNANT
WINNERS

HOPE— Beloved daughter of Mr. and Mrs. Fan of this city departed this life yesterday afternoon at the West Side Ball Park after a lingering illness of nine innings. She was attended by thirty thousand physicians who did all in their power to save her, but with comparatively little success. She rallied a little in the second inning but a terrific relapse in the third defied the most heroic measures and reduced her pulse, respiration and temperature until they were perceptible to only the most prejudiced observers. The heartless conduct of nine conspirators from a place called Philadelphia hastened her untimely end. The remains will lie in state today at the park, weather permitting, and the funeral will probably be later. She leaves two sisters, Faith and Charity, neither of whom was present yesterday. Philadelphia papers please copy.

PHILADELPHIA ATHLETICS ———1910
CHICAGO CUBS

Mr. Mack's College Kids
Surprise the Beer Drinkers

For the fourth time in five years Frank Chance and his Cubs won the National League pennant. But as in 1906, when they were surprised by the weak-hitting White Sox, the veteran Cubs were upset, this time by a young and speedy Philadelphia team that had been assembled with care and cunning by Connie Mack. He toured college campuses looking for intelligent and quick ballplayers, for as he often said, "This game is like the railroads—faster than 25 years ago and getting faster." In three years he had built a powerful machine sparked by Frank (Home Run) Baker and Eddie Collins. They clubbed the renowned Cub pitchers for a .316 average, a Series mark that stood until 1960. After the A's took the first two games in Philadelphia, the glum Cubs, many of them German-speaking and most of them good beer drinkers, stayed up late in the night on the train to Chicago, muttering Teutonic curses into their cups. The beer didn't help: The A's won two of the next three to capture the Series, four games to one.

Eddie Collins:
". . . as scarce as molars in a hen . . ."

A ball game is a funny affair, said the A's second baseman, Eddie Collins, in a story in the *Sporting News* of December 21, 1910. *There are never two games alike. In the World Series just past, it is a cinch you will all agree with me there was never a series of games where the national title was at stake that were more peculiarly contrasted. Peculiarly, I mean, in the sense that opportunities were sometimes lavishly presented to both clubs and then again were as scarce as molars in a hen. . . . It ofttimes happens in a game that the team to which is presented the most opportunities will not emerge from a conflict a winner. Particularly was this true in the second game of the big Series in which the Cubs had something like 20 men reach first base . . . still they were able to amass a total of three runs. Likewise was this true of the Athletics in the fourth stanza when the Cubs triumphed 4-3. Time and again we had a man on third base with none out or one down and we couldn't get him in. As our opportunities came and went unheeded . . . a fountain of confidence arose . . . in the Cubs . . . became more pronounced and culminated in their favor in the tenth.*

The expiration of the Chicago Cubs was mourned in an ad in the *Tribune.* But even in defeat Evers and his partner sold shoes. And in victory there is always an ad man on the scene.

41

Philadelphia fans crowd the housetops ringing Shibe Park to watch a game. Opposite page: Connie Mack and his stalwarts. Below (l. to r.) are three of his stars: pitcher Jack Coombs, second baseman Eddie Collins, pitcher Chief Bender. In Chicago $3 box seats were sold by scalpers for $12. Fans who had sent checks to the Cubs but hadn't received tickets—the games sold out—stormed the Cubs' office. In Philadelphia throngs jammed the streets near newspaper offices to hear reports of the games bellowed by a man with a megaphone. Motion-picture cameramen, filming the games, had to be shooed off the field.

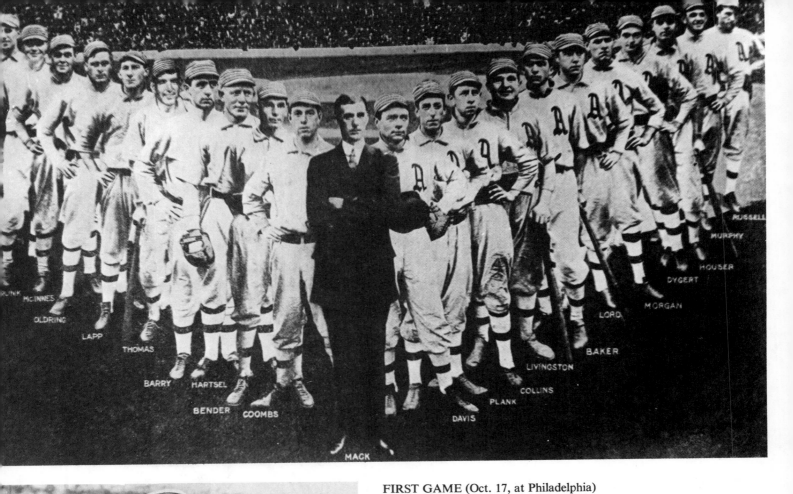

PLUNK McINNES
OLDRING
LAPP
THOMAS
BARRY HARTSEL
BENDER COOMBS

RUSSELL
MURPHY
HOUSER
DYGERT
MORGAN
LORD
BAKER
LIVINGSTON
COLLINS
PLANK
DAVIS

MACK

FIRST GAME (Oct. 17, at Philadelphia)

CHICAGO .000 000 001 1 3 1
PHILADELPHIA 021 000 01x 4 7 2
Overall, McIntire (4th)
Bender

SECOND GAME (Oct. 18, at Philadelphia)

CHICAGO 100 000 101 3 8 3
PHILADELPHIA 002 010 60x 9 14 4
Brown, Richie (8th)
Coombs

THIRD GAME (Oct. 20, at Chicago)

PHILADELPHIA 125 000 400 12 15 1
CHICAGO 120 000 020 5 6 5
Coombs
Reulbach, McIntire (3d), Pfiester (3d)

FOURTH GAME (Oct. 22, at Chicago)

PHILADELPHIA 001 200 000 0 3 11 3
CHICAGO 100 100 001 1 4 9 1
Bender
Cole, Brown (9th)

FIFTH GAME (Oct. 23, at Chicago)

PHILADELPHIA 100 010 050 7 9 1
CHICAGO 010 000 010 2 9 2
Coombs
Brown

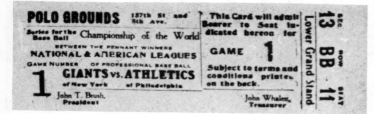

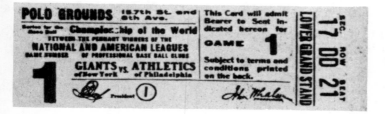

PHILADELPHIA ATHLETICS
NEW YORK GIANTS
1911

For Connie Mack and the A's,
a Chance To Avenge '05

Few, if any, sports events in America up to this time were more widely anticipated and warmly debated than the 1911 Series between the Giants and the A's. With both teams clinching the pennants early, millions of fans took sides in arguments over which team was better. For the A's, Connie Mack had good pitching—Chief Bender, Jack Coombs, Eddie Plank—and his "$100,000 infield": Frank Baker at third, Jack Barry at shortstop, Eddie Collins at second, Stuffy McInnis at first (Stuffy, however, missed most of the Series with an injury). For the Giants, John McGraw had Christy Mathewson, Rube Marquard, and speed: The team had stolen more than 300 bases during the season. The biggest crowd in World Series history up to then, 38,381, filled the Polo Grounds for the first game and watched Matty beat Bender, 2-1. But the Giants could not run on the A's, stealing only four bases; in one game alone four Giants were caught stealing. And Frank (Home Run) Baker lived up to his nickname in this Series, hitting a home run in the second game to beat Marquard, and another home run in the ninth inning of the third game to help beat Matty. The A's won in six, four games to two, and Mack gained revenge for his loss in '05 to his managerial rival, McGraw. The tension that had built between the two men, each hailed by

their followers as a genius, eased when McGraw came into the A's dugout after the final game and shook Mack's hand.

John McGraw:
Better than Tinker and Evers

After the Series, McGraw credited the A's shortstop and second baseman, Jack Barry and Eddie Collins, for the failure of the Giants to run the way they had during the season. *They showed as perfect teamwork between them as I ever saw. If I signed for the hit and run expecting Collins to cover second base and leave the space open between first and second, why Barry would be at the bag to cover the runner on a throw from the catcher and if Barry looked to be the most likely man to run to the bag, Collins dug over there and Barry would be at shortstop to block that anticipated open territory. I had my players try to detect what signs they had between them to denote who was to cover second on steals but I had to give it up. I came to the conclusion it must have been intuition. I don't think Tinker and Evers, in their best days with the Cubs, excelled them in teamwork and in guessing out defensive plays.*

Rival captains, Larry Doyle (l.) and Harry Davis, meet before the first game, won by New York. The victory was hailed by a cartoonist, but his "so far" was prophetic. Genuine tickets (top) were forged (bottom). Giants got a trophy for winning the flag; their fans, travel tips.

FIRST GAME (Oct. 14, at New York)
PHILADELPHIA..............010 000 000   1 6 2
NEW YORK.................000 100 10x   2 5 0
Bender
Mathewson

SECOND GAME (Oct. 16, at Philadelphia)
NEW YORK.................010 000 000   1 5 3
PHILADELPHIA.............100 002 00x   3 4 0
Marquard, Crandall (8th)
Plank

THIRD GAME (Oct. 17, at New York)
PHILADELPHIA...........000 000 001 02   3 9 2
NEW YORK..............001 000 000 01   2 3 5
Coombs
Mathewson

FOURTH GAME (Oct. 24, at Philadelphia)
NEW YORK.................200 000 000   2 7 3
PHILADELPHIA............000 310 00x   4 11 1
Mathewson, Wiltse (8th)
Bender

FIFTH GAME (Oct. 25, at New York)
PHILADELPHIA...........003 000 000 0   3 7 1
NEW YORK.................000 000 102 1   4 9 2
Coombs, Plank (10th)
Marquard, Ames (4th), Crandall (8th)

SIXTH GAME (Oct. 26, at Philadelphia)
NEW YORK.................100 000 001   2 4 3
PHILADELPHIA............001 401 70x   13 13 5
Ames, Wiltse (5th), Marquard (7th)
Bender

The A's Bris Lord is tagged out by diving Buck Herzog in a run-down between second and third. Helping on the play are shortstop Art Fletcher and Christy Mathewson (r.). Below: A mighty swing by the mighty Home Run Baker. He hit nine that season to lead the American League.

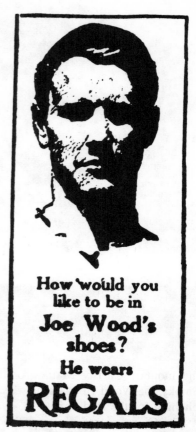

BOSTON RED SOX
NEW YORK GIANTS
1912

In Los Angeles a Lady Faints as the Giants Swoon

This Giant-Red Sox Series is usually rated among the most thrilling of all time. With one game ending in a tie, the two teams struggled to an eighth and final game, tied three games apiece.

After nine innings of the decisive game the score was tied, 1-1, the ace of each staff now on the mound: Christy Mathewson for the Giants, Smoky Joe Wood (a 34-game winner that season) pitching for the Red Sox.

The Giants scored a run off Wood in the top of the 10th to lead, 2-1. Pinch-hitter Clyde Engle led off the bottom of the 10th for the Sox and popped a soft fly into centerfield. The Giants' Fred Snodgrass camped under the ball, then dropped it, Engle sliding safely into second on the error. Harry Hooper, who had saved the game for the Sox a few innings earlier with a miracle catch of Larry Doyle's seemingly sure homer, hit a long drive, but Snodgrass raced back and caught the ball, atoning for his muff. The next batter walked, putting runners on first and second. Up came Hall-of-Famer Tris Speaker. He looped a short pop foul near the first-base coach's box. First baseman Fred Merkle stared, as though entranced, not moving toward the pop, and it dropped untouched a dozen feet away from the box. With a second chance Speaker hit a single, scoring the tying run and sending Stephen Yerkes to third. From there Yerkes scored on a long fly, the Sox winning the Series, four games to three. For John McGraw the loss was a galling one; his Giants had come back after trailing, three games to one, to tie the Series, only to lose it on two sandlot plays. "I know errors are a part of baseball," Giant captain Larry Doyle said later of Snodgrass'

muff. "But I wish he had caught it. He feels worse than any of us and that is saying something."

A Fan:
The Long Wait

"Baseball Viewed from the Boston Bleachers" was the title put on this letter from a fan to the *Sporting News*. On a cloudy, wet day the fan arrived in Boston to see one of the Series games. Here is his account:

Upon our arrival at Fenway Park, after a hasty breakfast, we scouted around the grandstand entrance in an effort to buy some tickets. 'Nothing doing,' was all the encouragement given. We went around to the bleacher entrances, and got into one of the many 'bread lines' which were at that early hour over 100 yards long and about a dozen of them.

Scattered along the sidelines were boxes, barrels and boards, the evidences of the camp of those who had spent the night in the line. Boys with choice positions sold their places at a premium.

After a wait the ticket offices were opened and the long lines began to move. They looked like long snakes disappearing into a large stadium. . . . In a short while I had at last a ticket for $1 and was passing through the turnstiles to see a World Series game.

We hurried into the bleachers and our long vigil began. It was then about 10 o'clock. Four hours to wait for the game to start and the worst of it was there wasn't a moment that we did not expect

An alert advertiser put his shoes onto the feet of both Giant and Red Sox stars. Below: Boston's Royal Rooters wave pennants and megaphones as their band toots. The Rooters marched onto the field before each game led by Mayor John (Honey Fitz) Fitzgerald, Rose Kennedy's father.

Opposite page: Long lines of fans curl under the "El" outside the Polo Grounds, waiting to buy $3 grandstand tickets for the first game. Left: Smoky Joe Wood, winner of three games, helped his teammates to a winner's share of $4,024 each—then a record. Also a record was the total attendance: 252,037. The players demanded a cut of the receipts of the first five games, arguing that the tie second game was not a complete game. When the owners refused, Matty and other players on both sides briefly considered a strike but then gave in and played out the Series.

Christy Mathewson: After his loss in the final game, when the Giants let two easy flyballs get away, Matty was as outwardly relaxed, said writers of the time, as he would have been in victory. In the club-house he consoled the unhappy Snodgrass, then went over to a table and joined in a game of bridge. But in Los Angeles a lady watching the game on an electric board took the loss much more dramatically. Fred Snodgrass' mother fainted.

51

to hear the announcement that there would be no
game. . . . The crowd was prepared for the long
wait. Papers and magazines were everywhere. Evidently their supply ran short because they [the
crowd] sought other amusements. First peanuts
began to bounce off stiff hats and folded newspapers began to fly down the stands. 'Everybody's
doin' it,' and no one seemed to mind. Then a
small crowd of fellows gave an impromptu con-
cert in which the crowd joined in with a will. . . .
'Tessie,' 'Sweet Adeline,' 'I want to be down in
Dixie,' were the favorites and concluded with a
'Star Spangled Banner' and everybody stood up
and cheered like mad.

About that time many people brought forth
their lunches and sandwiches, cakes and even pies
were being handed about among friends and it
looked like a regular picnic. . . . By 12 the stands
were well-filled . . . and every woman who passed
in front of the centerfield bleachers received an
ovation. . . .

At one o'clock the New York Giants made
their first appearance. . . . In New York's practice
session an incident occurred which showed New
York's love for Boston fans. Snodgrass raced into
centerfield for a fly and a few fans tried to get
the ball. Snodgrass beat them to it and as they
scrambled back over the partition he threw the
ball at one of them and hit him in the leg. . . .

At last the game is about to begin and the
crowd . . . who had spent from two to four hours
in those stands almost hoping against hope for a
game were rewarded. . . .

Left: The Giants' Buck Herzog slides
into third with a triple. Above: New
York's Josh Devore hooks a foot
back into first base after a pick-off
throw nearly caught him looking.
Opposite page: Boston star Tris
Speaker (The Grey Eagle) swings
outside the batting cage. Stuffed in
Speaker's rear pocket is his glove,
a puny thing compared to today's
leather traps.

52

Harry Hooper tosses away his bat on a low pitch for ball four. He saved the Series for the Red Sox in the final game with a leaping catch of a seemingly sure homer by Larry Doyle—the greatest catch, McGraw said later, he had ever seen.

FIRST GAME (Oct. 8, at New York)

```
BOSTON.....................000 001 300   4 6 1
NEW YORK..................002 000 001   3 8 1
```
Wood
Tesreau, Crandall (8th)

SECOND GAME (Oct. 9, at Boston)

```
NEW YORK.............010 100 030 10   6 11 5
BOSTON..................300 010 010 10   6 10 1
```
Mathewson
Collins, Hall (8th), Bedient (11th)

THIRD GAME (Oct. 10, at Boston)

```
NEW YORK..................010 010 000   2 7 1
BOSTON.....................000 000 001   1 7 0
```
Marquard
O'Brien, Bedient (9th)

FOURTH GAME (Oct. 11, at New York)

```
BOSTON.....................010 100 001   3 8 1
NEW YORK..................000 000 100   1 9 1
```
Wood
Tesreau, Ames (8th)

FIFTH GAME (Oct. 12, at Boston)

```
NEW YORK..................000 000 100   1 3 1
BOSTON.....................002 000 00x   2 5 1
```
Mathewson
Bedient

SIXTH GAME (Oct. 14, at New York)

```
BOSTON.....................020 000 000   2  7 2
NEW YORK..................500 000 00x   5 11 2
```
O'Brien, Collins (2d)
Marquard

SEVENTH GAME (Oct. 15, at Boston)

```
NEW YORK.............610 002 101   11 16 4
BOSTON..................010 000 210    4  9 3
```
Tesreau
Wood, Hall (2d)

EIGHTH GAME (Oct. 16, at Boston)

```
NEW YORK.............001 000 000 1   2 9 2
BOSTON..................000 000 100 2   3 8 5
```
Mathewson
Bedient, Wood (8th)

PHILADELPHIA ATHLETICS
NEW YORK GIANTS
1913

The A's Take the Rubber Series and Matty Walks Off a Loser

In this third World Series between the A's and the Giants, Connie Mack and his A's won for the second time—by a decisive four games to one. Before the Series began, a controversy erupted when Garry Herrmann, a member of the National Commission, argued that the Series should be abolished. He proposed that all 16 teams participate in an interleague round robin to pick the best team—an obvious way of allowing the poorer teams to dip their hands into the postseason pot of gold. "Losers always hate to see the victors get the spoils," John McGraw said. "There isn't a chance of the World Series being dropped. It's too great an event in baseball."

It was so great, argued some, that it could hurt baseball. "Sociologists and other half-baked kind of people," wrote a *Sporting Life* editorialist, "are questioning if the World Series craze is not a sign of national decadence." Newspapers and magazines, he declared, could harp on the issue to hurt baseball. But Ban Johnson, also a member of the commission, defended the Series. "While I recognize many of the necessary evils of the World Series," he said, citing the betting and the ticket scalping, "the one great big point in its favor is that it arouses tremendous interest in every city, village and community in the whole country." In his final appearance in a Series, Christy Mathewson lost to Eddie Plank—the first time Plank had defeated Matty in a pitching rivalry that dated back to their college days.

Connie Mack:
Looking at the Series from a commercial—and dishonest—standpoint

In an article in the *Saturday Evening Post,* titled "Honesty in Baseball," Connie Mack wrote: *This brings me . . . to the last game of the World Series that was, played in New York on Saturday. There were many reasons why I wanted this game, wanted it badly. One of these, and not the least important reason, was that I knew the gamblers expected us to lose it—and were betting on what they thought was a certainty. You see, before the Series opened, we sold tickets for three games in Philadelphia, with the understanding that if the third game were not played, the money would be refunded. . . . Everybody knew approximately how much money was at stake. With the exception of the bleachers every seat in Shibe Park had been sold for Monday's game, and the money was actually in the treasury of the club. The amount, to give the exact figure, was $45,639. Looking at it from a commercial angle—from the dishonest standpoint—there was every inducement for our club—not the players—to lose Saturday's game. We won the game, 3-1. We paid back in cash to holders of tickets $45,639. Compare this with any business you know intimately and then tell me if you find any evidence of downright dishonesty. . . .*

Christy Mathewson and William Courtney, an actor who played the lead in *The Girl and the Pennant,* cowritten (the ads claimed) by Matty, chat before the Series. Cabs to the games were horseless, and some of the rooters pretty.

PHILADELPHIA AMERICANS
1913
CHAMPIONS OF THE WORLD

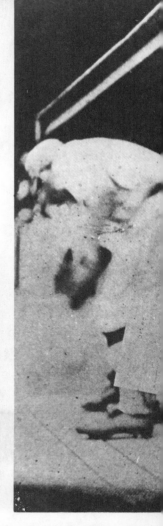

Giant catcher Larry McLean tags out A's Amos Strunk at the plate in the second game. The run would have won the game for the A's, who lost it in the tenth to Matty, 3–0. Opposite page: Straw-hatted Connie Mack in the dugout, in his hand the scorecard he used to wave his fielders into position. Bottom: Mack's "$100,000 infield"— first baseman Stuffy McInnis (l.), second baseman Eddie Collins (far r.), shortstop Jack Barry (second from r.), and third baseman Home Run Baker (third from r.)—pose with reserve Danny Murphy (second from l.). Opposite page: Baker is tagged out by Giant third baseman Buck Herzog. After the Series the Giants began an around-the-world tour that took them from Japan to England, playing games against the Chicago White Sox.

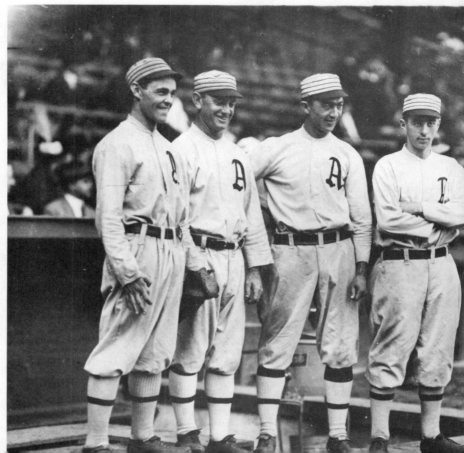

FIRST GAME (Oct. 7, at New York)

PHILADELPHIA............000 320 010 6 11 1
NEW YORK................001 030 000 4 11 0
Bender
Marquard, Crandall (6th), Tesreau (8th)

SECOND GAME (Oct. 8, at Philadelphia)

NEW YORK................000 000 000 3 3 7 2
PHILADELPHIA............000 000 000 0 0 8 2
Mathewson
Plank

THIRD GAME (Oct. 9, at New York)

PHILADELPHIA............320 000 210 8 12 1
NEW YORK................000 010 100 2 5 1
Bush
Tesreau, Crandall (7th)

FOURTH GAME (Oct. 10, at Philadelphia)

NEW YORK................000 000 320 5 8 2
PHILADELPHIA............010 320 00x 6 9 0
Demaree, Marquard (5th)
Bender

FIFTH GAME (Oct. 11, at New York)

PHILADELPHIA............102 000 000 3 6 1
NEW YORK................000 010 000 1 2 2
Plank
Mathewson

BOSTON BRAVES

PHILADELPHIA ATHLETICS **1914**

The Miracle Braves
Tell the Chief Who They Are

George Stallings' Boston Braves were baseball's first "miracle team," coming from last place in July to win the National League pennant. In the American League Connie Mack's A's were considered a near-unbeatable dynasty as they won their fourth American League pennant in five years. "The A's," said John McGraw, "have become a menace to the World's Series and to my league."

Stallings and his Braves worked one more miracle: They beat Connie Mack's proud A's in the biggest upset in Series history up to then and perhaps since. Not only did they beat the heavily favored A's; they won in four straight, a Series first.

Before the Series, Mack told Chief Bender to go to Boston to scout the Braves. The next day Mack saw Bender and asked him why he wasn't in Boston. "What's the good of looking over a bush league outfit?" Bender growled. During the first game of the Series, Mack looked up at the crestfallen Chief as he came into the dugout after being batted out of the box and rasped, "Pretty good hitting, isn't it, for a bush league team?"

Later Mack claimed that the A's players were concentrating more on attractive offers from the Federal League, the new third league, than on the Braves. So by the following season he had dismembered this team, the one he had built so carefully, and gone were Bender, Plank, Jack Coombs, Home Run Baker, Eddie Collins, and Bob Shawkey.

The miracle Braves were a collection of unwanted players picked off the baseball scrap heap by Stallings. But in that 1914 Series three of the unwanteds—catcher Hank Gowdy, a Giant reject, who hit .545; second baseman Johnny Evers, the old Cub, who hit .438; and pitcher Dick Rudolph, another Giant reject who won two games—made

Stallings seem like baseball's newest genius. The peppery Stallings spoke bitingly of Mack's managing, and at the end of the Series the proud Cornelius Alexander McGillicuddy—Connie Mack—sat in the A's dugout, refusing to cross the field to shake Stallings' hand.

Dick Rudolph:
Thinking about a baby in the Bronx

Before the Series, Dick Rudolph told his friends to bet on the Braves if he pitched the first game. Rudolph himself bet heavily on the Braves to win. Before the last game he was concerned about his wife back in the Bronx, where she had given birth a few days earlier to a 10-pound girl. Seated on a porch of his house in the Bronx, he spoke to Bozeman Bulger of the *Sporting News* a few weeks after the end of the Series: *I was thinking about home and that baby all the time. To get my mind as easy as possible I called up my home on the long-distance phone just before the game and they told me everything was fine and dandy. Still I wanted to be there. George Stallings offered to let me go, but as long as everything was all right at home, I knew it wouldn't be fair to the rest of the boys.*

I heard that John McGraw bet $1,000 that I'd win the first World Series game I pitched. That really made me feel good because, being from the Bronx and all, I wanted to pitch for the Giants. They never gave me a chance when I trained with them and I'll tell you I pitched as well with the Giants as I did in that World Series and maybe Mr. McGraw knew it.

I don't know how those Athletics played in the past, but they were the worst suckers on a curve ball I ever pitched against in my life.

A's captain Ira Thomas and the umpires listen before the first game as Brave captain Johnny Evers points out a ground rule at Fenway Park, loaned by the Red Sox to the Braves for the Series. Below: Boston's Royal Rooters.

The Miracle 1914 Braves—First row (l. to r.): Joseph Connolly, coach Mitchell, bat boy Conner, Dick Rudolph, Rabbit Maranville, Dick Crutcher, Bill Martin, Johnny Evers. Second row: George Whitted, Oscar Dugey, George Tyler, Paul Strand, Josh Devore, Larry Gilbert, Carlisle Smith, Herb Moran. Third row: Bill James, Ted Cather, Charles Deal, George Davis, Ensign Cottrell, Gene Cocreham, Otto Hess, Leslie Mann, Hank Gowdy, Charles Schmidt, Al Whaling.

FIRST GAME (Oct. 9, at Philadelphia)

BOSTON....................020 013 010   7 11 2
PHILADELPHIA............010 000 000   1 5 0
Rudolph
Bender, Wyckoff (6th)

SECOND GAME (Oct. 10, at Philadelphia)

BOSTON.....................000 000 001   1 7 1
PHILADELPHIA.............000 000 000   0 2 1
James
Plank

THIRD GAME (Oct. 12, at Boston)

PHILADELPHIA.........100 100 000 200   4 8 2
BOSTON.................010 100 000 201   5 9 1
Bush
Tyler, James (11th)

FOURTH GAME (Oct. 13, at Boston)

PHILADELPHIA.............000 010 000   1 7 0
BOSTON......................000 120 00x   3 6 0
Shawkey, Pennock (6th)
Rudolph

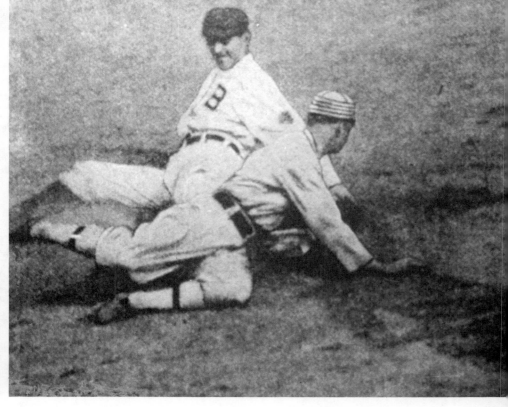

Above: George Stallings with pitchers Bill James (l.) and Dick Rudolph, each the winner of two games. After the Series Rudolph and Hank Gowdy "made fools of themselves," as one writer put it, on the vaudeville stage for a reported $1,500 a week. "The path of baseball glory leads only to the stage," wrote a *New York Sun* reporter. Right: Johnny Evers evades second baseman Eddie Collins' tag. Opposite page: Hank Gowdy plows into third with a triple. The umpire is Bill Klem.

BOSTON RED SOX
PHILADELPHIA PHILLIES
1915

A President Comes—
and Babe Ruth Is on the Bench

The previous year the winning Boston Braves had been invited by the Red Sox to play their Series games in Fenway Park. When the Red Sox won the pennant in 1915, the Braves returned the favor, inviting the Sox to play their games in the recently built Braves Field. The Sox accepted, playing the third and fourth games of the Series in the new park. The biggest World Series crowd up to then, 42,300, came to that third game and saw a tense duel between Boston's Dutch Leonard and the Phillies' Grover Cleveland Alexander, who had won 31 games that season, 12 by shutouts. Leonard gave up only three hits and won in the last of the ninth, 2-1. Each game in this five-game Series was a close battle, all but one being decided by a single run. The clutch hitting of Harry Hooper and Duffy Lewis, who knocked in 8 of the 12 runs scored by the Sox in the Series, gave Boston its winning margin.

The World Series received official recognition as a national event when Woodrow Wilson came from Washington to attend the second game in Philadelphia—the first United States president to attend a World Series game.

Watching most of the Series on the Boston bench was a young lefthanded pitcher, Babe Ruth, who got into the Series only as a pinch-hitter. Batting against Alexander, he rolled out to first base to end the first game. "The Philadelphia fans," wrote a *Sporting News* correspondent, "breathed a sigh of relief when Ruth made out. Babe is the hardest-hitting pitcher in the business." And then, unconsciously prophetic, the correspondent added, "Extra-base swats [are] his specialty."

Duffy Lewis:
"... Cobb ... the greatest until Ruth ..."

Duffy Lewis, the Red Sox outfielder, said: *I had five hits in eight at-bats off Alexander. I hit .444 in that '15 Series. But I was lucky against Alexander. He was a great pitcher, one of the best. I was just lucky the ball was going through the slot. He once pitched 12 shutouts in that little Baker Bowl and that was something. I remember I beat Alexander, 2-1, with a hit in the ninth. We had a man on second and they walked Speaker to get to me. They had a conference at the mound and their manager, Pat Moran, figured that since I already had two hits, they could get me out. I hit the first ball, a line drive into centerfield, to win the game.*

We played together in the outfield, Hooper, Speaker and me. Speaker was the king. He moved left, I moved left, Hooper moved left. He could do everything next to Cobb, who was the greatest until Ruth came along and stole his thunder. Cobb was never in a slump. When he wasn't hitting, he was dragging [bunting] to get on. Ruth, as a pitcher, struck out a lot, he swung so hard, and one time [Bill] Carrigan [Boston manager] told me to pinch-hit for him and I got a hit, I was the only one ever to pinch-hit for Ruth.

It was a funny thing about the homers Hooper hit. Both of them bounced into the stands. Today that would be a double but in those days they counted for a home run. We were behind 4-2 in the eighth, with a man on base, and I hit a home run high up into the stands. Then in the ninth Hooper hit another one of those homers that bounced into the stands and we won the last game. He and I, we had a hell of a Series.

Loud-voiced entertainers sing for the crowd before the games. The check is for the winning Red Sox players, each of whom received $3,780. Bottom: Smoke billows from diamond in Philadelphia before the first game as gasoline is burned to dry out the field.

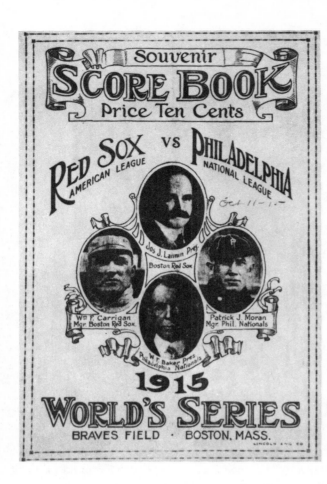

FIRST GAME (Oct. 8, at Philadelphia)

BOSTON........................000 000 010   1 8 1
PHILADELPHIA..............000 100 02x   3 5 1
Shore
Alexander

SECOND GAME (Oct. 9, at Philadelphia)

BOSTON........................100 000 001   2 10 0
PHILADELPHIA..............000 010 000   1 3 1
Foster
Mayer

THIRD GAME (Oct. 11, at Boston)

PHILADELPHIA..............001 000 000   1 3 0
BOSTON........................000 100 001   2 6 1
Alexander
Leonard

FOURTH GAME (Oct. 12, at Boston)

PHILADELPHIA..............000 000 010   1 7 0
BOSTON........................001 001 00x   2 8 1
Chalmers
Shore

FIFTH GAME (Oct. 13, at Philadelphia)

BOSTON........................011 000 021   5 10 1
PHILADELPHIA..............200 200 000   4 9 1
Foster
Mayer, Rixey (3d)

Right: President Wilson, his wife-to-be giggling on his right, poses to throw out the first ball. Top: Duffy Lewis at bat and tagged in rundown. Bottom: Phils' Ed Burns scores. The catcher is Red Sox player-manager Bill Carrigan.

BOSTON RED SOX
BROOKLYN DODGERS
1916

Casey, Babe, and the $100,000 Hit

"The $100,000 hit," the batting of Casey Stengel, and the pitching of Babe Ruth were the moments to remember of this Series, played as the shadow of World War I crept across the Atlantic from the trenches of France. ("Six Ships Sunk off Nantucket by U-Boats," headlines proclaimed as the Series opened in Boston, fewer than 50 miles from the torpedoings.) "The $100,000 hit" came in the second game, which stretched through 14 innings, the longest World Series game ever played. Babe Ruth dueled with Brooklyn's Sherry Smith in that match. After giving up a home run in the first, Ruth shut out the Dodgers for 13 innings, beginning a streak of scoreless Series innings that would reach 29⅔, a record that stood for nearly a half-century until snapped by Whitey Ford in 1961. In the last of the 14th, with darkness descending, Boston's Del Gainor doubled home the winning run. If Gainor's hit had not broken the tie and the game had to be replayed the next day, it would have drawn gate receipts of at least $100,000. The most comfort the Dodgers, or Superbas, as they were also called, got out of the Series was the hitting of

their spindly-legged outfielder, Casey Stengel, who batted .364. The Red Sox won in five games, the last game in Boston drawing 42,620—until 1923 and the opening of Yankee Stadium a Series attendance record.

Babe Ruth:
"When in doubt, hit to Ivy"

Babe Ruth, in his autobiography (*The Babe Ruth Story;* as told to Bob Considine, 1948), wrote: *Brooklyn played a terrible fielding game against us all through the Series, which helped us over the rough spots. The shortstop for the Dodgers was Ivan Olson, who had played in the American League with Cleveland. Ivy had a terrible Series and we didn't do anything to help him. We used to yell out, 'When in doubt, hit to Ivy.' We had him crazy before it was over. At one stage of the Series he said he'd lick our whole ball club. Of course we only greeted him with laughs, and the more we laughed, the madder he became and the madder he became the worse he played.*

Babe Ruth, the pitcher. In this Series he batted .000 in five at-bats, but his earned-run average was 0.64, the best of all the starting pitchers for both clubs.

FIRST GAME (Oct. 7, at Boston)

BROOKLYN................000 100 004 5 10 4
BOSTON....................001 010 31x 6 8 1
Marquard, Pfeffer (8th)
Shore, Mays (9th)

SECOND GAME (Oct. 9, at Boston)

BROOKLYN..........100 000 000 000 00 1 6 2
BOSTON.............001 000 000 000 01 2 7 1
Smith
Ruth

THIRD GAME (Oct. 10, at Brooklyn)

BOSTON....................000 002 100 3 7 1
BROOKLYN................001 120 00x 4 10 0
Mays, Foster (6th)
Coombs, Pfeffer (7th)

FOURTH GAME (Oct. 11, at Brooklyn)

BOSTON....................030 110 100 6 10 1
BROOKLYN................200 000 000 2 5 4
Leonard
Marquard, Cheney (5th), Rucker (8th)

FIFTH GAME (Oct. 12, at Boston)

BROOKLYN................010 000 000 1 3 3
BOSTON....................012 010 00x 4 7 2
Pfeffer, Dell (8th)
Shore

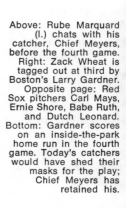

Above: Rube Marquard (l.) chats with his catcher, Chief Meyers, before the fourth game. Right: Zack Wheat is tagged out at third by Boston's Larry Gardner. Opposite page: Red Sox pitchers Carl Mays, Ernie Shore, Babe Ruth, and Dutch Leonard. Bottom: Gardner scores on an inside-the-park home run in the fourth game. Today's catchers would have shed their masks for the play; Chief Meyers has retained his.

72

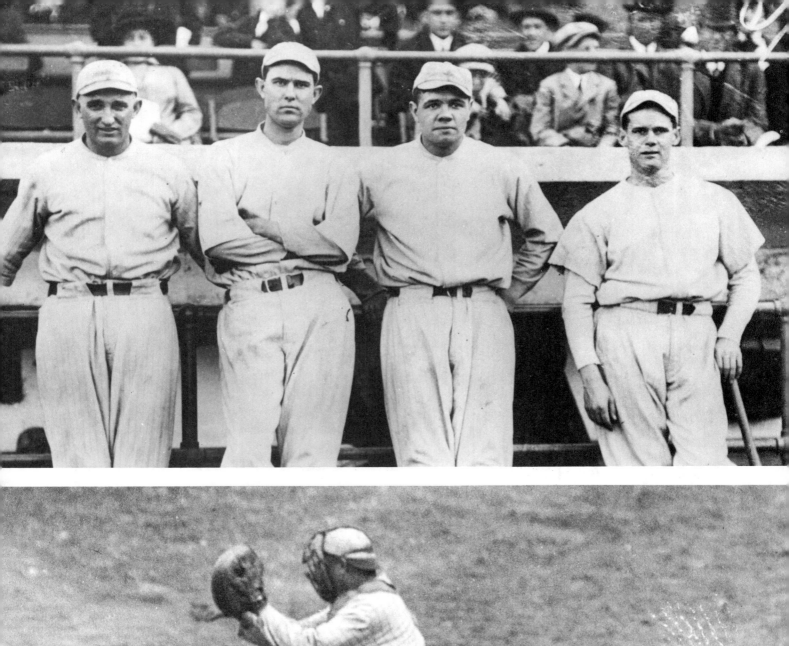

Papa Rooter Says: "Here's The

ONE BEST GIFT

FOR A

FELLOW FAN"

—or for any one of your family

"Papa Rooter"

PRICE 75¢

WORLD'S SERIES Parlor Baseball

TRADE MARK REGISTERED

Scientifically Based On

BIG LEAGUE AVERAGES

You can replay the big league decisions and get barrels of real baseball practice, and hilarious fun. Allows you to sacrifice, steal bases, do all the stunts of the diamond—even *pitch a curved ball.*

Anybody can play it

from the children to the old folks. No baseball knowledge needed; but if you do know baseball, it's all the better. Played on the table. 75 cents at dealer's, 85 cents by mail. A peach of a Christmas or Birthday Gift.

FREE—One of the Players

Give us the name of your dealer in games and we will send you one of the "base runners" and full details.

UNITED GAMES CO.

29 Chestnut Hill Ave., Athol, Mass.

Our Daddy is fighting at the Front for You—Back him up—Buy a United States Govt Bond of the

2nd LIBERTY LOAN

of 1917

HELP KNOCK THE KAISER OUT OF THE BOX

CHICAGO WHITE SOX
NEW YORK GIANTS
1917

Who's on Third? Zim.
Who's at Home? Nobody

The first wartime World Series opened in Chicago with fans made aware of the grimness of the time by the sight of 1,500 khaki-clad soldiers seated in a clump behind the first base line. When the teams moved to New York, signs in the Polo Grounds asked, "The Giants Have Bought Their Liberty Bonds—Have You?" But the Series itself gave a war-conscious America something to laugh about, for it was filled with mistakes and came to an end with a boner.

In one game the White Sox committed six errors. In the sixth and final game the Giants made two errors and committed the boner, all in one fateful inning—the fourth. With the game scoreless, Eddie Collins tapped a grounder to Giant third baseman Heinie Zimmerman, who threw wild to first while Collins scampered to second. Joe Jackson popped to right but the Giant rightfielder dropped the ball, so runners were now on first and third. The next batter hit to the pitcher, Rube Benton, who saw Collins halfway off third. Instead of throwing home he threw to Zimmerman at third. Heinie, instead of throwing home, advanced on Collins. The catcher, Bill Rariden, crept up on Collins, who saw neither the pitcher nor the first baseman covering home. Collins dashed for home, beating the slower Zimmerman in a footrace to the plate. The boner—perhaps unfairly—was labeled "Zim's boner," although he said, accurately enough, "Who was

I supposed to throw the ball to—myself?" In any case the White Sox scored three runs in the inning, and the Giants lost the sixth and final game, 4-2. Eddie Collins was the Chicago star with a .409 average, the old Athletic playing in his 5th Series and 26th Series game, more than anyone before him.

Jim Thorpe:
One day pro football teams could be big in the East, too

Jim Thorpe, the former Olympic champion and college football All-American, was a part-time player for the Giants in 1917, pinch-hitting once —unsuccessfully—in the Series. After the 1917 Series he told a reporter he was going back to the West from where he had sprung to become a professional football player. *I know professional football has never been big in the East,* he said. *But in the Middle West and out in Oklahoma there are a lot of good teams. I am going back to Oklahoma and organize, coach and I'll play for a professional team. Maybe we'll bring two teams east and play a game on Thanksgiving Day in the Polo Grounds. One day professional football teams could be as big in New York as the Giants are now.* [Three years later Thorpe became the head of what is now the National Football League.]

Rival managers Pants Rowland (l.) and John McGraw confer with the umpires. Armchair managers could play World's Series Parlor Baseball. A sign (l.) at the Polo Grounds was another reminder to buy Liberty Bonds.

FIRST GAME (Oct. 6, at Chicago)

NEW YORK 000 010 000   1 7 1
CHICAGO 001 100 00x   2 7 1
Sallee
Cicotte

SECOND GAME (Oct. 7, at Chicago)

NEW YORK 020 000 000   2 8 1
CHICAGO 020 500 00x   7 14 1
Schupp, Anderson (2d), Perritt (4th), Tesreau (8th)
Faber

THIRD GAME (Oct. 10, at New York)

CHICAGO 000 000 000   0 5 3
NEW YORK 000 200 00x   2 8 2
Cicotte
Benton

FOURTH GAME (Oct. 11, at New York)

CHICAGO 000 000 000   0 7 0
NEW YORK 000 110 12x   5 10 1
Faber, Danforth (8th)
Schupp

FIFTH GAME (Oct. 13, at Chicago)

NEW YORK 200 200 100   5 12 3
CHICAGO 001 001 33x   8 14 6
Sallee, Perritt (8th)
Russell, Cicotte (1st), Williams (7th), Faber (8th)

SIXTH GAME (Oct. 15, at New York)

CHICAGO 000 300 001   4 7 1
NEW YORK 000 020 000   2 6 3
Faber
Benton, Perritt (6th)

Above: Jim Thorpe, the greatest athlete of his time, who had only one fault as a baseball player: He couldn't hit the curve ball. Right: "Zim's boner," the unfortunate Heinie flying high over the plate, finishing second in the footrace to home with the sliding Eddie Collins. Opposite page (top): The White Sox stars (l. to r.)—Nemo Leibold, Eddie Murphy, John F. Collins, Shoeless Joe Jackson, and Happy Felsch. Bottom: The Sox pitchers— Mellie Wolfgang, Dave Danforth, Urban (Red) Faber, Joe (Blitzen) Benz, Reb Russell, Lefty Williams, and Eddie Cicotte.

76

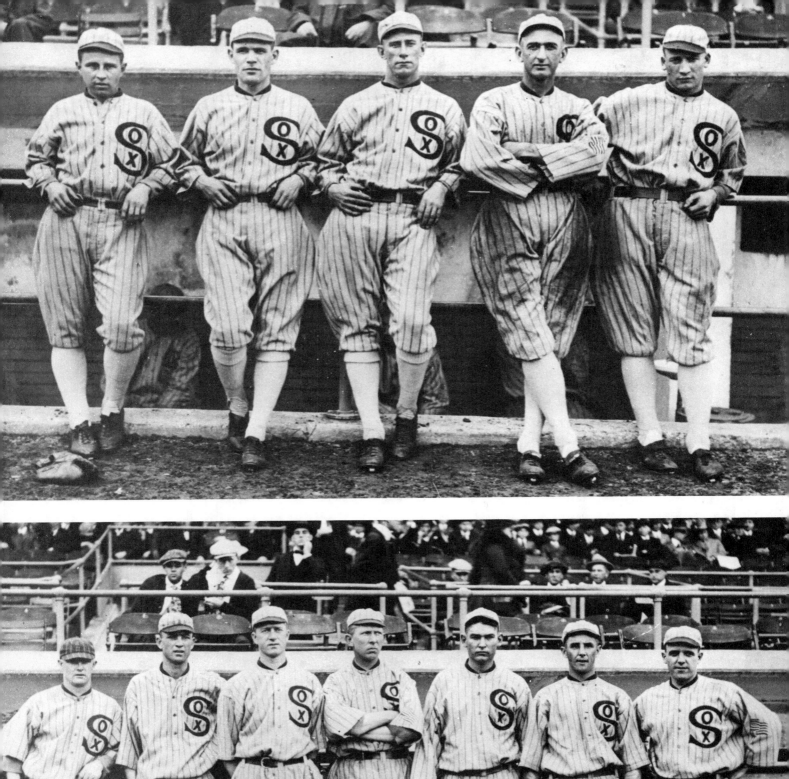

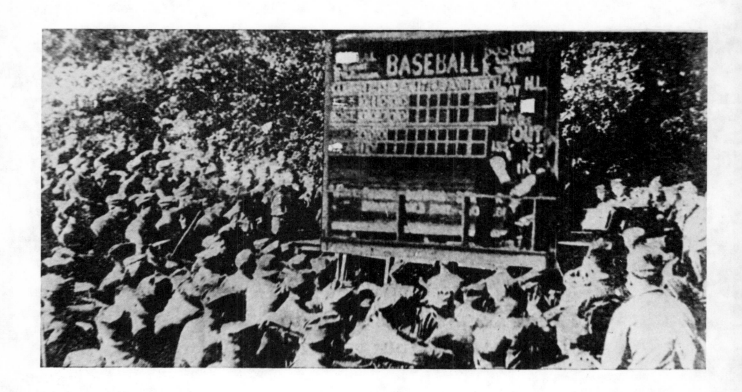

BOSTON RED SOX
CHICAGO CUBS ——1918

Even in France They Watched

A sit-down strike by the players delayed the start of the fifth game of the Series. The Series was held in September because the government had halted the regular season on Labor Day under its Work-or-Fight rule; the players had to enlist or work in a factory or shipyard. For the first time the teams finishing second, third, and fourth were sharing in the Series receipts. As a result the Boston and Chicago players heard that each winning share, with a deduction for war charities, would be less than $1,000. (The winning Red Sox actually got $890, the Cubs $535—the lowest Series winnings ever.) Before the fifth game, the players, led by Harry Hooper, sat in their clubhouses, refusing to take the field unless they were promised more. National Commission officials appealed to their loyalty to baseball and the country. The players would not budge, while on the field the band serenaded the restive crowd, including a contingent of wounded veterans, with songs like "Over There" and "Dixie."

The players finally relented, and the Red Sox went on to win their fifth straight World Series. They were led by Babe Ruth and Carl Mays, each winning two games. That year manager Ed Barrow had been playing Ruth in leftfield when he wasn't pitching, and Ruth had led the team in runs-batted-in. In the fourth game he cracked his first Series hit—a triple.

Some 25,000 came to the fifth game in Boston, but only 15,000 appeared for the final game, and there was talk in the newspapers that the fans were angered at the players for being "spoiled slackers." But newspaper stories from the camps in France told of hundreds of soldiers grouped around electric boards that re-created the games play-by-play.

Harry Hooper:
The emblems that never came

At his home in Santa Cruz, Calif., Harry Hooper commented on the player strike. *We demanded a meeting with the National Commission,* he said, *but after hearing us in the hotel in Boston, Mr. Ban Johnson* [head of the American League] *said there was nothing we could do about it, just go out and play. So we went back to the ball park and had a meeting between the two teams, and the teams decided not to play. There were a lot of people in the stands already. Leslie Mann represented the National League players, I represented the Boston team. Leslie and I waited for the National Commission, which was composed of three men, Ban Johnson, John Heydler, and Garry Herrmann. I guess we waited for pretty nearly an hour and the stands were nearly full. Finally the three of them came in. They had evidently celebrated their victory over us in the hotel by cocktails and so forth. Garry Herrmann started to talk about what a great man he had been for baseball in front of Mann, myself, and the newspapermen. Then Ban Johnson got up and shoved him aside and in a big pompous voice he started to talk for about a minute and then he broke down and started to cry. He came over and put his hand on my shoulder and he said, 'Harry, you know I love you, go out there and play that game.' He kept repeating that, 'Go out there and play that game.'*

American soldiers in France watch a scoreboard recording the progress of one of the games. Far left: Boston Mayor Peters throws out the first ball of the fourth game; Babe Ruth then took over the pitching for Boston. Left: Boston manager Ed Barrow and pitcher Sad Sam Jones.

Top: Cubs' Max Flack takes the low road into third. A rightfielder, he was the goat of the Series. He muffed a flyball in the final game, two Red Sox runners scoring to beat the Cubs, 2–1. Above: Cubs' Dode Paskert is run down between third and home. Right: Flack takes the high road into third as the Red Sox make a play at first. Opposite page: Cubs' Charlie Hollocher is safe at second. Despite Flack's error, a sportswriter of the time called this Series "the best ever for defensive work . . ."

80

We looked at the newspapermen and said it was very apparent we have no one here to argue with. John Heydler was the one sober man on the commission and he never opened his mouth. Mann and I excused ourselves and went back and told the players what had happened. We had decided not to play and give what we had earned to the Red Cross, if our demands were not met. But now the players decided, 'Well, the fans are out there, we can't punish them, we will go ahead and play. But only under one condition: that they won't take any action against us.' So I happened to be the talker for the two teams so I went back to the room, still full of newspapermen, and I told them that the players had decided to go ahead and finish the Series, but only under the condition that no action would be taken against any ballplayer. Ban Johnson said, 'That's fine, Harry, go on out there and play that game for the honor and glory of the American League,' that's what he kept saying, his words still ring in my ears.

We won the Series. About a week before Christmas we got a letter from Mr. Heydler and he said, 'Owing to the disgraceful actions of the ballplayers, [in] the strike in Boston, they were fined their World Series emblems,' which was a diamond lapel pin. And to this day they have never given us our emblems, even though they promised us no action would be taken, and to this day baseball owes all those fellows those emblems.

FIRST GAME (Sept. 5, at Chicago)

BOSTON	.000 100 000	1 5 0
CHICAGO	.000 000 000	0 6 0

Ruth
Vaughn

SECOND GAME (Sept. 6, at Chicago)

BOSTON	.000 000 001	1 6 1
CHICAGO	.030 000 00x	3 7 1

Bush
Tyler

THIRD GAME (Sept. 7, at Chicago)

BOSTON	.000 200 000	2 7 0
CHICAGO	.000 010 000	1 7 1

Mays
Vaughn

FOURTH GAME (Sept. 9, at Boston)

CHICAGO	.000 000 020	2 7 1
BOSTON	.000 200 01x	3 4 0

Tyler, Douglas (8th)
Ruth, Bush (9th)

FIFTH GAME (Sept. 10, at Boston)

CHICAGO	.001 000 020	3 7 0
BOSTON	.000 000 000	0 5 0

Vaughn
Jones

SIXTH GAME (Sept. 11, at Boston)

CHICAGO	.000 100 000	1 3 2
BOSTON	.002 000 00x	2 5 0

Tyler, Hendrix (8th)
Mays

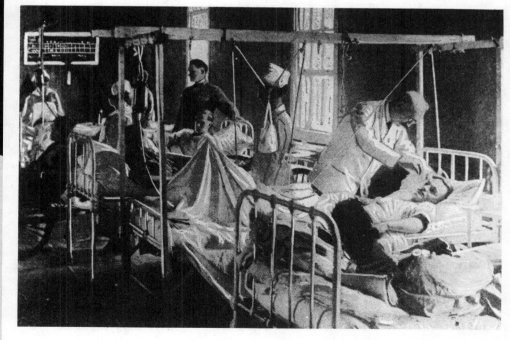

CINCINNATI REDS
CHICAGO WHITE SOX
1919

The White Sox Turn Black

With boom times coming to America as the boys came marching home, crowds were filling ball parks, and the Golden Age of American Sport began. Taking advantage of the postwar enthusiasm, the National Commission again made the Series a best-of-nine affair. The White Sox were favored as the Series began; but after the first game a sudden deluge of money was bet on Cincinnati, especially by New York gambler Arnold Rothstein and friends. White Sox pitcher Ed Cicotte hit the first Cincinnati batter with the pitch, and that was the signal to rings of gamblers across the nation that some of the White Sox players had accepted bribes to throw the Series.

The White Sox did win three games, two with the incorruptible Dickie Kerr on the mound. After the Series some officials, including Ban Johnson and White Sox owner Charles (The Old Roman) Comiskey, tried to pooh-pooh the rumors, now being published, of a fixed Series. Late in the 1920 season a Chicago grand jury reported its findings; it indicted eight White Sox players for taking bribes. Among them were Shoeless Joe Jackson and Buck Weaver, who had led their team in hitting with averages of .375 and .324. Also indicted were pitchers Ed Cicotte and Claude Williams. Cicotte, Williams, and Jackson confessed but later repudiated their confessions. All the players were acquitted by a jury.

But baseball's new commissioner, Kenesaw Mountain Landis, whom the owners had selected in 1921 to replace the three-man National Commission, partly as the result of the fix rumors, banned all eight players from the game. Much-criticized in the press was Charles Comiskey, who seemed to have known of the conspiracy but, it was alleged, attempted to hush it up because he had invested so much money in acquiring stars like Jackson and Weaver.

Wrote one minor league manager in the *Sporting News:* "Let us know the truth, as bitter as it may be. It will be better for baseball in the long run." And, indeed, even though the truth leaked out very slowly, baseball not only survived the bitter truth, it found a strong man—Judge Landis—who would clean up the blemishes that had marred the World Series during its growing years. Like American sport, the World Series was entering a Golden Decade that would make it unquestionably the nation's prime sports event.

Edd Roush:
"They weren't laying that ball in there with nothing on it for me . . ."

Edd Roush was the National League batting champion in 1919, with a .321 average. In the Series he hit only .214, but he made his six hits count, scoring six runs and driving in seven. He was living in Bradenton, Fla., when he recalled the only fixed Series. *I was told about it after the second ball game. A friend of mine told me before we were going to Chicago, he stopped me in front of our hotel . . . and he said, 'Roush, you hear about the squabble the White Sox got in last night?' I said no, what squabble? He said, 'Well, they were supposed to throw the Series to the Cincinnati ball club and they didn't get their money after the first game. They had a meeting up in Cicotte's room, and they agreed to go out and try to cross the gamblers.' I didn't pay any attention to it, just one of those things that happen, see?*

I'm satisfied they tried to win after that first game. They told that themselves. Cicotte told that. The writers never would print it that way. . . . I don't care how hard you try, it's pretty damn hard to throw a ball game. The pitcher can lay that ball

in there, that doesn't mean the hitter is going to hit it. That Williams, in the last game, he was putting everything on it that I could see. There were two men on in the first inning and I hit a curve ball off Williams—he was a lefthanded pitcher and I was a lefthanded hitter—and it went right over the first base bag.... It was a curve ball. I was reading a piece the other day in a book, Eight Men Out, where a fellow said Williams was just laying the ball in there, he didn't throw a curve ball. Now I know what I hit—it was a curve ball. We scored four runs in the first inning, I think, and we beat them ten to five.

Cicotte may have lost that first ball game, I don't know, but the rest of them were pretty damn tight ball games, I'll tell you that. They weren't laying that ball in there with nothing on it for me, I'll tell you that. I don't know what they were doing for the other fellows. But if they were we should have beat them by bigger scores.

Right: Chicago's Chick Gandil, another of the accused White Sox players, is caught stealing second base. The Reds' shortstop (l.) is Larry Kopf; the second baseman about to wing the ball to third is Morrie Rath. After the Series, with rumors of a scandal abounding, White Sox owner Charles Comiskey said he would make an investigation; near the end of 1919 he said he had found no evidence incriminating any of the players.

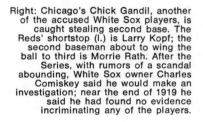

Left: Reds' Edd Roush is safe at second. The shortstop (l.) is Swede Risberg, the second baseman Eddie Collins. Middle: The Reds' Heinie Groh tumbles into third ahead of the throw to Buck Weaver, one of the Sox later banned from baseball.

FIRST GAME (Oct. 1, at Cincinnati)

		R	H	E
CHICAGO	010 000 000	1	6	1
CINCINNATI	100 500 21x	9	14	1

Cicotte, Wilkinson (4th), Lowdermilk (8th)
Ruether

SECOND GAME (Oct. 2, at Cincinnati)

		R	H	E
CHICAGO	000 000 200	2	10	1
CINCINNATI	000 301 00x	4	4	2

Williams
Sallee

THIRD GAME (Oct. 3, at Chicago)

		R	H	E
CINCINNATI	000 000 000	0	3	1
CHICAGO	020 100 00x	3	7	0

Fisher, Luque (8th)
Kerr

FOURTH GAME (Oct. 4, at Chicago)

		R	H	E
CINCINNATI	000 020 000	2	5	2
CHICAGO	000 000 000	0	3	2

Ring
Cicotte

FIFTH GAME (Oct. 6, at Chicago)

		R	H	E
CINCINNATI	000 004 001	5	4	0
CHICAGO	000 000 000	0	3	3

Eller
Williams, Mayer (9th)

SIXTH GAME (Oct. 7, at Cincinnati)

		R	H	E
CHICAGO	000 013 000 1	5	10	3
CINCINNATI	002 200 000 0	4	11	0

Kerr
Ruether, Ring (6th)

SEVENTH GAME (Oct. 8, at Cincinnati)

		R	H	E
CHICAGO	101 020 000	4	10	1
CINCINNATI	000 001 000	1	7	4

Cicotte
Sallee, Fisher (5th), Luque (6th)

EIGHTH GAME (Oct. 9, at Chicago)

		R	H	E
CINCINNATI	410 013 010	10	16	2
CHICAGO	001 000 040	5	10	1

Eller
Williams, James (1st), Wilkinson (6th)

Photos on This Page Courtesy Chicago Historical Society

Just When Your Favorite Fruit Is Right

—From *The Indianapolis News*

"Step Lively"

—From *The Philadelphia Evening Ledger*

Contrast in Black and White

—From *The Chicago News*

CLEVELAND INDIANS
BROOKLYN DODGERS 1920

Three by Wamby and Four by Smith

The 1920 Series opened under the pall of the Black Sox scandal. Each day's newspapers reported a shocking new revelation as a Chicago grand jury investigated the briberies. But once inside the ball park, the fans seemed to forget the scandal.

The underdog Dodgers won two of three at Ebbets Field, and there was hope in Brooklyn that the beloved Flock might beat Cleveland and its 31-game winner, Jim Bagby. The Indians squelched the hopes by reeling off four straight victories in Cleveland to win their first championship in their first Series. The hero was wiry Stan Coveleski, who pitched three complete-game victories and gave up only two runs in 27 innings.

Two feats helped the fans to forget the scandal. Both occurred in the fifth game. In the first inning Cleveland's Elmer Smith hit the first grand-slam World Series homer. In the fifth inning the Dodgers put runners on first and second and Clarence Mitchell came to bat. With both runners taking off on the hit-and-run play, Mitchell sliced a low liner toward right centerfield. Cleveland second baseman Billy (Wamby) Wambsganss leaped and speared the ball in his glove. Seeing the runner off second base he ran over and tagged the base for the second out. He turned to throw to first and saw the runner, Otto Miller, braking to turn and run back to first base. Wambsganss ran over and tagged Miller to complete the only unassisted triple-play in Series history and one of the few in the history of big league baseball.

The Dodgers, failing to score a run for the last 18 innings of the Series, were embarrassed further when one of their pitchers, Rube Marquard, was arrested for scalping tickets.

Stan Coveleski:
There was no stopping Zack

Many years later, Stan Coveleski, winner of three Series games, remembered: *Before the Series they told me, if you want to beat Brooklyn, you got to stop Zack Wheat. Well I think he got more hits off me than anybody on their team. But I kept the hitters ahead of him off the bases and I won the three games. I had a good spitball that you could use in those days, and so did Burleigh Grimes for their team. In fact, they had four good pitchers and we had only two, Jim Bagby and me, and they were big favorites before the Series started. But after I won the first game the odds got lower and when I started the last game, the odds were favoring us. But I never bet on the games. I never bet on anything in my life.*

Cartoonists of 1920 portray the fan as astounded and outraged by the scandal but willing to forgive a cleaned-up baseball. Also not forgotten by the fan: most players were honest.

Cleveland's Billy Wambsganss (far r.) completes his unassisted triple-play, in a view from third base, as he tags out Otto Miller, who appeared, said writers, "befuddled" by what was happening. Fans sat stunned and silent for several moments, then burst into applause and were still talking about the play innings later. It was only the third unassisted triple-play in baseball history, dating back to 1878. Bottom: In the seventh game Cleveland's Charlie Jamieson helps to nail down the defeat of Brooklyn by stealing second, the ball bounding into centerfield between Dodger second baseman Pete Kilduff and shortstop Ivy Olson.

FIRST GAME (Oct. 5, at Brooklyn)

CLEVELAND.................020 100 000 3 5 0
BROOKLYN.................000 000 100 1 5 1
Coveleski
Marquard, Mamaux (7th), Cadore (9th)

SECOND GAME (Oct. 6, at Brooklyn)

CLEVELAND.................000 000 000 0 7 1
BROOKLYN.................101 010 00x 3 7 0
Bagby, Uhle (7th)
Grimes

THIRD GAME (Oct. 7, at Brooklyn)

CLEVELAND.................000 100 000 1 3 1
BROOKLYN.................200 000 00x 2 6 1
Caldwell, Mails (1st), Uhle (8th)
Smith

FOURTH GAME (Oct. 9, at Cleveland)

BROOKLYN.................000 100 000 1 5 1
CLEVELAND...............202 001 00x 5 12 2
Cadore, Mamaux (2d), Marquard (3d), Pfeffer (6th)
Coveleski

FIFTH GAME (Oct. 10, at Cleveland)

BROOKLYN.................000 000 001 1 13 1
CLEVELAND................400 310 00x 8 12 2
Grimes, Mitchell (4th)
Bagby

SIXTH GAME (Oct. 11, at Cleveland)

BROOKLYN.................000 000 000 0 3 0
CLEVELAND.................000 001 00x 1 7 3
Smith
Mails

SEVENTH GAME (Oct. 12, at Cleveland)

BROOKLYN.................000 000 000 0 5 2
CLEVELAND.................000 110 10x 3 7 3
Grimes, Mamaux (8th)
Coveleski

NEW YORK GIANTS
NEW YORK YANKEES
1921

Johnny on the Spot
for Muggsy and the Giants

This was a Series of firsts: the first Series overseen by the new commissioner, Judge Landis; the first Series to be played in one ball park, the Polo Grounds, occupied then by both the Giants and Yankees; the first Series in which a team won the first two games and lost the Series; the first Series in which Babe Ruth, now with the Yankees, hit a home run (in the fourth game); the first of 29 World Series duels for the Yankees during the next 43 years; and the first Series in five tries to be won by John J. (Muggsy) McGraw and the Giants since their victory in 1905.

The pitching hero was the Yankees' Waite Hoyt, who would, oddly, also be the hard-luck guy of the Series. A dashing 21-year-old gay blade, Hoyt won two games and allowed no earned runs in 27 innings of pitching, tying Christy Mathewson's 1905 record. But he lost the eighth and decisive game, 1-0, when a runner scored from second on an error by Yankee shortstop Roger Peckinpaugh.

That final game, and the Series, ended on a dramatic fielding play. With the Yankees' Aaron Ward on first and one out, the veteran Home Run Baker slammed a ball toward the hole in right-field. But Giant second baseman Johnny Rawlings knocked down the ball, picked it up, and threw to George Kelly at first to get Baker. Aaron Ward, meanwhile, rounded second base and, for no good reason, took off for third. Kelly lined a perfect throw into the glove of third baseman Frankie Frisch, who tagged out Ward. The game was over, and Muggsy McGraw had won his second World Series.

Frankie Frisch:
All you need is four good ones

I got four of the five hits the Giants got in that first game, said Frankie Frisch in 1972. (He died in 1973.) *Three of the hits were singles and one was a triple. I was nervous, sure I was; those fellows who tell you they're not nervous before a Series game, especially your first one, your first Series, there has to be something wrong with them.*

On that play at third, I imagine Ward thought the ball had gone through to rightfield. Rawlings made a hell of a play on the ball. He dove at the ball and I think he threw the ball to Kelly on his knees. What kept Ward from making it was Kelly's great arm. He could throw that ball like a bullet. Ward jumped into me, he tumbled me over pretty good, trying to knock the ball out of my hands. They all did in those days. I don't know about these days.

It was a close-scoring Series. Art Nehf was a big help to us. He had great control, a lefthander, and he was fast. We only used four pitchers in that Series—Nehf, Phil Douglas, Jesse Barnes, and Fred Toney. Four is all you need when you have four good ones.

At the dawn of the
Golden Age of Sport,
the Bambino is king.

Opposite page: Yankee third baseman Mike McNally beats a throw to the plate in the fifth game, tying the score. The Giant catcher is Earl Smith. The player toeing the third-base line may be pitcher Art Nehf. Left: Casey Stengel's strong arms help center a ragged pyramid of Giant players. On Casey's right is Frankie Frisch. The smallish crowd of only 25,410 at the eighth game impelled Judge Landis to suggest a seven-game Series so as not to "overtax the patience of the public." Ruth, an arm and knee injured, missed two of the games, watching one from the press box. He had hit 59 homers in 1921 and was a national idol, going off after the Series for 15 weeks of personal appearances.

FIRST GAME (Oct. 5, at Polo Grounds)

YANKEES....................100 011 000   3 7 0
GIANTS.......................000 000 000   0 5 0
Mays
Douglas, J. Barnes (9th)

SECOND GAME (Oct. 6, at Polo Grounds)

GIANTS.......................000 000 000   0 2 3
YANKEES....................000 100 02x   3 3 0
Nehf
Hoyt

THIRD GAME (Oct. 7, at Polo Grounds)

YANKEES..................004 000 010   5 8 0
GIANTS....................004 000 81x   13 20 0
Shawkey, Quinn (3d), Collins (7th), Rogers (7th)
Toney, J. Barnes (3d)

FOURTH GAME (Oct. 9, at Polo Grounds)

GIANTS.......................000 000 031   4 9 1
YANKEES....................000 010 001   2 7 1
Douglas
Mays

FIFTH GAME (Oct. 10, at Polo Grounds)

YANKEES....................001 200 000   3 6 1
GIANTS.......................100 000 000   1 10 1
Hoyt
Nehf

SIXTH GAME (Oct. 11, at Polo Grounds)

GIANTS.......................030 401 000   8 13 0
YANKEES....................320 000 000   5 7 2
Toney, J. Barnes (1st)
Harper, Shawkey (2d), Piercy (9th)

SEVENTH GAME (Oct. 12, at Polo Grounds)

YANKEES....................010 000 000   1 8 1
GIANTS.......................000 100 10x   2 6 0
Mays
Douglas

EIGHTH GAME (Oct. 13, at Polo Grounds)

GIANTS.......................100 000 000   1 6 0
YANKEES....................000 000 000   0 4 1
Nehf
Hoyt

Hear the Crowd Roar!

at the World Series Games
with the Radiola

Grantland Rice

famous sports editor of the New York Tribune

will describe every game personally, play by play, direct from the Polo Grounds.

His story, word by word, as each exciting play is made by Yankees or Giants, will be Broadcasted from famous Radio-Corporation-Westinghouse Station

W. J. Z.

There's an RCA set for every home and every purse. As low as $25, ranging upward according to type of set.

Owners of RCA sets are sure of broadcasting results from the World Series.

Prepare for the big event by buying your RCA set from your nearest dealer and ask him for the Radiola Score Sheet which will enable you to mark up every move on a convenient chart of the field.

You can get all the thrills of being at all the World Series games and have a Radiola that will give entertainment for the whole family all year round by going to an RCA dealer today.

This symbol of quality is your protection

233 Broadway, New York

Grantland Rice at the "radiophone" for the first game and first Series broadcast from a ball park. (In 1921 Rice gave an inning-by-inning report by telephone to an announcer in Newark; the announcer then relayed Rice's description over the radio.) In 1922 Rice's broadcast was heard by an estimated million people in a 300-mile area around New York. Crowds stood outside radio stores to hear the games on loudspeakers. "Out over the ether," wrote one critic, "there came even the cries of the peanut vendors."

NEW YORK GIANTS
NEW YORK YANKEES —1922

Bottles for the Judge, Dusty Curves for the Babe

With the Series again a best-of-seven affair, a format that has continued since, the second game ended after 10 innings in a 3-3 tie. The umpires called the game because of darkness, although the time was only 4:45 p.m., and there was at least a half hour of light remaining. Umpire Bill Klem had reminded the other umpires that if the 11th inning were prolonged, it might be played in dusk, the batters unable to see the pitches. But the players were shocked and the fans enraged.

Mobs of spectators, howling they had been gypped, encircled Judge Landis in his box. Thinking that he had called the game, they hurled bottles, sticks, and curses at him. The stony-faced judge calmly walked out of the box and across the field, ignoring the fans and their threats. But he was as angry as the fans by the decision. The next day he ordered both clubs to contribute all of the first-game receipts—roughly $120,000—to a charity for the war-wounded. And the umpires had learned not to be so quick in stopping a game —the next day's game was played in a murky drizzle, the field darker than it had been the day before when the game had been called. But this time the game went on. Art Nehf won two games for the Giants, who limited Babe Ruth, by now baseball's premier hitter, to a .118 average. On McGraw's orders the pitchers threw curve balls in the dust to Ruth, and the overeager Babe could loft only two of them for hits, one a single, the other a pop-fly double.

For McGraw, long envious of the success of his Yankee neighbors and their new star, Babe Ruth, this World Series triumph could not have tasted more delicious. However, it would be his last World Series championship.

Joe Dugan:
"... None of this crazy business ..."

The Yankee third baseman, Jumping Joe Dugan, at his home in Norwood, Mass., recalled the game that was called on account of darkness. *The sun was out just as it is right now, it was crazy. The people were milling around, yelling, they were mad at everybody. They could have played another inning or two anyway. We dressed out in centerfield and as I was walking off—we wanted to get out of there before someone killed us—I found myself next to John McGraw. He said to me, 'What's it all about?' I said 'I don't know, Mr. McGraw.' I think that umpire blew his top or something. It was broad daylight. Everyone was laughing, it was a joke among the players.*

The game had only been played for a little over two hours, two and a half hours. We used to play ball in those days, none of this crazy business of looking for signs. We just got the ball and played ball, none of this stepping off the mound. The fans are getting a little tired of it, it gets boring, all that talking, the conferences on the mound. We'd take two hours to complete a game. Listen, one game, Grover Cleveland Alexander and Adolph Luque, they played against each other in Cincinnati and Alexander shut them out, 1-0. You know how long it took to play that game—58 minutes. Get the ball and play ball. That's why pro football has got the people. They give you action, they don't fool around, they just line up and play football, that's the way to do it, kiddo.

Emil (Irish) Meusel slams a home run for the Giants. The Yankee catcher is Wally Schang. This was the game at the Polo Grounds called "on account of darkness." Emil Meusel was the Giant leftfielder, his brother Bob the Yankee leftfielder. Bottom (l. to r.): Giant second baseman Frankie Frisch, Yankee third baseman Joe Dugan, Giant third baseman Heinie Groh.

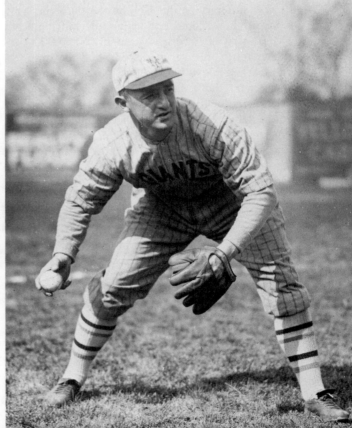

96

FIRST GAME (Oct. 4, at Polo Grounds)

YANKEES	000 001 100	2	7	0
GIANTS	000 000 03x	3	11	3

Bush, Hoyt (8th)
Nehf, Ryan (8th)

SECOND GAME (Oct. 5, at Polo Grounds)

GIANTS	300 000 000 0	3	8	1
YANKEES	100 100 010 0	3	8	0

J. Barnes
Shawkey

THIRD GAME (Oct. 6, at Polo Grounds)

YANKEES	000 000 000	0	4	1
GIANTS	002 000 10x	3	12	1

Hoyt, Jones (8th)
J. Scott

FOURTH GAME (Oct. 7, at Polo Grounds)

GIANTS	000 040 000	4	9	1
YANKEES	200 000 100	3	8	0

McQuillan
Mays, Jones (9th)

FIFTH GAME (Oct. 8, at Polo Grounds)

YANKEES	100 010 100	3	5	0
GIANTS	020 000 03x	5	10	0

Bush
Nehf

NEW YORK YANKEES
NEW YORK GIANTS
1923

Casey the Comic Sends 'em Home

The first World Series game ever played at the new Yankee Stadium was won by the Giants in the ninth when their bandy-legged centerfielder, 33-year-old Casey Stengel, hit an inside-the-park home run. Casey came back two days later to hit another home run, this time over the head of Babe Ruth and into the rightfield seats for a 1-0 Giant triumph. That game was watched by 62,817 people crammed into the stadium, the biggest crowd to date, not only for a World Series but for any game of baseball.

This was the first "million-dollar Series," the total receipts coming to $1,063,815, with a record crowd of 301,430 watching the six games. But despite the two Stengel home runs and the troubles of the Yankees in their new stadium—they lost two of three at home—the Yankees won their first world championship, the first of 20 during the next 40 years. In the final game their graceful control artist, Herb Pennock, outpitched Art Nehf, long a Yankee killer. Nehf went into the eighth inning ahead, 4-1, then was driven from the mound by the big Yankee hitters. In this Series Babe Ruth refrained from chasing those curve balls that the Giant pitchers were throwing into the dust. He walked eight times. When he saw good pitches he whacked three home runs, two in a row in the second game, and batted .368. But the crowds went away talking about the caprices of Casey: his monkeyshine antics on the bases, his ribald gestures to the Yankee pitchers; and how he had slid home with his home run, then rose on one knee and waved to the crowd in a way that said, "That's it folks, the game's over, now you can go home." After the game he wisecracked to reporters, one of whom wrote, "Casey simply refuses to be serious."

Casey Stengel:
Out of the shoe came the cushion

Before an Oldtimers' Day game in Shea Stadium in 1971, Casey Stengel said: *What a lotta people forget about that inside-the-park home run was that I hit it between Bob Meusel and Whitey Witt, and that I ran home ahead of the best arm in baseball. Anyone will tell you that Bob Meusel could throw the ball farther than anyone who ever played this game. In fact he could throw it too hard and the ball on one bounce would skip by the catcher, unless that catcher was someone like Mr. Dickey here.* [He pointed to former Yankee catcher Bill Dickey.] *I was coming to third base and then I had this cushion in my shoe here* [he pointed to his heel] *half the foot was hurting me and I had this cushion to protect it, and when I'm running the cushion comes out of the shoe, and now the foot hurts when I'm running, and I am running against the best arm in baseball, so it showed you how speedy I was, how fast I could go around those bases, he threw it home and I had it beat, and the catcher that day was Wally Schang, and he. . . .*

Casey Stengel scores the winning run on his inside-the-park homer in the ninth inning of the first game. Casey later made a gesture at a Yankee pitcher "that shocked some people," a reporter wrote.

Above: Casey at the bat. At 33, he was near the end of his playing career. Two years earlier he had been a sub with the last-place Phils, "and what could be more humbling?" wrote one reporter. Above right: Babe Ruth is tagged out trying to score from third on a flyball. The Giant catcher is Frank (Pancho) Snyder. Right: Herb Pennock, winner of two games for the Yankees in this Series. In three World Series he won five games without a defeat. Opposite page: The Babe hook-slides away from a tag by the Giants' Heinie Groh for a triple in the first game.

100

FIRST GAME (Oct. 10, at Yankee Stadium)

GIANTS....................004 000 001   5   8 0
YANKEES..................120 000 100   4 12 1
Watson, Ryan (3d)
Hoyt, Bush (3d)

SECOND GAME (Oct. 11, at Polo Grounds)

YANKEES..................010 210 000   4 10 0
GIANTS....................010 001 000   2   9 2
Pennock
McQuillan, Bentley (4th)

THIRD GAME (Oct. 12, at Yankee Stadium)

GIANTS....................000 000 100   1   4 0
YANKEES..................000 000 000   0   6 1
Nehf
Jones, Bush (9th)

FOURTH GAME (Oct. 13, at Polo Grounds)

YANKEES..................061 100 000   8 13 1
GIANTS....................000 000 031   4 13 1
Shawkey, Pennock (8th)
J. Scott, Ryan (2d), McQuillan (2d), Jonnard (8th), V.
    Barnes (9th)

FIFTH GAME (Oct. 14, at Yankee Stadium)

GIANTS....................010 000 000   1   3 2
YANKEES..................340 100 00x   8 14 0
Bentley, J. Scott (2d), V. Barnes (4th), Jonnard (8th)
Bush

SIXTH GAME (Oct. 15, at Polo Grounds)

YANKEES..................100 000 050   6   5 0
GIANTS....................100 111 000   4 10 1
Pennock, Jones (8th)
Nehf, Ryan (8th)

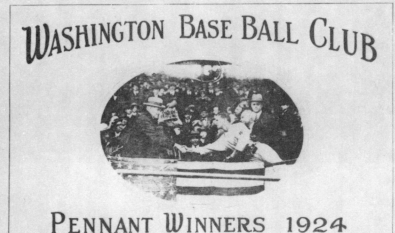

OFFICIAL SCORE CARD   Price 25 cents

WASHINGTON BASE BALL CLUB

PENNANT WINNERS 1924

WORLD SERIES 1924   WASHINGTON vs. NEW YORK

WASHINGTON SENATORS
NEW YORK GIANTS
1924

Sometimes a Ball
Will Take a Funny Bounce

Two bad-luck bounces, almost incredibly similar, cost the Giants the seventh game, climaxing what was probably the most exciting Series since the 1912 battle between the Giants and the Red Sox. In his first World Series game, the fastballing Walter (The Big Train) Johnson was clubbed for 14 hits by the Giants and lost, 4-3. He tried again in the fifth game and lost, 6-2, battered by 13 hits.

The plucky Senators, led by their "boy manager," 28-year-old second baseman Bucky Harris, rallied behind southpaw Tom Zachary, who won two games, and the Series came down to a seventh and final game in Washington. Watching were President Calvin Coolidge and his wife—she was a fan, he wasn't. By the eighth inning the Giants, ahead 3-1, seemed to have the game and the Series won. In the Senators' eighth, with runners on second and third, Bucky Harris tapped a bouncing ball right at 18-year-old Freddie Lindstrom, who was filling in at third base for the injured Heinie Groh. The ball bounced over Lindstrom's head, the two runners raced around to score, and the game was tied, 3-3.

Walter Johnson came in to pitch, and he held off the Giants through the top of the 12th. In the bottom of the 12th, Washington's Muddy Ruel hit a pop foul. Circling under the ball, Giant catcher Hank (Old Sarge) Gowdy stepped into his discarded mask and missed the ball. Given this second chance, Ruel doubled. Earl McNeely rapped another hopping ground ball at Lindstrom.

Again the ball, at the last moment, bounced perversely over his head, and Ruel scored with the run that won the game for The Big Train and the Series for the Senators. It was the last of nine World Series for John McGraw.

Ossie Bluege:
"...he...stuck it in his pocket..."

The whole strategy of that last game was in our starting Curly Ogden, said Ossie Bluege, the Senators' third baseman and shortstop. *McGraw's strategy was to get all his lefthand hitters against our righthand pitchers and vice versa. McGraw and our owner, Mr. [Clark] Griffith, were always at each other, you know, outflanking each other. But McGraw moved too quick. We started Ogden, a righthander, and he put in all his lefthanded hitters. And then we shot in George Mogridge [a lefthander], and that made McGraw switch again to all his righthand hitters. [Righthander Fred] Marberry then came in and McGraw had exhausted his entire bench. Then, about the ninth inning, when the shades of night were falling, we brought in The Big Train. So that was a pivotal piece of strategy right there ... Walter had tough going up to then against the Giants. In the 11th, I think it was, Frankie Frisch tripled, leading off with no one out. But Walter got the next three men in a row. He struck out Ross Youngs, he struck out George Kelly, and he got Bob*

103

Giant shortstop Travis Jackson comes
down to earth after missing a high
throw that is caught by Frankie Frisch,
Nemo Leibold sliding into second.
Right: Senator owner Clark Griffith
and his 28-year-old manager
Bucky Harris.

Below: Comedian Will Rogers grins in his folksy way at the second game. He is accompanied by Mrs. Edward McLean, the wife of a publisher. Bottom: An ad for a car given to Walter Johnson during the Series.

The Public Is Cordially Invited
to Inspect

Walter Johnson's Car

On Display at

1132 Connecticut Avenue

The gift from the Fans, selected by the
Walter Johnson Testimonial Committee.

105

FIRST GAME (Oct. 4, at Washington)

NEW YORK 010 100 000 002   4 14 1
WASHINGTON 000 001 001 001   3 10 1
Nehf
Johnson

SECOND GAME (Oct. 5, at Washington)

NEW YORK 000 000 102   3 6 0
WASHINGTON 200 010 001   4 6 1
Bentley
Zachary, Marberry (9th)

THIRD GAME (Oct. 6, at New York)

WASHINGTON 000 200 011   4 9 2
NEW YORK 021 101 01x   6 12 0
Marberry, Russell (4th), Martina (7th), Speece (8th)
McQuillan, Ryan (4th), Jonnard (9th), Watson (9th)

FOURTH GAME (Oct. 7, at New York)

WASHINGTON 003 020 020   7 13 3
NEW YORK 100 001 011   4 6 1
Mogridge, Marberry (8th)
V. Barnes, Baldwin (6th), Dean (8th)

FIFTH GAME (Oct. 8, at New York)

WASHINGTON 000 100 010   2 9 1
NEW YORK 001 020 03x   6 13 0
Johnson
Bentley, McQuillan (8th)

SIXTH GAME (Oct. 9, at Washington)

NEW YORK 100 000 000   1 7 1
WASHINGTON 000 020 00x   2 4 0
Nehf, Ryan (8th)
Zachary

SEVENTH GAME (Oct. 10, at Washington)

NEW YORK 000 003 000 000   3 8 3
WASHINGTON 000 100 020 001   4 10 4
V. Barnes, Nehf (8th), McQuillan (9th), Bentley (11th)
Ogden, Mogridge (1st), Marberry (6th), Johnson (9th)

Meusel I guess on a popout. Then in the 12th we scored by a lucky bounder. The ball that went over Lindstrom's head earlier, it should have been fielded. In the 12th we had Muddy Ruel on second and he wasn't too fast as most catchers are. Earl's grounder over Lindstrom, it wasn't hit very hard. [Irish] Meusel picked up the ball, he had a great arm and with Muddy running . . . but he just picked up the ball and stuck it in his pocket, walked off the field and Muddy scored. He didn't have a chance maybe, Muddy was almost in, but the guy could drop dead between third and home. Meusel should have picked up the ball and thrown, that's your last shot if you don't get him. But he walked off the field with the ball in his pocket, and that was that, the end of the Series.

Opposite page: It is the end of the affair as Ruel scores the winning run in the 12th inning of the seventh game. John McGraw, in street clothes, puts on his hat as he leads the losing Giants out of their dugout. The catcher, still waiting for the throw that never came, is Hank Gowdy. Below: Bucky Harris slams into third base ahead of a throw to luckless Lindstrom.

Washington
Baseball Club
1925

Bucky Harris — Bill McKee c

World Championship Series
Washington vs Pittsburgh

Published by National Print Co.

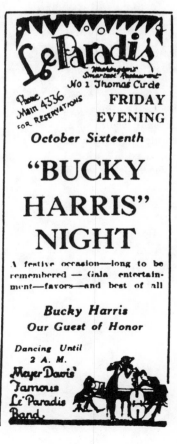

Le Paradis
Washington's Smartest Restaurant
No 1 Thomas Circle

Phone Main 4336 for Reservations

FRIDAY EVENING

October Sixteenth

"BUCKY HARRIS" NIGHT

A festive occasion—long to be remembered — Gala entertainment—favors—and best of all

Bucky Harris
Our Guest of Honor

Dancing Until 2 A.M.

Mayer Davis' Famous Le Paradis Band.

PITTSBURGH PIRATES
WASHINGTON SENATORS
1925

Sam Told It the Way It Was

For the first time in the history of a seven-game World Series, a team came back to win the championship after being down three games to one. The Pirates, in fact, were never ahead in this Series until the eighth inning of the final game. Then they smashed across three runs against the great Walter Johnson on a muddy, fog-bound field, The Big Train betrayed by the slickness of the rain-spattered ball and by the fielding lapses of shortstop Roger Peckinpaugh.

The third game of the Series was enlivened by controversy when Washington centerfielder Sam Rice leaped into the seats in right centerfield while chasing a drive, disappeared for several moments, then came up clutching the ball. The umpires ruled he'd caught the ball; the Pirates screamed, "It's a homer," claiming that Rice had picked up the ball in the seats. The catch saved the game, Washington winning, 4-3, to take a two-game to one-game lead in the Series. The next day Judge Landis asked Rice if he had caught the ball. "The umpire said I did," Sam answered truthfully, and Landis said, "That's a good answer, Sam."

Despite the Pirate rally after being down three games to one, Pittsburgh's hopes seemed dashed in the seventh game when the Senators scored four runs in the first inning and took the field behind Johnson's fastballs. But Johnson could not grip the wet ball properly, and he was slipping on the muddy mound. Behind him Peckinpaugh made two costly muffs—he made eight errors on 40 chances, a Series record—and in the eighth the Pirates tied the score, 7-7, filling the bases with two out. Young outfielder Kiki Cuyler slapped a double past the first baseman, two runs scored, and Pittsburgh had the lead, 9-7, and a few minutes later, the world championship.

Pirate fans applauded the veteran Stuffy McInnis, the old A's first baseman, who took over at first when the Pirates trailed, three games to

one, and who hit .286 to spark the comeback. The two teams hit a dozen homers, a Series record up to then, which may have amazed 43-year-old Babe Adams, the Pittsburgh pitching hero of the 1909 Series, who was still with the team. There had been only four in the 1909 Series.

Pie Traynor:
And after that, he was home free

Pie Traynor, the former Pirate third baseman, was reminiscing about this Series at his home in Pittsburgh. *A lot of people,* he said, *criticized Bucky Harris for leaving Walter Johnson in so long in that last game, but Harris said he was the best pitcher he had and it wasn't his fault anyway. Peckinpaugh, he was a great shortstop but he was all bandaged up, his legs were bothering him. He dropped a couple of balls. Still after we tied the game six to six, Peckinpaugh came up in the eighth—he was having the bad time—and he hit a home run to make it seven to six. We got just one run off Johnson in the first two games . . . one run in 18 innings. We were due. Remember, we won the last three games, the first time that it had ever been done. We were just in a groove then and we thought we could beat any club 10 straight. We were never down at all, we had the confidence. It was just like this Pittsburgh team [of 1971], it lost the first two games and they came back and said they could win and they did.*

I was nervous but after you get the first chance, it's just another ball game. My first chance was a tough chance. It was in the first inning of the first game. It was a topped ball. Bucky Harris was running. I went halfway to the plate on the line. I got a hold of it, I threw him out and I was home free after that.

Honus Wagner, Bill McKechnie, John McGraw, Walter Johnson, Babe Ruth, Nick Altrock, and writer Christy Walsh line up before the second game to honor Christy Mathewson, who had died a day earlier. Harris was criticized for staying with Johnson so long in the final game, but loyal fans honored the manager.

Three of the Series stars: Walter Johnson pitching in the first game, which he won; Pittsburgh third baseman Pie Traynor warming up; Washington's Goose Goslin rapping a fly to center. The Goose hit three homers, but the Washington star was Sam Rice, who collected 12 hits and made the controversial catch by diving into the stands. In 1972 Rice said he would disclose in his will, to be opened after his death, whether he caught the ball or not.

FIRST GAME (Oct. 7, at Pittsburgh)

WASHINGTON..............010 020 001 4 8 1
PITTSBURGH...............000 010 000 1 5 0

Johnson
Meadows, Morrison (9th)

SECOND GAME (Oct. 8, at Pittsburgh)

WASHINGTON..............010 000 001 2 8 2
PITTSBURGH...............000 100 02x 3 7 0

Coveleski
Aldridge

THIRD GAME (Oct. 10, at Washington)

PITTSBURGH..............010 101 000 3 8 3
WASHINGTON.............001 001 20x 4 10 1

Kremer
Ferguson, Marberry (8th)

FOURTH GAME (Oct. 11, at Washington)

PITTSBURGH...............000 000 000 0 6 1
WASHINGTON.............004 000 00x 4 12 0

Yde, Morrison (3d), Adams (8th)
Johnson

FIFTH GAME (Oct. 12, at Washington)

PITTSBURGH................002 000 211 6 13 0
WASHINGTON.............100 100 100 3 8 1

Aldridge
Coveleski, Ballou (7th), Zachary (8th), Marberry (9th)

SIXTH GAME (Oct. 13, at Pittsburgh)

WASHINGTON..............110 000 000 2 6 2
PITTSBURGH...............002 010 00x 3 7 1

Ferguson, Ballou (8th)
Kremer

SEVENTH GAME (Oct. 15, at Pittsburgh)

WASHINGTON.............400 200 010 7 7 2
PITTSBURGH...............003 010 23x 9 15 2

Johnson
Aldridge, Morrison (1st), Kremer (5th), Oldham (9th)

Alex Comes in To Put Out the Fire

In perhaps the most dramatic moment of World Series history, 39-year-old Grover Cleveland (Old Pete) Alexander strode in from the bullpen in the seventh inning of the seventh game. The Cardinals led, 3-2, but the Yankees were threatening to win the game and the Series, with the bases loaded and two out. At bat stood Tony Lazzeri, second only to Babe Ruth that season on the Yankee roster in runs-batted-in. The day before, Old Pete had stopped the Yankees, 10-2, and that night, as was his custom, he had celebrated his second victory of the Series with some heavy drinking.

Now he was being called on by Cardinal manager Rogers Hornsby to stop this Yankee attempt to wrest the game and the Series away from St. Louis. Hornsby met Alexander near the shortstop position and looked into his eyes, trying to determine how clearly Old Pete could see after his night of celebrating. Satisfied, Hornsby handed the ball to Alexander. After warming up he threw a ball, then a strike to Lazzeri. On the next pitch Lazzeri lined a foul down the leftfield line, the count now one ball and two strikes. Alex threw again, and Lazzeri swung and missed, striking out to end the inning and the threat.

Alexander put down the Yankees in the eighth. In the ninth, with two out, Ruth walked. In what Yankee executive Ed Barrow later called "Ruth's only dumb play of his life," the Babe tried to steal second and was thrown out, ending the game and the Series.

Babe again had been the hitting hero of the Series for the Yankees. He clubbed four home runs, three of them in the fourth game, one of them the longest home run seen up to that time in St. Louis' Sportsman's Park.

Pop Haines:
"Aleck was always calm..."

Jesse (Pop) Haines was the Cardinals' starting pitcher in the seventh game. At his home in Phillipsburg, Ohio, he recalled how he felt when he was relieved by Alexander in the seventh inning with the bases loaded. *I had a blister on my finger and after I walked a man to fill the bases, Hornsby came over and looked at the finger and saw how it was. He said, 'Well, I guess I'll have to relieve you.' I don't know whether he mentioned Aleck's name or not. I just went on into the clubhouse to have my finger taken care of, and I heard the rest of the game on the radio.*

I felt pretty good when I heard he struck out Lazzeri. After the game I talked to him. He looked all right to me. I always say: He pitched two good innings, didn't he, and he couldn't be drunk if he pitched two good innings. I got to give the old fellow credit. Aleck was always calm, no matter what the game was. He was never jubilant, that's the way he was. I would never say a word against him. A man comes out and pitches two and one-third innings and then they accuse him of being drunk. I would never do that because he couldn't do that, pitch like that, if he was drunk.

In St. Louis Babe Ruth (lower r.) poses with children in front of a window decorated by one of his home runs.

FIRST GAME (Oct. 2, at New York)

ST. LOUIS 100 000 000   1 3 1
NEW YORK 100 001 00x   2 6 0
Sherdel, Haines (8th)
Pennock

SECOND GAME (Oct. 3, at New York)

ST. LOUIS 002 000 301   6 12 1
NEW YORK 020 000 000   2 4 0
Alexander
Shocker, Shawkey (8th), Jones (9th)

THIRD GAME (Oct. 5, at St. Louis)

NEW YORK 000 000 000   0 5 1
ST. LOUIS 000 310 00x   4 8 0
Ruether, Shawkey (5th), Thomas (8th)
Haines

FOURTH GAME (Oct. 6, at St. Louis)

NEW YORK 101 142 100   10 14 1
ST. LOUIS 100 300 001   5 14 0
Hoyt
Rhem, Reinhart (5th), H. Bell (5th), Hallahan (7th),
   Keen (9th)

FIFTH GAME (Oct. 7, at St. Louis)

NEW YORK 000 001 001 1   3 9 1
ST. LOUIS 000 100 100 0   2 7 1
Pennock
Sherdel

SIXTH GAME (Oct. 9, at New York)

ST. LOUIS 300 010 501   10 13 2
NEW YORK 000 100 100   2 8 1
Alexander
Shawkey, Shocker (7th), Thomas (8th)

SEVENTH GAME (Oct. 10, at New York)

ST. LOUIS 000 300 000   3 8 0
NEW YORK 001 001 000   2 8 3
Haines, Alexander (7th)
Hoyt, Pennock (7th)

Grover Cleveland
Alexander warms up at
the stadium during
the Series. "Poosh 'em
Up" Tony, as the fans
called Lazzeri, is struck
out by Old Pete. The
catcher is Bob
O'Farrell.

114

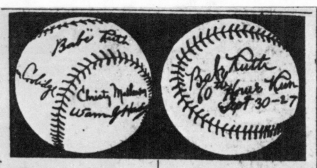

BABE KNICKERBOCKER

NEW YORK YANKEES
PITTSBURGH PIRATES
1927

The Antidote for Poison
Was a Dose of Pitching

With 20 million people listening on their radios to the first coast-to-coast broadcast of the World Series—Graham McNamee reporting on NBC and J. Andrew White on CBS—the overpowering Yankee machine, which had won the pennant by 19 games, crushed the Pirates in four games. The Bronx Bombers and their Murderers' Row—Babe Ruth, Lou Gehrig, Bob Meusel, and Tony Lazzeri —had come to full stature, and they were supported by a tight-fisted pitching staff: Herb Pennock, Waite Hoyt, George Pipgras, and Wilcy Moore. This was the year that Babe Ruth hit 60 home runs, a feat that can best be measured when one realizes that no other *team* in the American League hit 60 home runs that year.

The Pirates had won the pennant with the steady hitting of Paul (Big Poison) Waner, and Lloyd (Little Poison) Waner, and Kiki Cuyler. But Cuyler, feuding with manager Donie Bush, did not play in the Series, despite the chanting of Forbes Field crowds, "We want Cuyler, we want Cuyler." The Waners outhit Ruth and Gehrig, 11 hits to 10, and the Murderers' Row boomed out only two homers, both by Ruth. But steady Yankee pitching limited the Pirates to only 10 runs in the four games.

The fourth game was the most exciting. With the score tied going into the bottom of the ninth, the Yankees filled the bases with nobody out. Pirate reliever John Miljus courageously struck out Gehrig and Meusel but threw an outside pitch to the next batter, Tony Lazzeri, which flew by catcher Johnny Gooch. Earle Combs sped home from third with the run that ended the game and the Series.

The players split up the biggest player pool up to that time; $5,592 to each Yankee, $3,728 to each Pirate. The day after the Series ended, Gehrig and Ruth showed up on a Bronx school field to play an exhibition game.

Lloyd Waner:
There is always one like Koenig

Lloyd Waner said in Florida: *I had a good Series. I hit .400 and my brother hit .333—I still remember the exact figures. The Yankees had a good ball club. But it's funny, Mark Koenig, he was the weakest hitter on their ball club and we couldn't get him out.* [Koenig led the Yankees with nine hits in 18 at-bats.] *Babe Ruth hit a couple of home runs but Lou Gehrig and the rest, they didn't get that many hits. If we could have kept Koenig off the bases. . . . but that always happens in a Series, someone like Koenig will come along and hit like hell. Still, the Yankees were great and if you made a mistake they beat you. In the first game there was a double play ball that went right through our second baseman's legs and they scored a bunch of runs and beat us, 5-4. There was only one game—the one Herb Pennock won—that they beat us bad and he was quite a pitcher.*

Earle Combs touches home plate with the winning run for the Yankees in the final game. Pitcher John Miljus watches his catcher run down his wild pitch. Above: The name of the Babe dominates the game and the World Series.

The 1927 World Champion Yankees:
Front row (l. to r.): Julie Wera, Mike
Gazella, Pat Collins, mascot Eddie
Bennett, Benny Bengough, Walter
Beall, unknown, Cedric Durst.
Middle row: Urban Shocker, Joe
Dugan, Earle Combs, coach Charlie
O'Leary, manager Miller Huggins,
coach Art Fletcher, Mark Koenig,
Dutch Ruether, Johnny Grabowski,
George Pipgras. Back row: Lou
Gehrig, Herb Pennock, Tony Lazzeri,
Wilcy Moore, Babe Ruth, Ray Morehart,
Bob Meusel, Bob Shawkey, Waite Hoyt,
Joe Giard, Ben Paschal, Myles Thomas,
and trainer Doc Woods.

FIRST GAME (Oct. 5, at Pittsburgh)

NEW YORK	103 010 000	5	6	1
PITTSBURGH	101 010 010	4	9	2

Hoyt, Moore (8th)
Kremer, Miljus (6th)

SECOND GAME (Oct. 6, at Pittsburgh)

NEW YORK	003 000 030	6	11	0
PITTSBURGH	100 000 010	2	7	2

Pipgras
Aldridge, Cvengros (8th), Dawson (9th)

THIRD GAME (Oct. 7, at New York)

PITTSBURGH	000 000 010	1	3	1
NEW YORK	200 000 60x	8	9	0

Meadows, Cvengros (7th)
Pennock

FOURTH GAME (Oct. 8, at New York)

PITTSBURGH	100 000 200	3	10	1
NEW YORK	100 020 001	4	12	2

Hill, Miljus (7th)
Moore

NEW YORK YANKEES
ST. LOUIS CARDINALS
1928

Bill's Mistake:
He Pitched To the Babe

The Yankees won their eighth World Series game in a row as they trimmed the Cardinals in four straight, surprising even their followers, for the Yankees had limped into the Series. Herb Pennock's arm was lame and he never pitched. Lazzeri also had a sore arm and had to be replaced late in each game by a brash young rookie, Leo Durocher. The Babe was slowed down by aching legs.

Perhaps thinking that Ruth's hitting would suffer because of his injuries, Cardinal manager Bill McKechnie told his pitchers to pitch to Ruth rather than walk him, as the Cardinals of 1926 had done when they gave him 11 bases on balls. Ruth hit three home runs in the fourth game and collected 10 hits in 16 at-bats for a .625 average, still an all-time Series high some 45 years later.

Lou Gehrig hit four homers and batted .545, while the Yankees' Waite Hoyt won two games to collect his sixth Series triumph. The Yankees' pitching splintered the Cardinal bats, St. Louis hitting at only a .206 average. After the Series the infuriated Cardinal owner, Sam Breadon, fired Bill McKechnie, a move he later termed the worst mistake of his life.

Al Schacht:
The way Babe Ruth's shoulders would shake when he laughed

Al Schacht, once the Clown Prince of Baseball, performed with his partner, Nick Altrock, at 27 World Series games from 1921 to 1951, entertaining fans before the games with pantomime stunts. Schacht, a former Senator pitcher, would wind up in slow motion, then pretend to throw to Altrock, who would swing in comical slow motion. Looking back four decades to the 1928 Series, Schacht said: *I remember Ruth in that Series, he was watching us, and he had a way of laughing that made his shoulders shake. He would be making a million, six hundred thousand dollars a year if he was playing today because he filled the parks wherever he went. He looked better striking out than most guys look hitting a home run. People used to love to watch him swing and they yelled as loud when he struck out as when he hit a home run. I remember before one Series game, I don't know what year it was, I saw him eat 10 frankfurters after taking batting practice. He could do everything an ordinary guy couldn't do.*

Yankees politick for Presidential candidate Al Smith, led by the bat boy and Babe Ruth. Third from the end of the line is Lou Gehrig. And in an ad a pre-TV sponsor tries to get sight as well as sound into the Series broadcasts.

FIRST GAME (Oct. 4, at New York)

ST. LOUIS 000 000 100   1 3 1
NEW YORK 100 200 01x   4 7 0
Sherdel, Johnson (8th)
Hoyt

SECOND GAME (Oct. 5, at New York)

ST. LOUIS 030 000 000   3 4 1
NEW YORK 314 000 10x   9 8 2
Alexander, Mitchell (3d)
Pipgras

THIRD GAME (Oct. 7, at St. Louis)

NEW YORK 010 203 100   7 7 2
ST. LOUIS 200 010 000   3 9 3
Zachary
Haines, Johnson (7th), Rhem (8th)

FOURTH GAME (Oct. 9, at St. Louis)

NEW YORK 000 100 420   7 15 2
ST. LOUIS 001 100 001   3 11 0
Hoyt
Sherdel, Alexander (7th)

The crowd (top) deluges the field with hats to salute the Babe as he trots across home after his third homer—"a hat trick"—in the fourth game. He is congratulated by Lou Gehrig, with whom he poses (r.).

WRIGLEY FIELD BLUES

New words set to old music.
(Slow—with feeling.)

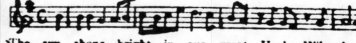

The sun shone bright in our great Hack Wilson's eyes— 'Tis Sunday, the Mack men are gay—

The third game's won, and Cub pitching's gone astray-- As our series title fades far away.

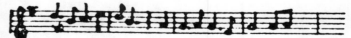

Weep no more, Dear Cub fan. Oh, weep no more today; for we'll

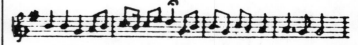

Sing one song for the game and fighting Cubs. For the record whiffing Cubs far away.

PHILADELPHIA ATHLETICS ──── 1929
CHICAGO CUBS

Ehmke Was the First Surprise;
That Seventh Inning, the Second

"Stocks trended sharply upward (yesterday) with gains of 5 to more than 10 points established in the leaders . . . ." said the *New York Times* as the 1929 World Series opened.

It opened with a surprise. Connie Mack sent 35-year-old Howard Ehmke to the mound to face the Cubs, with the Cub fans murmuring astonishment. Ehmke had pitched only 55 innings all season and had won only seven games. But Mack figured that the Cubs, with power hitters like Rogers Hornsby, Kiki Cuyler, and Hack Wilson, would blast a speed pitcher like the A's ace, Lefty Grove. He thought Ehmke's slow stuff might throw the Cubs off-balance. He was right. Ehmke weathered a Cub rally in the ninth to win, 3-1, striking out 13, a record that stood for 24 years.

Mack had built a high-scoring club to enter his first Series since 1914. He had assembled power hitters like Jimmy Foxx ("the righthanded Babe Ruth"), Al Simmons, Mickey Cochrane, Mule Haas, and Jimmy Dykes. His pitching staff was bolstered by Grove and George Earnshaw. The A's won the second game but lost the third. In the fourth the Cubs seemed certain to tie the Series at two games apiece, leading 8-0 behind Charley Root as the A's came to bat in the seventh inning. The A's crashed 10 runs across the plate, still a World Series mark for one inning. The Cubs did not quit, going into the bottom of the ninth of the fifth game leading, 2-0. Again the A's exploded, this time scoring three runs and winning the championship, Connie Mack's fourth.

"The stocks of almost every group were driven downward, the selling movement gaining momentum as the day wore on . . . ." said the *New York Times* three days after the end of the Series.

Lefty Grove:
"Yup"

Robert Moses (Lefty) Grove, at his home in Norwalk, Ohio, discussed the Series in which he, a 20-game winner that season and almost every other season, did not start a game. Instead he came in from the bullpen to relieve in two games. *I don't know what Mr. Mack's thinking was in doing that. That was his decision. Yup. I just went in, that's all, it was my duty. Yup. I relieved in that game in which we scored the 10 runs. I had seen that before. Once we scored 14 runs in one inning in a game against Cleveland. Naturally we were tickled when we scored the 10 runs, we knew we had them beat then. I pitched the same against Chicago as I did during the regular season. The hitters, they all look the same. Yup.*

Connie Mack was the greatest manager in the world. He never came into the clubhouse, hardly ever. Yup. After a game he went on up to his office. Sometimes we'd have a meeting in the clubhouse and he'd go over the hitters, that was the only time we ever saw him, except in the dugout during the game. Yup. Greatest manager in the world. Yup.

To the tune of "My Old Kentucky Home," Cub fans sang this dirge. The hitting of the Cubs' Hack Wilson (l.) and Rogers Hornsby was stifled by the A's pitching (top, l. to r.): Rube Walberg, Lefty Grove, and George Earnshaw. Rogers Hornsby struck out eight times.

FIRST GAME (Oct. 8, at Chicago)

PHILADELPHIA 000 000 102   3 6 1
CHICAGO 000 000 001   1 8 2
Ehmke
Root, Bush (8th)

SECOND GAME (Oct. 9, at Chicago)

PHILADELPHIA 003 300 120   9 12 0
CHICAGO 000 030 000   3 11 1
Earnshaw, Grove (5th)
Malone, Blake (4th), Carlson (6th), Nehf (9th)

THIRD GAME (Oct. 11, at Philadelphia)

CHICAGO 000 003 000   3 6 1
PHILADELPHIA 000 010 000   1 9 1
Bush
Earnshaw

FOURTH GAME (Oct. 12, at Philadelphia)

CHICAGO 000 205 1 00   8 10 2
PHILADELPHIA 000 000 10 0x   10 15 2
Root, Nehf (7th), Blake (7th), Malone (7th), Carlson
     (8th)
Quinn, Walberg (6th), Rommel (7th), Grove (8th)

FIFTH GAME (Oct. 14, at Philadelphia)

CHICAGO 000 200 000   2 8 1
PHILADELPHIA 000 000 003   3 6 0
Malone
Ehmke, Walberg (4th)

Fans—and at least four photographers
—cram bleachers erected on roofs
behind Philadelphia's Shibe Park by
some enterprising individual. Others
watch from windows. The lineup is
for the third game, won 3–1 by the
Cubs. No one in that game won the
$500. Bleachers had been built on the
roofs as early as 1910. Bottom: Mickey
Cochrane pats Al Simmons after both
scored what proved to be the winning
runs in the ninth inning of the first
game, won 3–1 by the A's. Both
came home on a single by Bing Miller.

126

$500. To the Player that Hits this Sign with a Fairly Batted Ball
CHEVROLET VOICE MOTOR CO.

BE A GOOD SPORTSMAN DON'T THROW CUSHIONS OR PAPER

PHILADELPHIA ATHLETICS
ST. LOUIS CARDINALS
1930

For Some People
Herbert Hoover Was Good Luck

Although far from being the most popular man in the United States as the depression deepened, President Herbert Hoover was greeted enthusiastically by Connie Mack and the A's when he arrived for the first game. Hoover had watched the A's in three games in 1929 and 1930, and the A's had won all three times. A superstitious man who believed in all sorts of good omens and bad omens, Connie Mack told the president, "I'm glad to see you here because we always win with you." Connie was so glad to see the president that he went over to shake his hand. He rarely left the dugout before a game—he considered it bad luck.

Hoover continued to be good luck for the A's as they won the first game behind Lefty Grove. Mack's other ace, George Earnshaw, won the second game. But then Wild Bill Hallahan and Jesse (Pop) Haines won successive games for the Cardinals to tie the Series at two games apiece. In the fifth game Earnshaw and spitballer Burleigh Grimes started, and neither gave up a run through the first seven innings. Lefty Grove relieved Earnshaw in the eighth, and the 0-0 deadlock continued into the ninth. In the ninth Grimes walked Mickey Cochrane, and with one out, Jimmy Foxx stepped to the plate. He hit a home run into the left centerfield seats. Grove blanked the Cardinals in the bottom of the ninth and the A's were 2-0 winners. Two days later George Earnshaw beat the Cardinals with a five-hitter for a 7-1 triumph, and a proud Mack strode off the field with a record fifth world championship.

The Cardinals could find some solace even in defeat. During the Series film star Buster Keaton

had entertained them at a dinner he gave for the entire team. And Frankie Frisch knocked out his 48th Series hit—a record.

Chick Hafey:
"...my heart nearly stopped..."

Chick Hafey* was the National League batting champion in 1931 with a .349 average, and he had a career average of .317. Yet he hit only .205 in four World Series, but managed to set a record in the 1930 Series by hitting five doubles. *I never hit worth a darn in the Series,* said Chick, *not for average. I don't know why, you're a little tight, and they bear down on you, too. It's a funny thing, I remember way back in 1926 we had this Tommy Thevenow at shortstop. I don't think he hit .240 for the season. He gets in the World Series and they couldn't get him out. The pitchers just don't bear down on them or something. They bear down on the better hitters. They sort of relax against the lesser fellows. I remember old Burleigh Grimes, he'd say he hated like hell to see a .250 hitter get a hit off him. In a Series the pitchers don't give the good hitters anything good. I remember before that '30 Series we'd go over the A's hitters in the clubhouse and they'd say they'd rather walk someone like [Al] Simmons than let him get a hit off you.*

Ruth. They'd rather give him a walk than let him get a hold of one. Oh boy, do you remember that 1926 Series when he tried to steal second and was thrown out in the last of the ninth. Oh, boy, was I relieved out there [in leftfield]. Big Meusel

*He died, at 70, in the summer of 1973.

Al Simmons outruns a throw to Cardinal first baseman Jim Bottomley. Simmons was one of three A's interviewed after the final game by a radio interviewer—the first broadcast from a Series clubhouse.

was hitting when Ruth tried to steal and he could hit to leftfield a lot, and that was a tough field. I couldn't see nothing from out there, that was the worst sunfield I ever played in, that Yankee ball park.

That drive that Lazzeri hit foul off old Aleck, my heart nearly stopped. It went into the stands foul by a good 20 or 30 feet, but boy it looked bad when it started out, though it kept hooking away from me, oh boy. I was surprised Hornsby brought old Aleck in, but as Hornsby said, he knew he wouldn't walk anybody. He was always on the corners, even in batting practice, the inside corner, the outside corner, he never gave you anything good to hit at. . . .

I never really had a good Series. But I hit that Lefty Grove a couple of times [in 1930]. Boy, was he fast. I was a dead pull hitter to left, but he made me hit to right a few times, and I guess that's how I got those doubles, but I really don't remember them. . . .

A's Mickey Cochrane drills a home run in the second game. Middle: The A's Jimmy Foxx swings high and cracks a single. Bottom: President Hoover autographs a ball for Cardinal manager Gabby Street. Said the Cardinals' Jimmy Wilson of the A's pitching: "Those boys sent them too fast for us to hit." The Cards hit .200, the A's only .197, lowest for a winner since the Red Sox' .186 in 1918.

FIRST GAME (Oct. 1, at Philadelphia)

ST. LOUIS .002 000 000   2 9 0
PHILADELPHIA 010 101 11x   5 5 0
Grimes
Grove

SECOND GAME (Oct. 2, at Philadelphia)

ST. LOUIS .010 000 000   1 6 2
PHILADELPHIA 202 200 00x   6 7 2
Rhem, Lindsey (4th), Johnson (7th)
Earnshaw

THIRD GAME (Oct. 4, at St. Louis)

PHILADELPHIA 000 000 000   0   7 0
ST. LOUIS .000 110 21x   5 10 0
Walberg, Shores (5th), Quinn (7th)
Hallahan

FOURTH GAME (Oct. 5, at St. Louis)

PHILADELPHIA 100 000 000   1 4 1
ST. LOUIS .001 200 00x   3 5 1
Grove
Haines

FIFTH GAME (Oct. 6, at St. Louis)

PHILADELPHIA 000 000 002   2 5 0
ST. LOUIS .000 000 000   0 3 1
Earnshaw, Grove (8th)
Grimes

SIXTH GAME (Oct. 8, at Philadelphia)

ST. LOUIS .000 000 001   1 5 1
PHILADELPHIA 201 211 00x   7 7 0
Hallahan, Johnson (3d), Lindsey (6th), Bell (8th)
Earnshaw

131

ST. LOUIS CARDINALS
PHILADELPHIA ATHLETICS
1931

The Wild Horse Drives Mickey Wild

"We can sure use the money," Mickey Cochrane was saying, "and we want the record."

Mickey and some of the other A's needed the money after losing much of their previous Series winnings in the stock market collapse. And the proud A's wanted to set a record that had eluded the other great teams of the century—the Giants, Red Sox, White Sox, and Yankees, none of which had ever won three Series in a row.

The A's were stopped one game short of that record, mainly by the spectacular performances of a rookie centerfielder, John (Pepper) Martin, forever known after that Series as the Wild Horse of the Osage. Few World Series, before or since, have been so dominated by one man as this Series was dominated by Martin. That spring he'd come out of the West riding the rails like a hobo to report to the Cardinal camp. Hawk-nosed and bandy-legged, "he had the shoulders of a piano-carrier, a sprinter's speed, a fullback's fight," wrote one reporter. In the Series he stole five bases, one short of the record, knocked out 12 hits in 24 at-bats for a .500 average, scored five runs, and drove in five. During one game Connie Mack asked George Earnshaw, "What's he hitting, George?" and Earnshaw muttered, "Everything I throw up to him."

The A's won the first game despite Pepper's three hits, Grove beating Paul Derringer, 6-2. In the second game Pepper singled and doubled to score both runs in the Cardinals' 2-0 triumph. In the third game he again singled and doubled to score two runs in the 5-2 St. Louis victory. He doubled and singled and stole a base in the fourth game, but the Cardinals lost, 3-0. Slashing three

hits, including a home run, Pepper batted in four of the runs for the Cardinals' 5-1 victory in the fifth game.

The A's stopped Pepper in the sixth game, the Cardinals losing, 8-1. He walked and stole a base in the seventh game that the A's came close to winning in a heartthumper of a finish. Losing 4-0, the Athletics scored twice and loaded the bases with two out in the top of the ninth. But Wild Bill Hallahan, winner of two previous games, saved the game in relief for St. Louis by inducing Max Bishop to hit a high pop foul that first baseman Jim Bottomley caught near the box seats.

Pepper Martin:
"You country — — — —"

In a conversation published in 1959 in *True* magazine, Pepper Martin told W. C. Heinz: *When I come up in that third game, Grove said to me, 'You country — — — —, I'm gonna throw this right through your head.' I said: 'You country — — — —, you do that.' Cochrane had to laugh and I hit the pitch out to the scoreboard in right center. You know, they blamed Cochrane for my stealing, but that wasn't right. It wasn't a question of me studyin' the motion of the pitchers, either. I guess it was the subconscious brain that told me to go. I only got the steal sign once in that Series but you steal in the first ten steps, and I always knew I had the base stole about the time I got under way. Really, I felt sorry for Cochrane. Once he said to me, 'Don't you ever make an out?'*

Jim Bottomley is out at first, Jimmy Foxx taking the throw. Then—and until the 1940s—there were other autumn baseball games besides the Series. The White Sox played the Cubs in a City Series; in the fall of 1931 Babe Ruth played for a Fort Lee, N.J., team, Lou Gehrig for the opposing team—West New York, N.J.

133

Pepper Martin, the Wild
Horse of the Osage,
slides home in the third
game. The A's catcher
is Mickey Cochrane.

FIRST GAME (Oct. 1, at St. Louis)

PHILADELPHIA.............004 000 200 6 11 0
ST. LOUIS................200 000 000 2 12 0
Grove
Derringer, Johnson (8th)

SECOND GAME (Oct. 2, at St. Louis)

PHILADELPHIA.............000 000 000 0 3 0
ST. LOUIS................010 000 10x 2 6 1
Earnshaw
Hallahan

THIRD GAME (Oct. 5, at Philadelphia)

ST. LOUIS................020 200 001 5 12 0
PHILADELPHIA.............000 000 002 2 2 0
Grimes
Grove, Mahaffey (9th)

FOURTH GAME (Oct. 6, at Philadelphia)

ST. LOUIS................000 000 000 0 2 1
PHILADELPHIA.............100 002 00x 3 10 0
Johnson, Lindsey (6th), Derringer (8th)
Earnshaw

FIFTH GAME (Oct. 7, at Philadelphia)

ST. LOUIS................100 002 011 5 12 0
PHILADELPHIA.............000 000 100 1 9 0
Hallahan
Hoyt, Walberg (7th), Rommel (9th)

SIXTH GAME (Oct. 9, at St. Louis)

PHILADELPHIA.............000 040 400 8 8 1
ST. LOUIS................000 001 000 1 5 2
Grove
Derringer, Johnson (5th), Lindsey (7th), Rhem (9th)

SEVENTH GAME (Oct. 10, at St. Louis)

PHILADELPHIA.............000 000 002 2 7 1
ST. LOUIS................202 000 00x 4 5 0
Earnshaw, Walberg (8th)
Grimes, Hallahan (9th)

BASES LOADED, IT'S TIME TO DO SOMETHING

NEW YORK YANKEES
CHICAGO CUBS
1932

The Babe Calls His Last Shot

In this last Series appearance of the remnants of Murderers' Row—Gehrig, Lazzeri and Ruth together for the last time—it was Lou Gehrig who dominated the Series statistically as the Yankees rolled over the Cubs in four straight. Larrupin' Lou hit .529, rapping nine hits in four games, three of them home runs. But, characteristically, it was Babe Ruth who provided this Series with its melodrama, standing at home plate and pointing a finger toward the centerfield wall, a moment that is probably the most discussed incident in World Series history.

It happened in the fifth inning of the third game. During the first two games the Cub players had insulted Ruth's ancestry while he laughed and called them cheapskates because the Cubs had voted only a half-share of their Series winnings to ex-Yankee shortstop Mark Koenig, traded to Chicago in the last part of the season. Before the third game, the first in Chicago, Cub fans had pelted Ruth with lemons and he had good-naturedly thrown them back.

When he came to bat against Charley Root in the fifth, after homering earlier, he heard the yapping of the Cub bench and saw a lemon roll toward him. Grinning, he snapped words at the Cubs. Root threw two strikes by the Babe. Then the Babe pointed toward center. *New York Times* writer John Drebinger, reporting the game, wrote that "in no mistaken motion the Babe notified the crowd that the nature of his retaliation would be a wallop right out of the confines of the park."

Root wound up and threw. Babe hooked his bat into the pitch and drove it on a high arc into the right-centerfield bleachers, his 15th and last Series homer (the most ever up to that time).

The next batter was Gehrig, who hit the first pitch for another homer. But the dazed crowd, and baseball fans ever since, took little notice, awed by the brazenness of a man who would tell a hostile crowd of 50,000 he would hit a home run in a World Series game—and then do it.

Zack Taylor:
I saw the Babe call his shot

Zack Taylor was a catcher with Chicago, Brooklyn, and Boston. At an Oldtimers' Day game in St. Petersburg, Fla., three weeks before his death, he said: *They say the Babe didn't really call that home run but don't you believe it because I was sitting on the Cub bench and I saw it happen. Charley Root always denied it but what happened was this: Charley had a habit of turning around to touch the rosin bag after he'd thrown a strike, and he had his back turned to the Babe and he didn't see Babe point to the fence. There was a lot more bench jockeying in those days, you know, than there is today. I don't know why . . . maybe because the dugouts are farther apart. The Cubs were saying awful things to Babe. He'd called us cheapskates because we hadn't cut in Koenig and that was embarrassing to me because I roomed with Mark. Our bench was yelling just awful things, I don't even want to talk about them . . . about Babe's personal life. Anyway, he turned to us. He put up two fingers. Two strikes. Then he put up one finger, saying I got one left. And then he pointed to direct centerfield. He hit that pitch right into what must have been a 60-mile-an-hour wind coming off that lake and I don't know how he did it.*

A cartoonist at World Series time likened candidate FDR's strength around the country to a bases-loaded situation against President Herbert Hoover's GOP team. Mr. Roosevelt was among the attractions on Chicago radio for Series visitors. Far left: Zack Taylor (l.) with Rogers Hornsby, Bob Smith.

138

The Babe powers the pitch by Charley Root into the centerfield seats—the home run he'd called, the one that was his 15th and last in a Series. Above: Grinning after he'd made gestures at the Cub bench while rounding third, Babe shakes the hand of an obviously delighted Lou Gehrig. It was the tenth Series for Ruth and the sixth in which he had batted over .300. For the Yankees the victory in the fourth game was their 12th straight in a Series—still a record.

FIRST GAME (Sept. 28, at New York)

CHICAGO 200 000 220 6 10 1
NEW YORK 000 305 31x 12 8 2
Bush, Grimes (6th), Smith (8th)
Ruffing

SECOND GAME (Sept. 29, at New York)

CHICAGO 101 000 000 2 9 0
NEW YORK 202 010 00x 5 10 1
Warneke
Gomez

THIRD GAME (Oct. 1, at Chicago)

NEW YORK 301 020 001 7 8 1
CHICAGO 102 100 001 5 9 4
Pipgras, Pennock (9th)
Root, Malone (5th), May (8th), Tinning (9th)

FOURTH GAME (Oct. 2, at Chicago)

NEW YORK 102 002 404 13 19 4
CHICAGO 400 001 001 6 9 1
Allen, W. Moore (1st), Pennock (7th)
Bush, Warneke (1st), May (4th), Tinning (7th), Grimes (9th)

NEW YORK GIANTS
WASHINGTON SENATORS ——1933

A King and a Prince
Are Too Much for FDR and the Senators

The Giants entered their 10th World Series, but this time the ruddy face and beer-barrel body of John McGraw were missing from the New York dugout. He had quit as manager a year earlier, naming first baseman Bill Terry to replace him. In his first full season as manager, Terry won the National League pennant, helped in large part by a rawboned lefthander out of Oklahoma, Carl Owen Hubbell, who won 23 games, 10 by shutouts.

King Carl won the Series opener, and the Giants' No. 2 pitcher, Prince Hal Schumacher, won the second. President Franklin D. Roosevelt attended the third game in Washington and seemed to improve the weather and the Senators with his famous "Roosevelt luck." The game began in showers and ended in sunshine, and the Senators won their only game of the Series.

A young slugger, 24-year-old Mel Ott, won the fifth and final game as he would win so many for the Giants in the Thirties—with a home run. In the top of the 10th he slugged a low line drive into left centerfield. The Senators' Fred Schulte raced toward the low temporary seats, leaped for the ball, and touched it with his glove. Schulte toppled into the seats, and the ball bounced away from him down an aisle. At first one umpire ruled the hit a double. The Giants protested, and after a conference among the umpires Ott was waved home with the run that won the championship. Muggsy McGraw watched from the press box, nibbling peanuts—"a study in reverie," wrote one reporter. Four months later he was dead.

Joe Cronin:
All I could do was say something quick

I saw Schulte leap for the ball, said Joe Cronin, president of the American League and the former shortstop who was player-manager for the Senators. *It hit his fingertips and fell into the seats. I knew that it was a home run but you like to say something quick to the umpires in a situation like that, hoping you'll get them to call the play your way. Like on a close play at second I'd make a swipe with the glove and holler, 'I got him' even before the ump could signal safe or out. With a lot of umpires you can get them to make a quick decision in your favor. Anyway I ran out to where the umpire, Cy Pfirman, was standing and I was yelling, 'It's two bases! Two bases!' Pfirman started to wave Ott back toward second base and then he said, 'Oh, no, that's a home run.' It was all I could do in that situation, say something quick.*

Displaying that jaunty FDR grin, the President tosses out the first ball. On his left are Joe Cronin and Bill Terry. The players fought for the ball. Washington's Heinie Manush won it and gave it to winning pitcher Earl Whitehill.

Joe Cronin skids on his belly back into
first base, his opposing player-manager,
the Giants' Bill Terry, putting on
a tag too late. Both managers played
well, Cronin hitting .318, Terry .273.
After the Series the Giants asked for
rings instead of watches, which had
been the usual Series gift to the
players. They may have been the first
to get rings, which have since
become a tradition.

FIRST GAME (Oct. 3, at New York)

WASHINGTON 000 100 001 2 5 3
NEW YORK 202 000 00x 4 10 2
Stewart, Russell (3d), Thomas (8th)
Hubbell

SECOND GAME (Oct. 4, at New York)

WASHINGTON 001 000 000 1 5 0
NEW YORK 000 006 00x 6 10 0
Crowder, Thomas (6th), McColl (7th)
Schumacher

THIRD GAME (Oct. 5, at Washington)

NEW YORK 000 000 000 0 5 0
WASHINGTON 210 000 10x 4 9 1
Fitzsimmons, Bell (8th)
Whitehill

FOURTH GAME (Oct. 6, at Washington)

NEW YORK 000 100 000 01 2 11 1
WASHINGTON 000 000 100 00 1 8 0
Hubbell
Weaver, Russell (11th)

FIFTH GAME (Oct. 7, at Washington)

NEW YORK 020 001 000 1 4 11 1
WASHINGTON 000 003 000 0 3 10 0
Schumacher, Luque (6th)
Crowder, Russell (6th)

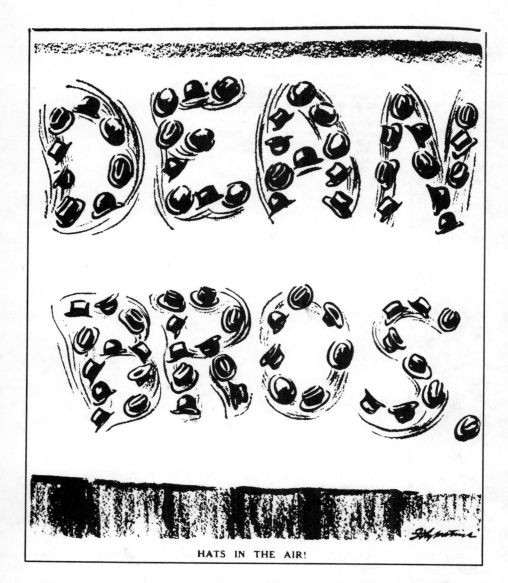

HATS IN THE AIR!

ST. LOUIS CARDINALS
DETROIT TIGERS
1934

Dizzy Wins but Ducky Has To Take a Walk

The irrepressible Jerome (Dizzy) Dean dominated this Series with his pitching and his personality. During the year he had won 30 games for the Cardinals while his brother, Paul (Daffy) Dean, won 19. The Gashouse Gang, as the Cardinals would be called, were now managed by Frankie Frisch, who had played in more World Series games, 42, than anyone up to that time. Pepper Martin was back and he would smack 11 hits in this Series for a .355 average. He stole two bases as Mickey Cochrane, now the Tiger catcher and manager, still couldn't throw him out.

"Leave it to us," Dean told Cardinal fans before the Series. "We'll make pussy cats out of those Tigers." With Ducky Medwick, the Cardinal leftfielder, chipping in four hits, Dizzy won the first game. But Lynwood (Schoolboy) Rowe won the second for Detroit. With Charley Gehringer and Hank Greenberg doing most of the hitting, the Tigers took a three-game to two-game lead as the teams returned to Detroit, the Tigers needing only one victory for the championship. The Cardinals won the sixth game, 4-3, shortstop Leo Durocher sliding home with the winning run on a hit by Paul Dean. Durocher had been known as the All-American Out, and Cochrane growled after the game, "Imagine getting beat on hits by Durocher and Dean."

Dizzy Dean started the last game. Before the game he watched Eldon Auker warm up for Detroit, then shouted at Cochrane, "He won't do, Mickey." He wouldn't. The Cardinals chased him in the third with a seven-run explosion, and they went on to win the game, 11-0, and the championship. In the sixth inning Medwick hit a triple and, sliding into third, jostled Marv Owen. When Medwick took the field the glum Detroit fans pelted

him with garbage and bottles. Judge Landis appeased the crowd by ordering Medwick out of the game—a decision often called the only bad one he ever made.

Joe Medwick:
"Well, ——you, too"

Joe Medwick, the former Cardinal leftfielder and later a part-time Cardinal batting instructor, recalled that: *There was hard feeling between the teams even before the Series. I remember we got to Detroit before the first game and we went to the ball park. The Tigers were taking hitting [practice]. Hank Greenberg had a bat. Dizzy [Dean] said to him, 'Hey Moe,' he always called him Moe, 'Hey, Moe, gimme that bat.' Then Diz swung at a pitch and knocked it out of the park. 'That's the way to hit a ball, Moe,' Diz said, and right there we almost had a fight. What a lot of the sportswriters never realized about my slide into third was this: I got the standup sign from my coach. But as I got near the bag, I saw Owen make a motion to tag me. So I slid from in close. But he didn't have the ball; it was a phantom tag. Anyway I stuck up my hand to show that I hadn't meant to hurt him, and he said something and I said, 'Well, —— you, too.' But years later we talked on the telephone and he admitted he had forced me to slide with that phantom tag. And then we saw some movies and I proved to the sportswriters what I had been saying for years: that the throw had been cut off by the shortstop and that Owen's phantom tag motion had forced me to make the slide that caused all the fuss.*

Ticket holders for the fourth game saw Dizzy knocked "dizzy" by a throw from shortstop Billy Rogell. After the Series the hero-brothers pitched exhibition games against black teams like the Kansas City Monarchs.

Ducky Medwick slides into third, cracking into Marv Owen's right leg. The ball doesn't seem to be on its way to Owen, judging from his stance, adding evidence to Medwick's claim that he slid because Owen had made a motion to tag him. Below: Dizzy the great throwing the hard one.

FIRST GAME (Oct. 3, at Detroit)

ST. LOUIS....................021 014 000 8 13 2
DETROIT.....................001 001 010 3 8 5
J. Dean
Crowder, Marberry (6th), Hogsett (6th)

SECOND GAME (Oct. 4, at Detroit)

ST. LOUIS...............011 000 000 000 2 7 3
DETROIT................000 100 001 001 3 7 0
Hallahan, W. Walker (9th)
Rowe

THIRD GAME (Oct. 5, at St. Louis)

DETROIT.....................000 000 001 1 8 2
ST. LOUIS...................110 020 00x 4 9 1
Bridges, Hogsett (5th)
P. Dean

FOURTH GAME (Oct. 6, at St. Louis)

DETROIT..................003 100 150 10 13 1
ST. LOUIS................011 200 000   4 10 5
Auker
Carleton, Vance (3d), W. Walker (5th), Haines (8th),
   Mooney (9th)

FIFTH GAME (Oct. 7, at St. Louis)

DETROIT.....................010 002 000 3 7 0
ST. LOUIS...................000 000 100 1 7 1
Bridges
J. Dean, Carleton (9th)

SIXTH GAME (Oct. 8, at Detroit)

ST. LOUIS...................100 020 100 4 10 2
DETROIT.....................001 002 000 3 7 1
P. Dean
Rowe

SEVENTH GAME (Oct. 9, at Detroit)

ST. LOUIS.................007 002 200 11 17 1
DETROIT..................000 000 000   0 6 3
J. Dean
Auker, Rowe (3d), Hogsett (3d), Bridges (3d), Mar-
   berry (8th), Crowder (9th)

DETROIT TIGERS
CHICAGO CUBS
1935

What the Tigers Need Is a Goose

"Yeah, Goose . . . Yeah, Goose . . ."

That chant echoed across Cadillac Square and reverberated in a thousand Detroit taverns after Leon (Goose) Goslin won the sixth game of the Series for the Tigers with a line drive single. As the ball bounced along the grass in rightfield, Detroit player-manager Mickey Cochrane galloped home with the run that won the Tigers' first championship. Delirious fans celebrated in the streets until dawn, a victory party that ranks with Pittsburgh's celebration in 1971 as among the wildest Series victory parties of all time.

The fans toasted Goslin, pitcher Tommy Bridges, who won two games, second baseman Charley Gehringer, who hit .375, and Cochrane, all heroes of that climactic sixth game. For eight innings, with 50,000 tense Tiger fans watching in Navin Field, Bridges and the Cubs' Larry French dueled, time after time getting the third out with men on base. As the Cubs came to bat in the top of the ninth the score was tied, 3-3.

Cub third baseman Stan Hack drilled a triple, and the Detroit crowd, recalling the disappointing sixth and seventh games of a year before, sat hushed, watching Bill Jurges come to bat. A fly-ball would put the Cubs ahead. But the slim Bridges, always coolly tough in delicate situations, struck out Jurges. Cub manager Charley Grimm let French bat. The pitcher tapped back to Bridges, who threw him out, while Hack held at third. Then Augie Galan lofted a fly for the third out, the crowd standing to applaud Bridges.

In the bottom of the ninth Cochrane singled and went to second on a fielder's choice. The crowd now roaring, Goslin stepped up to the plate. He stroked a line drive single to right. "Black Mike" Cochrane sped around third and dashed for home. In the Tiger dugout shortstop Billy Rogell shouted what Detroit fans would be shrieking most of the night: "We're world champions . . . we're world champions . . . ."

Charley Gehringer:
What they thought of the ump's vision

Charley Gehringer hit .379 and scored five runs in the 1934 World Series. *But,* the former Tiger second baseman said later, *I will always remember that Series in 1935 because I hit the hardest ball I ever hit in baseball in that Series. It was off Charley Root in the second game. It went over the temporary scoreboard in rightfield. I didn't usually hit for very good distance, but this one went out. The only trouble was, it was foul. Root finally walked me—it was in the first inning—and Greenberg came up after me and hit a home run. Later in the Series I slid into third base—I recall I stole the base—and the Cubs thought I was out. The Cub infielders—Hack, Jurges, Woody English—they told umpire George Moriarty what they thought of his vision. If it hadn't been a Series, he would have thrown them out. They didn't use any cuss words—if they had he would have thrown them out, Series or no Series—but they got on Moriarty pretty good and after the Series Judge Landis fined them all.*

Detroit pitcher Tommy Bridges twists to retrieve a wide throw from first baseman Hank Greenberg, but Phil Cavarretta is safe on the error in the second game. Unfazed, Bridges won, 8–3.

Cub first baseman Phil Cavarretta gloves a throw from third baseman Stan Hack to retire Flea Clifton in the final game. Right: Cubs' Gabby Hartnett tags out Hank Greenberg. Opposite page: Umpire George Moriarty threatens to eject Cub manager Charley Grimm and substitutes Woody English and Tuck Stainback. Judging from grins on Cubs, Grimm seems to have gotten the last laugh.

150

FIRST GAME (Oct. 2, at Detroit)

CHICAGO....................200 000 001 3 7 0
DETROIT....................000 000 000 0 4 3
Warneke
Rowe

SECOND GAME (Oct. 3, at Detroit)

CHICAGO....................000 010 200 3 6 1
DETROIT....................400 300 10x 8 9 2
Root, Henshaw (1st), Kowalik (4th)
Bridges

THIRD GAME (Oct. 4, at Chicago)

DETROIT................000 001 040 01 6 12 2
CHICAGO...............020 010 002 00 5 10 3
Auker, Hogsett (7th), Rowe (8th)
Lee, Warneke (8th), French (10th)

FOURTH GAME (Oct. 5, at Chicago)

DETROIT....................001 001 000 2 7 0
CHICAGO....................010 000 000 1 5 2
Crowder
Carleton, Root (8th)

FIFTH GAME (Oct. 6, at Chicago)

DETROIT....................000 000 001 1 7 1
CHICAGO....................002 000 10x 3 8 0
Rowe
Warneke, Lee (7th)

SIXTH GAME (Oct. 7, at Detroit)

CHICAGO...................001 020 000 3 12 0
DETROIT....................100 101 001 4 12 1
French
Bridges

NEW YORK YANKEES
NEW YORK GIANTS 1936

From FDR To DiMag, a Wave

This was the pit of the depression, and a man of his time was Tony Albano, an unemployed Brooklyn chauffeur. For 12 days he stood in line outside the Polo Grounds to be the first to buy a ticket. On the 12th day he offered to sell his spot for $150. This also told of the times: He got no offers.

Despite the hard times, big crowds filled the two ball parks that squatted across from each other on the Harlem River—the double-decked Polo Grounds and the triple-tiered Yankee Stadium. The receipts, counting a radio fee of around $100,000, came to $1,204,399, the highest ever. This was the fourth "nickel" Series, 5¢ being the cost of a subway ride to the Polo Grounds or to Yankee Stadium. For the second time the Yankees won, beating the Giants in six games.

This was the first Series for the Yankees without Babe Ruth in their lineup. And it was the first Series for a lanky, shy centerfielder, then only 21, named Joe DiMaggio. As in almost every Series he played in, Joltin' Joe distinguished himself, this time hitting .346.

The Giants' King Carl Hubbell halted the Yankee machine in the first game with a 6-1 victory, his 17th straight triumph. He had not lost a game since the Cubs' Bill Lee beat him 1-0, in July. The Yankees evened the Series with an 18-4 massacre, the most lopsided win in Series history. The Yankees then rolled to victory, even beating Hubbell on the way. With President Franklin Roosevelt watching from a box seat at the Polo Grounds, the second game ended with Hank Leiber hitting a soaring drive to deep centerfield. Joe DiMaggio raced toward the bleacher wall and speared the ball for the final out. Then he stood at attention as Mr. Roosevelt, in his limousine, was driven out of the ball park through the centerfield exit, the President waving to DiMag as he passed by.

Carl Hubbell:
Suppose a fan saw me talking to Gehrig

Carl Hubbell, the Giant pitcher and later the team's director of player development, recalled that: *We had a book on all the Yankee hitters. Our scouts had watched the Yankees and they told us the usual things: pitch so-and-so inside, that sort of thing. But I have always thought that those books on hitters were vastly overrated. Before each World's Series you will hear how one team is going to pitch so-and-so high and tight and this other guy low and away. But no two pitchers can pitch alike. A book could have told me and [Fred] Fitzsimmons to pitch tight to a certain hitter. But a hitter might murder a tight pitch by me while a tight pitch by Fitz might get him out. . . . In those days we didn't talk to the players on the other team—especially before a Series. I never believed in it. Suppose a fan saw me talking to Lou Gehrig before a game. Then in a game Gehrig hits one up into the seats off me. The average fan, he's got to think, Hey is there something going on here or what?*

Sequence photos show Giants' King Carl Hubbell twisting off his famous screwball during the first game of the Series. In the rain-swept Polo Grounds Hubbell stopped the Yankees, 6–1.

FIRST GAME (Sept. 30, at Polo Grounds)

| YANKEES | 001 000 000 | 1 | 7 | 2 |
| GIANTS | 000 011 04x | 6 | 9 | 1 |

Ruffing
Hubbell

SECOND GAME (Oct. 2, at Polo Grounds)

| YANKEES | 207 001 206 | 18 | 17 | 0 |
| GIANTS | 010 300 000 | 4 | 6 | 1 |

Gomez
Schumacher, Smith (3d), Coffman (3d), Gabler (5th), Gumbert (9th)

THIRD GAME (Oct. 3, at Yankee Stadium)

| GIANTS | 000 010 000 | 1 | 11 | 0 |
| YANKEES | 010 000 01x | 2 | 4 | 0 |

Fitzsimmons
Hadley, Malone (9th)

FOURTH GAME (Oct. 4, at Yankee Stadium)

| GIANTS | 000 100 010 | 2 | 7 | 1 |
| YANKEES | 013 000 01x | 5 | 10 | 1 |

Hubbell, Gabler (8th)
Pearson

FIFTH GAME (Oct. 5, at Yankee Stadium)

| GIANTS | 300 001 000 1 | 5 | 8 | 3 |
| YANKEES | 011 002 000 0 | 4 | 10 | 1 |

Schumacher
Ruffing, Malone (7th)

SIXTH GAME (Oct. 6, at Polo Grounds)

| YANKEES | 021 200 017 | 13 | 17 | 2 |
| GIANTS | 200 010 110 | 5 | 9 | 1 |

Gomez, Murphy (7th)
Fitzsimmons, Castleman (4th), Coffman (9th), Gumbert (9th)

Sequence photos (opposite page) show Yankees' Lou Gehrig hitting a home run in the third inning of the fourth game. Left: Another sequence shows DiMaggio scoring the first of seven runs in the ninth inning of the last game. With DiMag on third, Bill Dickey hit to the Giants' Bill Terry at first, who threw to third to trap DiMaggio. Joe (No. 9—he would later switch to No. 5) ran for home, and the throw bounded out of Harry Danning's mitt, Joe scoring chin first. No. 3—the Babe's old number and later retired—is George Selkirk.

155

NEW YORK YANKEES
NEW YORK GIANTS ━━1937

A First for Joe
and a Last Hurrah for Lou

During this Series, Hearst newspaper columnist Bill Corum was talking to Giant manager Bill Terry in Terry's hotel suite. Corum offered Terry a bet that the Yankees would beat the Giants. Terry refused to bet. "I'm no sucker," Terry told him, according to Corum.

Not many were betting on the Giants, who were three-to-one underdogs. The wise money was right. The Yankee hitting demolished the Giant pitching with such methodical force that Terry got a telegram from a Giant fan who informed him, tongue in cheek, to "change your signals. The Yankees know them."

The Yankees served up the bad news early, driving Carl Hubbell, winner of 22 that season, from the mound with a seven-run barrage in the sixth inning of the first game. But only Hub could stop a Yankee sweep, beating the Yankees, 7-3, in the fourth game. Lefty Gomez won the final game, his fifth Series victory without a defeat, matching the record of the Yanks' Herb Pennock of the Twenties.

In this Series there was a demonstration of the passing of strength in the Yankee lineup. Young Joe DiMaggio hit his first World Series home run, a towering drive that struck a flagpole above the leftfield roof of the Polo Grounds. And Lou Gehrig hit his 10th Series home run—his last.

After the final game one wag summed up the Series this way: "The Giants won one game and the Yankees won the Series and that's the way it should have been."

Joe DiMaggio:
A home run a kid might dream of

Joe DiMaggio was reminiscing not long ago at an Oldtimers' Day game at Shea Stadium in New York City. *When I think about World Series,* said Joe, *I always remember the 1937 Series because that was the one where I hit my first Series home run. It was off Cliff Melton in the Polo Grounds. It was always a dream I'd had, as a kid, you know, standing on the street corner [in San Francisco] and watching while they showed the play by play of a Series game on a big board. It would be a game in a place like the Polo Grounds or the Yankee Stadium or somewhere and I'd stand there and imagine myself hitting a home run in a World Series. I don't know if you remember this, but they had lights that showed the play by play on the boards. . . . And what impressed me always was a home run in a World Series game. And when I hit that home run off Melton, I thought, 'Now it's happened for me.' It was one of the hardest-hit balls I ever hit. It hit the flagpole on top of the roof. But that's not why I remember it, not because it was a hard-hit ball, but because it was my first in a Series.*

Young Joltin' Joe crossing home plate after hitting his first Series homer in the fifth game. The Giant catcher is Harry Danning. The Yankee sluggers were now labeled the Ruppert Rifles, their owner being Jacob Ruppert, a New York beer baron.

157

158

Opposite page: (l. to r.) Tony Lazzeri, Lefty Gomez, and Joe DiMaggio celebrate Yankees' victory in the first game. This was "Poosh 'em Up" Tony's sixth and last Series with the Yanks. He led both teams with a .400 average. A year later he was playing for the Cubs against the Yankees in the Series. Right: Lou Gehrig strides across the plate after hitting a homer —his last Series homer—off Carl Hubbell in the fourth game.

FIRST GAME (Oct. 6, at Yankee Stadium)

```
GIANTS.....................000 010 000  1 6 2
YANKEES...................000 007 01x  8 7 0
```
Hubbell, Gumbert (6th), Coffman (6th), Smith (8th)
Gomez

SECOND GAME (Oct. 7, at Yankee Stadium)

```
GIANTS...................100 000 000  1  7 0
YANKEES..................000 024 20x  8 12 0
```
Melton, Gumbert (5th), Coffman (6th)
Ruffing

THIRD GAME (Oct. 8, at Polo Grounds)

```
YANKEES..................012 110 000  5 9 0
GIANTS...................000 000 100  1 5 4
```
Pearson, Murphy (9th)
Schumacher, Melton (7th), Brennan (9th)

FOURTH GAME (Oct. 9, at Polo Grounds)

```
YANKEES..................101 000 001  3  6 0
GIANTS...................060 000 10x  7 12 3
```
Hadley, Andrews (2d), Wicker (8th)
Hubbell

FIFTH GAME (Oct. 10, at Polo Grounds)

```
YANKEES..................011 020 000  4  8 0
GIANTS...................002 000 000  2 10 0
```
Gomez
Melton, Smith (6th), Brennan (8th)

NEW YORK YANKEES
CHICAGO CUBS
1938

Again It's Dizzy Who Steals the Show

Joe McCarthy later called this Yankee team of 1938 his greatest. "We are the greatest ball club ever assembled, I believe," he said after the Yankees trampled the Cubs in four straight games. "We have the pitching, the power and the defensive play."

That kind of strength overpowered the Cubs, who had clinched the pennant on the last day of the season when Gabby Hartnett, their catcher-manager, hit a ninth-inning home run in the dusk at Wrigley Field. The man who gave this Series its drama, however, was Dizzy Dean. Dean had been obtained from the Cardinals in mid-season for $100,000, and though his arm ached, he'd won seven of eight games for the Cubs in their pennant drive.

Dizzy started the second game. His fastball a fat melon now, Dean mixed curves and off-speed pitches with cunning for seven innings. He went into the eighth with a 3-2 lead. George Selkirk singled, but Dean made Myril Hoag bounce into a force play. Now Frank Crosetti stepped into the batter's box. With the count two balls and two strikes Dean weaved a curve by Crosetti that Dizzy thought was strike three. The umpire called it a ball. On the next pitch Crosetti whacked a drive into the seats for a home run, and the Yankees, helped by another homer by DiMaggio in the ninth, won, 6-3.

Dean's pitching was called one of the most courageous performances in Series history. "My arm gave way," Dizzy said after the game. "It went out in the sixth inning and pained me from then on. At times it felt as if the bone was sticking out of the flesh. . . ."

And then the old, defiant Dean surfaced. "They're the luckiest bunch of ballplayers I ever pitched against," he said.

Dizzy Dean:
". . . I was suffering out there, boy . . ."

Dizzy Dean, a 30-game winner in 1934, remembered: *My arm was about to kill me. Gabby Hartnett, our catcher and manager, he came out to the mound in the seventh inning and he said, 'Diz, try to strike it through. If I take you out now with us ahead and something was to happen, they'd run me out of town.' 'I'll do all I can, Skip,' I said. Everytime I threw, it felt my arm was going to fall right off of me. I should have been leading 3-0 but Stanley Hack and Bill Jurges ran together on a little ground ball and it went through into leftfield. That scored a couple of runs. Gehrig scored all the way from first base on it and that made it 3-2 when Crosetti hit his home run. I had nothing on the ball. I couldn't have knocked a glass off a table. I was making a big motion, a big windmill motion, and then throwing off-speed balls. DiMaggio, Dickey, all those fellows, they was swinging off my motion, expecting more than I had, but I was suffering out there, boy. In the final game I relieved in the eighth and it was one of the biggest thrills I ever received in baseball. When they brought me in some 60,000 or 70,000 people in New York's Yankee Stadium, they roared.*

Old Diz, a-grinnin' and a-laughin'
before the Series, sore arm and all.
After the second game Yank manager
Joe McCarthy told reporters: "Dean
had plenty of heart in there, boys . . .
His arm may be gone but he was a
puzzle to us for seven innings."

162

Sequence photos taken from World Series motion-picture film show Dizzy pitching in the second game and Frank Crosetti hammering a Dean fastball on a 3-and-2 count for the home run that won the game. "It was my toughest defeat," Dean said after the game. Chicago's Mayor Kelly suffered another defeat, betting "a fine hog" against a New Yorker's box of "the best cigars."

FIRST GAME (Oct. 5, at Chicago)

NEW YORK	020 000 100	3	12	1
CHICAGO	001 000 000	1	9	1

Ruffing
Lee, Russell (9th)

SECOND GAME (Oct. 6, at Chicago)

NEW YORK	020 000 022	6	7	2
CHICAGO	102 000 000	3	11	0

Gomez, Murphy (8th)
J. Dean, French (9th)

THIRD GAME (Oct. 8, at New York)

CHICAGO	000 010 010	2	5	1
NEW YORK	000 022 01x	5	7	2

Bryant, Russell (6th), French (7th)
Pearson

FOURTH GAME (Oct. 9, at New York)

CHICAGO	000 100 020	3	8	1
NEW YORK	030 001 04x	8	11	1

Lee, Root (4th), Page (7th), French (8th), Carleton (8th), J. Dean (8th)
Ruffing

NEW YORK YANKEES 1939

CINCINNATI REDS

Break Up the Yankees

The Yankees were ruining baseball. They were ruining the World Series. They won all the time. Those were the complaints—in New York and elsewhere—as the Yankees easily won their fourth straight pennant, then swept by the Reds in four straight games, their fifth sweep in 13 years. It was the Yank's fourth straight world championship, their eighth in 17 years. Fans, writers, and baseball people offered all sorts of remedies for the same solution: Break up the Yankees.

No one would break up the Yankees until the big league draft of 20-odd years later, which allowed the teams with thin pocketbooks to bid equally with the richer clubs for young talent. But despite the flow of young talent from their farm clubs—King Kong Charlie Keller was their newest addition—the Yankees had to struggle to win two of the four games. And at least two games were ones to relish in the replaying in years to come.

In the second game the Yanks' Monte Pearson, like Herb Pennock in 1927, came within five outs of the first no-hit Series game. In the eighth Ernie Lombardi slapped a single to dash Pearson's hopes. In the ninth Bill Werber cracked another hit. But Pearson let neither man score and won his fourth Series game, a 4-0 shutout.

Those who saw the fourth and final game can still see the Reds' mammoth catcher, Ernie (Schnoz) Lombardi, sprawled helplessly near the plate, the ball nearby as Joe DiMaggio galloped home untouched. With the Yankees ahead, 5-4, in the top of the tenth, DiMaggio hit a sharp drive into left that bounced in front of Ival Goodman. When Goodman bobbled the ball, Charlie Keller tried to score all the way from first. The throw bounced in front of Lombardi as Keller slid home underneath him. The ball rolled a few feet away as Lombardi collapsed into a kneeling position. DiMaggio, who never stopped running, circled the bases and sped across the plate while Lombardi flopped helplessly next to the ball in what writers called "Ernie's Swoon" or "Ernie's Snooze."

The Yankees rode home jubilant, horseplaying in their special railroad cars. Watching over a game of bridge, a bemused smile on his face, was the Iron Horse, Yankee captain Lou Gehrig. His streak of 2,130 games had ended when he took himself out of the lineup earlier in the season. He was suffering from a terminal illness and had not played in the Series, watching in uniform from the bench. When the Yankees won that last game, 7-4, he took off for the last time the only uniform he'd ever worn on a big league baseball field.

Johnny Vander Meer:
The real story of Lombardi's "snooze"

The man who pitched two successive no-hitters for the Reds in 1938, Johnny Vander Meer, watched the 1939 Series from the bench after hurting his arm during the season. In St. Petersburg, Fla., he said: *The story has never been told of what happened when Lom collapsed. Lom was a very honest man and he had the reputation for telling the truth, but no one saw any reason for telling what happened because we'd lost the game whether DiMaggio scored or whether he didn't. His run made no difference. And Keller scored well ahead of the throw, so that was no fault of Lom's. What happened was that the throw bounced in late and it hit him in the [protective] cup. He wasn't able to move. It was ridiculous to blame Lom. They would have gotten DiMaggio if the pitcher [Bucky Walters] had been backing up the catcher, like he should, but he was on the mound. If anyone took a snooze, like they said Lom did, it was Bucky standing on the mound instead of backing up the throw.*

Joe Gordon flashes across the plate to score in the first game on a double by Babe Dahlgren. The Yankees won, 2–1. The Red catcher, missing the backhand tag, is Ernie Lombardi. Watching the play with the umpire is the Yanks' Frank Crosetti.

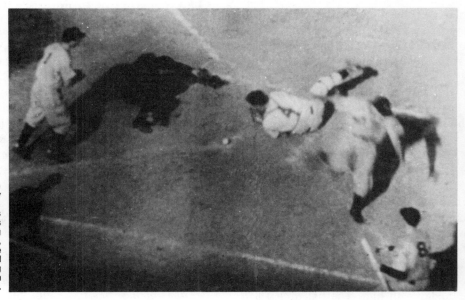

Keller scores as Ernie Lombardi is stunned by the low throw, the ball trickling by him. As the rest of the Reds stood rooted, watching the helpless Ernie, DiMaggio slides home with the Yanks' third run of the tenth inning in the final game, won 7–4 by New York.

FIRST GAME (Oct. 4, at New York)

CINCINNATI 000 100 000 1 4 0
NEW YORK 000 010 001 2 6 0
Derringer
Ruffing

SECOND GAME (Oct. 5, at New York)

CINCINNATI 000 000 000 0 2 0
NEW YORK 003 100 00x 4 9 0
Walters
Pearson

THIRD GAME (Oct. 7, at Cincinnati)

NEW YORK 202 030 000 7 5 1
CINCINNATI 120 000 000 3 10 0
Gomez, Hadley (2d)
Thompson, Grissom (5th), Moore (7th)

FOURTH GAME (Oct. 8, at Cincinnati)

NEW YORK 000 000 202 3 7 7 1
CINCINNATI 000 000 310 0 4 11 4
Hildebrand, Sundra (5th), Murphy (7th)
Derringer, Walters (8th)

CINCINNATI REDS
DETROIT TIGERS 1940

Dick, You Held the Ball Too Long

This World Series had a quality unique for the time: The Yankees were not there. Del Baker's Tigers had managed to finish ahead of the Bronx Bombers. Detroit's home-run-hitting pair, Hank Greenberg and Rudy York, had helped the team to nip out Cleveland and New York in a tight race.

The Reds, with Ernie Lombardi injured, had to put a 40-year-old coach, Jimmy Wilson, behind the plate for most of the games. Each night Jimmy soaked his aching limbs in hot baths and came back to hit .353, second highest among the Reds. He didn't allow a Tiger to steal a base, while he himself took off on his tired legs to steal the only base of the Series.

This was one of the most closely contested of Series, a happy change for fans bored by those Yankee sweeps. Neither team could lead by more than one game. Paul Derringer and Bucky Walters pitched well for the Reds, Bobo Newsom and Tommy Bridges for the Tigers. In the seventh game Derringer walked to the mound for the Reds, Newsom for the Tigers. Newsom was pitching with only one day's rest and after the sudden death of his father of a heart attack in a Cincinnati hotel room. After six innings he and the Tigers led, 1-0.

In the Red seventh Frank McCormick slammed a double. Then Jimmy Ripple hit a liner off the rightfield screen. McCormick, watching, started late because he thought the ball might be caught. A big, lumbering man, he rounded third as the throw came in to shortstop Dick Bartell, who had his back to the plate. Bartell did not hear the shouts of other Tigers to throw the ball home. When he did see McCormick halfway home, it was too late, McCormick scoring the run that tied

the game, 1-1. A little later Ripple, who had reached second on the hit and third on a bunt by Wilson, scored on a fly. The Reds and Derringer held on to win the game, 2-1, and the Series.

Bucky Walters:
He was the first since 1937

Bucky Walters, the former Red pitcher who now lives in Glenside, Pa., said: *It was a nice, well played Series. There was a lot of rivalry between the two teams. And the cities were close together —just an overnight sleeper jump on the train. I guess I was nervous in the first game I pitched. I walked the first two men and Charley Gehringer came up. Our sub catcher, Jimmy Wilson, he came out to talk to me. He told me to be myself out there. I guess he thought I was nervous. Gehringer hit a single to score one run. And now big Hank Greenberg stood up there. I always admired Hank, he was a great hitter. His record proved that. But Hank sure gave me a big break. He hit into a double play. Another run scored, but that double play was what I needed. If Hank had hit one out, that could have been the end for us. The Tigers would have been ahead two games to nothing. We won in seven games and it was the first time the National League had won in a long while. After the game they told me I was the first National League pitcher to win a Series game since 1937. Naturally I felt good. I hit a homer in the other game I pitched, the one I shut out the Tigers, and I still feel better about that home run than I do about the shutout. I was always a thwarted infielder. I wanted to play every day, you know.*

Top: Detroit's Bobo Newsom shakes hands with Paul Derringer before the first game. In the third game Red manager Bill McKechnie and Tigers Birdie Tebbetts, Pinky Higgins, and Dick Bartell (l. to r.) root for a ball to trickle fair or foul. It went foul.

Tiger shortstop Dick Bartell strains for a high throw from catcher Birdie Tebbetts, who was trying to pick off the sliding Eddie Joost. Also reaching for the throw is Charley Gehringer (l.). Both miss the ball, which bounded into centerfield, Joost going on to third in the second inning of the second game, won 5–3 by the Reds.

FIRST GAME (Oct. 2, at Cincinnati)

DETROIT....................050 020 000   7 10 1
CINCINNATI................000 100 010   2 8 3
Newsom
Derringer, Moore (2d), Riddle (9th)

SECOND GAME (Oct. 3, at Cincinnati)

DETROIT....................200 001 000   3 3 1
CINCINNATI................022 100 00x   5 9 0
Rowe, Gorsica (4th)
Walters

THIRD GAME (Oct. 4, at Detroit)

CINCINNATI................100 000 012   4 10 1
DETROIT....................000 100 42x   7 13 1
Turner, Moore (7th), Beggs (8th)
Bridges

FOURTH GAME (Oct. 5, at Detroit)

CINCINNATI................201 100 010   5 11 1
DETROIT....................001 001 000   2 5 1
Derringer
Trout, Smith (3d), McKain (7th)

FIFTH GAME (Oct. 6, at Detroit)

CINCINNATI................000 000 000   0 3 0
DETROIT....................003 400 01x   8 13 0
Thompson, Moore (4th), Vander Meer (5th), Hutch-
    ings (8th)
Newsom

SIXTH GAME (Oct. 7, at Cincinnati)

DETROIT....................000 000 000   0 5 0
CINCINNATI................200 001 01x   4 10 2
Rowe, Gorsica (1st), Hutchinson (8th)
Walters

SEVENTH GAME (Oct. 8, at Cincinnati)

DETROIT....................001 000 000   1 7 0
CINCINNATI................000 000 20x   2 7 1
Newsom
Derringer

NEW YORK YANKEES
BROOKLYN DODGERS ———1941

The Yanks Slip
the Dodgers a Mickey

In a Series filled with disappointments for the Dodgers, the Yankees won four games to one, manager Joe McCarthy winning his sixth World Series, breaking the record held by Connie Mack.

This would be no romp for the Yankees, however. In the first game Red Ruffing narrowly won his sixth Series game, 3-2, tying the number won by Chief Bender, Waite Hoyt, and Lefty Gomez. The Dodgers won the second game behind Whit Wyatt. In the third game Fat Freddie Fitzsimmons, now 40, went to the mound to try to win his first Series victory in four attempts. He and young Marius Russo pitched brilliantly for six shutout innings. With the score still 0-0 in the seventh, Russo came to bat and lined a pitch off Freddie's kneecap, chipping a bone. As his wife and daughter wept in a front-row seat, Fitz hobbled off the field, bent in pain, his last chance at a Series victory ended. The Yankees then went on to win, 2-1.

The ending of the fourth game was probably the weirdest of all Series games—and one of the most heartbreaking for a loser.

The Dodgers led, 4-3, in the top of the ninth, two men out, no one on base, victory seeming certain. With two strikes on Tommy Henrich, Hugh Casey threw a breaking ball. Henrich swung and missed for the third strike that would have ended the game. But catcher Mickey Owen missed the pitch. Henrich ran to first as Owen chased after the ball. A flood of cops burst out of the dugout, thinking the game was over, and they blocked whatever chance Owen had to throw to first.

At third base Brooklyn's Cookie Lavagetto thought to himself, "Oh, we can't give these guys a chance like that." He was right. The Yankees promptly blasted home four runs to win, 7-4.

After the game a white-faced Owen said, "I should have held the ball. It was my fault. I'm not sorry for myself. I'm sorry for what I've done to the other fellows."

Phil Rizzuto:
"It rocked old Ebbets Field"

I can still recall that look on Henrich's face when he struck out, said Phil Rizzuto, the former Yankee shortstop and now a CBS sportscaster. *He was looking back. He couldn't believe that Owen had missed it. I was sitting on the bench. I was holding the gloves of the guys who were batting that inning—DiMaggio, Keller, Dickey and [Joe] Gordon. In Brooklyn those kids would run down after the third out and take anything they could. When Henrich swung and missed that pitch, we all started for the runway in the dugout. Then all of a sudden—I couldn't believe it—people were jumping over the stands, Brooklyn fans. It looked like the third out and Brooklyn had won. Poor Casey, he had a hell of a spitball. Sure, that's what he threw. He threw that on the third strike. The ball exploded by Owen. When Henrich swung, Owen didn't get near the ball. He didn't even touch it. It exploded by him. Henrich couldn't believe it. It was a while before he started to run to first base. Then, when he ran, he had to run between people to get to first base. It took them a while to restore order. Then DiMaggio, Keller, Dickey and Gordon came up and what shots they hit—I never seen such shots in my life. That was exciting in itself but I'll never forget what happened the next day when Owen came to bat. The hand those Brooklyn fans gave him was unbelievable. They were telling him they didn't blame him. They stood and cheered. It rocked old Ebbets Field.*

Fitzsimmons (No. 14) leaves the field, spectators clapping, his wife hiding her tears. Japanese newspapers usually ran long accounts of Series, but this time ran little, "conditioning the populace for war," predicted a United Press correspondent.

173

Yanks' Charlie (King Kong) Keller lashes a drive off the rightfield wall (opposite page) at Ebbets Field, Dixie Walker chasing after the carom. On the other side of the wall, which angled upward and was topped by a screen, is Bedford Avenue. Dodger outfielders from Casey Stengel to Walker to Carl Furillo taught themselves how to play caroms off the wall or screen.

174

175

Hugh Casey, pitching what may or may not have been a spitter, throws to Tommy Henrich, who swings and misses. Mickey Owen has his mitt low on this sequence, taken from motion-picture film, as the ball flies by him. As plate umpire Larry Goetz signals a third out, Owen dashes after the ball. The real third out did not come until after the Yanks scored four more runs.

176

FIRST GAME (Oct. 1, at New York)
BROOKLYN.................000 010 100 2 6 0
NEW YORK.................010 101 00x 3 6 1
Davis, Casey (6th), Allen (7th)
Ruffing

SECOND GAME (Oct. 2, at New York)
BROOKLYN.................000 021 000 3 6 2
NEW YORK.................011 000 000 2 9 1
Wyatt
Chandler, Murphy (6th)

THIRD GAME (Oct. 4, at Brooklyn)
NEW YORK.................000 000 020 2 8 0
BROOKLYN.................000 000 010 1 4 0
Russo
Fitzsimmons, Casey (8th), French (8th), Allen (9th)

FOURTH GAME (Oct. 5, at Brooklyn)
NEW YORK.................100 200 004 7 12 0
BROOKLYN.................000 220 000 4 9 1
Donald, Breuer (5th), Murphy (8th)
Higbe, French (4th), Allen (5th), Casey (5th)

FIFTH GAME (Oct. 6, at Brooklyn)
NEW YORK.................020 010 000 3 6 0
BROOKLYN.................001 000 000 1 4 1
Bonham
Wyatt

ST. LOUIS CARDINALS
NEW YORK YANKEES
1942

To Be Young and Poor and Achin' To Be Rich

The Cardinals were the youngest team ever to play in a Series. The average age of the starters was 26; the oldest player, centerfielder Terry Moore, was not yet 30. In the other dugout the Yankees were their awesome selves: DiMaggio, Keller, Dickey, Gordon, Red Rolfe. When Red Ruffing shut out the young Cardinals for eight innings of the first game and was within a record four outs of the first Series no-hitter, ahead, 7-0, it seemed that the Yankees were on their way to their ninth successive world championship.

Then, in the ninth inning of that first game, the young Cardinals erupted, scoring four runs and showing a hunger to win and a lack of fear of the Yankees, but still losing, 7-4. Most of the Cardinals—Stan Musial, Country Slaughter, Walker and Mort Cooper, Marty Marion, Whitey Kurowski—had come from the dirt poor farms and the mill towns of the depression. By winning this Series some could win more money than the Cardinals had paid them for the entire season. Most were like Musial, who was a grocery-store clerk during the off-season in Donora, Pa., where he had grown up.

The Cardinals won four straight games to take the winners' purse. They won with their vaunted speed and unexpected power. "They might not be so hot at the plate," the Boston Braves' manager, Casey Stengel, had remarked, "but they sure got a lot of strength in their ankles." They showed strength at bat in the fourth game, whaling 12 hits to win, 9-6. And in the fifth and last game Country Slaughter and Whitey Kurowski clubbed home runs to give the Cardinals a 4-2 lead in the ninth.

The Yankees rallied in the last of the ninth, putting runners on first and second with no one out. Johnny Beazley, trying for his second Series victory, faced the next batter, Jerry Priddy. He threw. Catcher Walker Cooper grabbed the pitch and threw to Marty Marion at second base, who tagged out Joe Gordon. That pick-off play broke the back of the rally. Beazley retired the next two hitters, and the young Cardinals were world champions in the biggest upset since the Braves surprised the A's in 1914.

Stan Musial:
"For me . . . the greatest Series . . . beating the Yankees four games in a row"

Stan Musial, now an executive with the Cardinals: *The thing was, we were a young team—most of us had played only two or three years in the big*

The Cardinals' Whitey Kurowski collects a pop foul, Marty Marion behind him. Before the Series 1926 Card manager Rogers Hornsby said: "This Cardinal team couldn't carry our bats..."

FIRST GAME (Sept. 30, at St. Louis)

NEW YORK 000 110 032   7 11 0
ST. LOUIS 000 000 004   4 7 4
Ruffing, Chandler (9th)
M. Cooper, Gumbert (8th), Lanier (9th)

SECOND GAME (Oct. 1, at St. Louis)

NEW YORK 000 000 030   3 10 2
ST. LOUIS 200 000 11x   4 6 0
Bonham
Beazley

THIRD GAME (Oct. 3, at New York)

ST. LOUIS 001 000 001   2 5 1
NEW YORK 000 000 000   0 6 1
White
Chandler, Breuer (9th), Turner (9th)

FOURTH GAME (Oct. 4, at New York)

ST. LOUIS 000 600 201   9 12 1
NEW YORK 100 005 000   6 10 1
M. Cooper, Gumbert (6th), Pollet (6th), Lanier (7th)
Borowy, Donald (4th), Bonham (7th)

FIFTH GAME (Oct. 5, at New York)

ST. LOUIS 000 101 002   4 9 4
NEW YORK 100 100 000   2 7 1
Beazley
Ruffing

leagues and 1942 was my first full year. And the Yankees did have a hell of a ball club: DiMaggio, Ruffing, Rizzuto, Gordon, Keller, Dickey, all those great people. But I don't think we were nervous or awed by them or anything. In fact, that spring, we'd played them a city series in St. Petersburg and we'd beaten them in seven games. Then there was that first game. They were beating us pretty good and then we got four or five runs in the last of the ninth. We might have caught them, too, with that rally, I came up in the last of the ninth with the bases loaded and two out. A good long double might have tied the score. But I grounded out to first base. That rally really sparked us. After that Terry Moore made some great catches for us in centerfield. I was playing leftfield and that was the tough sun field at Yankee Stadium that time of the year. I could hardly see the ball. I lost one, it was hit by Di-Maggio, but Moore came over and made a great play to catch it. What also helped us, we had gone through a tough race with the Dodgers—we caught them late in September in a double-header at Brooklyn—and winning the pennant in a close race, I think, might have made us more aggressive—we might have been more up—than the Yankees were. For me it was the greatest Series I ever played in—being it was my first and then beating the Yankees four games in a row.

Right: Enos Slaughter crosses the plate in the seventh inning of the fourth game as the Cardinals break a 6–6 tie to score two runs and go on to win, 9–6. Bill Dickey is the catcher. In the fifth and final game (below), with the score tied 2–2 in the ninth and a runner on base, Whitey Kurowski socks a home run, and the Cardinals go on to win the game, 4–2, and the World Championship.

NEW YORK YANKEES
ST. LOUIS CARDINALS
1943

A Song for Momma,
a Cap for Pappy

Under their showers after the fifth game the Yankees sang the victory song they had been singing since way back in 1927—"The Sidewalks of New York": *East Side, West Side, all around the town . . . Boys and girls. . . .*

While flashbulbs glittered the Yankees swung into a wartime favorite, "Pistol Packin' Momma." The Yankees were singing with a special glee, for not only had they won the championship, New York's 10th, but they had upended those pesky Cardinals who had upset them the year before.

Both teams were minus a few stars, lost to the service for this second Series of World War II years. But Stan Musial—acclaimed by Dizzy Dean as "the greatest hitter I've ever seen come up in the National League"—was here for the Cardinals. Also returning for the Cardinals was the brother battery, Mort Cooper on the mound and Walker Cooper behind the plate. A few hours before Mort was to pitch in the second game, he and Walker learned of the sudden death of their father. Like Bobo Newsom in 1940, Mort went out to pitch. He beat the Yankees, 4-3, tying the Series at a game apiece. From that moment on the Yankees could not be stopped, winning the next three games and the Series, four games to one. It was Joe McCarthy's seventh and last championship.

After the Series many of the Cardinal and Yankee caps were shipped to the South Pacific, where Marine ace Major Gregory (Pappy) Boyington promised one to every flyer in his group who shot down a Japanese Zero.

Bill Dickey:
The tag on a shirt

It felt good beating them, said Bill Dickey, the former Yankee catcher. *I felt real good when I hit a home run, in the fifth game I think it was, with a man on base to beat Mort Cooper 2-0. That Series in 1942 was the only one I lost all the time I played with the team. We didn't have as good a team in 1943. We didn't have DiMaggio and [John] Lindell was playing center for DiMaggio. Funny, I'd always been a Cardinal fan having grown up in Little Rock, which was as close to St. Louis as any big league city. It was in 1943, I think, that Terry Moore slid home. The throw was off to the left and I got it and I dived at him. His shirt was flying out. He ran like a deer, you know. I grazed the shirt and I don't think the plate umpire could see me tag the shirt because the umpire was behind me when I dived. But he called Terry out anyway. Terry argued like hell. Anyway, you see Terry Moore today and you tell him I tagged him out and he'll say, 'The hell he did,' but I did.*

Yanks' Tuck Stainback puts down a bunt, which is chased by Walker Cooper. U.S. troops in North Africa had been getting only summaries of the games on radio. General Eisenhower asked for play-by-play broadcasts for the GI's—and got them.

Bill Dickey slams a two-run homer in the final game for a 2–0 Yankee victory. Manager Joe McCarthy called Dickey "the greatest World Series catcher" because he stayed loose under pressure and kept his team relaxed. Motion-picture film shows Mort Cooper and the No. 13 he liked to wear. Ten percent of the winning and losing purses was paid with War Bonds.

184

FIRST GAME (Oct. 5, at New York)

ST. LOUIS 010 010 000   2 7 2
NEW YORK 000 202 00x   4 8 2
Lanier, Brecheen (8th)
Chandler

SECOND GAME (Oct. 6, at New York)

ST. LOUIS 001 300 000   4 7 2
NEW YORK 000 100 002   3 6 0
M. Cooper
Bonham, Murphy (9th)

THIRD GAME (Oct. 7, at New York)

ST. LOUIS 000 200 000   2 6 4
NEW YORK 000 001 05x   6 8 0
Brazle, Krist (8th), Brecheen (8th)
Borowy, Murphy (9th)

FOURTH GAME (Oct. 10, at St. Louis)

NEW YORK 000 100 010   2 6 2
ST. LOUIS 000 000 100   1 7 1
Russo
Lanier, Brecheen (8th)

FIFTH GAME (Oct. 11, at St. Louis)

NEW YORK 000 002 000   2 7 1
ST. LOUIS 000 000 000   0 10 1
Chandler
M. Cooper, Lanier (8th), Dickson (9th)

185

ST. LOUIS CARDINALS
ST. LOUIS BROWNS
1944

8,247,918—and
an Unhappy Mrs. Verban

This was the first crosstown Series held anywhere except New York and Chicago. Reporters dubbed it the Trolley Series. For years the laughingstock of baseball, the pitiful St. Louis Browns came up with a wartime team of overage and underage ballplayers and won the pennant, proof again of a wartime song that declared, "They're either too young or too old. . . ."

The Cardinals, pennant winners for the third straight year, still had a handful of the young players who had won in 1942: Enos Slaughter, Whitey Kurowski, and Stan Musial. The Browns won two of the six games, their pitchers striking out 43 Cardinals; but they were betrayed by ten errors, seven of them leaking in runs.

At one point the underdog Browns led, two games to one. Denny Galehouse beat Mort Cooper in the first game, and Jack Kramer won the third. But then the strong-arm Cardinal pitching took control: Harry Brecheen, Mort Cooper, and Max Lanier won the last three games for the second Cardinal championship in three years.

After the Series someone did a little computing and concluded that 8,247,918 people had paid their way into Series games since 1903, paying a total of $27,857,404.11. One unhappy purchaser of a ticket to this Series was Cardinal second baseman Emil Verban. He had bought tickets for his wife, and she had found herself behind a post at the Browns' ball park. At the next game Verban

ran by the box of Brown president Don Barnes and shouted, "Fathead!"

Marty Marion:
" . . . you start to think, my God . . .
these guys are pretty good"

We thought the Browns would be pretty easy, says Marty Marion, the old Cardinal shortstop and now a restaurant executive in St. Louis. *But they turned out to be doggone tough. They were a very tough team to beat. We were a pretty cocky bunch and we'd seen the Browns play. In those days St. Louis was strictly a Cardinal town anyway. We didn't give it much of a thought they could beat us. But we wasn't near as good as the '42 club. That was the best team I ever played on. In '44, that was a war year and we had lost a lot of good ballplayers. Our second-string wasn't as strong. Denny Galehouse beat [Mort] Cooper in that first game, what was it, 2-1? And when you lose with your big guy like Cooper, you start to think, my God, these guys are pretty good. . . . That was the year there was some sort of strikeout record. We had hot weather and out in centerfield there was nothing but white shirts. That's why there were so many strikeouts. Nobody could see the ball very good. Back in those days they didn't worry about what it was like for the players. All they worried about was the turnstiles.*

Stan Musial skids safely into second base with a double, the Browns' Don Gutteridge looking for the ball. At the Series Dizzy Dean said Musial was "the best hitter I've ever seen come up in the National League."

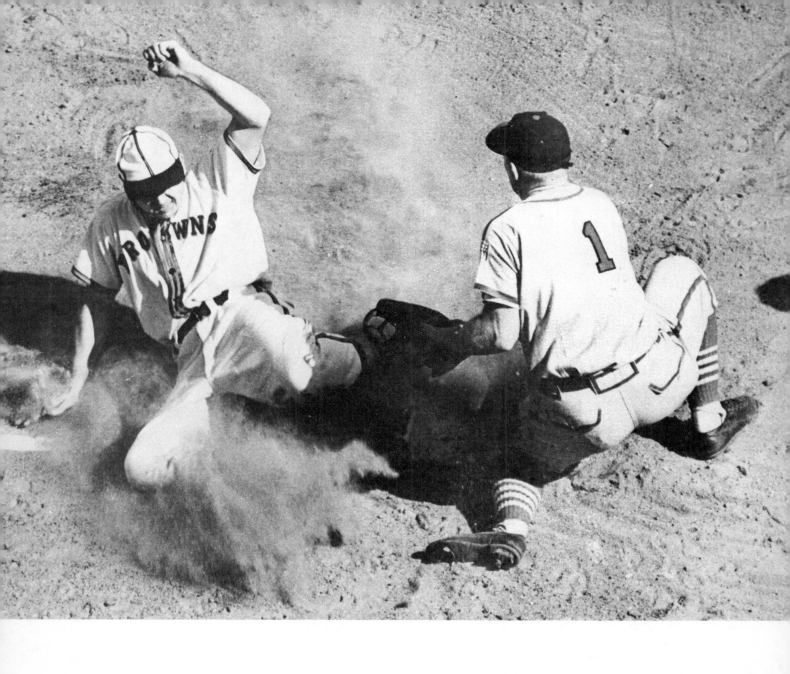

Browns' Al Zarilla slides into third ahead of a throw to Whitey Kurowski in the third game. The Series shared front pages with headlines like this: YANKS SMASH FOR COLOGNE. Attending the games was the Democratic Vice-Presidential candidate, Missouri Senator Harry S Truman.

FIRST GAME (Oct. 4, at Sportsman's Park)

BROWNS....................000 200 000 2 2 0
CARDINALS.................000 000 001 1 7 0
Galehouse
M. Cooper, Donnelly (8th)

SECOND GAME (Oct. 5, at Sportsman's Park)

BROWNS..................000 000 200 00 2 7 4
CARDINALS..............001 100 000 01 3 7 0
Potter, Muncrief (7th)
Lanier, Donnelly (8th)

THIRD GAME (Oct. 6, at Sportsman's Park)

CARDINALS.................100 000 100 2 7 0
BROWNS.....................004 000 20x 6 8 2
Wilks, Schmidt (3d), Jurisich (7th), Byerly (7th)
Kramer

FOURTH GAME (Oct. 7, at Sportsman's Park)

CARDINALS.................202 001 000 5 12 0
BROWNS....................000 000 010 1 9 1
Brecheen
Jakucki, Hollingsworth (4th), Shirley (8th)

FIFTH GAME (Oct. 8, at Sportsman's Park)

CARDINALS.................000 001 010 2 6 1
BROWNS....................000 000 000 0 7 1
M. Cooper
Galehouse

SIXTH GAME (Oct. 9, at Sportsman's Park)

BROWNS.....................010 000 000 1 3 2
CARDINALS................000 300 00x 3 10 0
Potter, Muncrief (4th), Kramer (7th)
Lanier, Wilks (6th)

DETROIT TIGERS
CHICAGO CUBS
1945

Oh, It May Have Been Bad but It Was Fun

Sportswriter Frank Graham called the fifth game "the worst game ever played" in a World Series. "It was the fat men against the tall men in a game of picnic baseball," Graham wrote, and another sportswriter declared, "Neither team can win this Series."

Whatever the skills of many of these wartime big leaguers, there were exciting moments and some excellent pitching in the seven games, supervised for the first time by A. B. "Happy" Chandler, who had succeeded the deceased Judge Landis as commissioner. Because homecoming troops were crowding trains, Series traveling was reduced to a minimum, the first three games played in Detroit, the remainder in Chicago.

Ex-Yankee Hank Borowy excelled for the Cubs in the opener with a 9-0 shutout. Virgil Trucks had shed his Navy blues only a week earlier, but he cranked up his right arm and brought the Tigers even with a 4-1 victory. The Cubs' Claude Passeau came back with a one-hit, 3-0 victory, the first Series one-hitter since Ed Reulbach's in 1906.

The Tigers won the next two games to go ahead, three games to two. The Cubs tied the Series when Hank Borowy pitched four shutout innings in relief, the game and the Series hovering in the balance until the 12th inning. In the Cub half of the 12th, with a runner on first, Stan Hack hit a sharp line drive to leftfield. Hank Greenberg ran in for the ball, but it hopped over his head for a double, the runner scoring all the way from first base to win the game, 8-7.

An arm-weary Borowy started the seventh game, his third successive game and his third start in the Series. The Tigers drove him to the clubhouse in the first inning. Paul Derringer came in to try to hush the Tiger bats, but catcher Paul Richards cracked a double with the bases loaded to drive in all three runners, the Tigers behind Hal Newhouser rolling to an easy 9-3 win and their second Series triumph. For the Cubs it was their seventh straight Series loss, their eighth in ten tries.

Hank Greenberg:
"There were a lot of errors..."

The year before I'd been in India in the service listening to the World Series on the radio, said Hank Greenberg, now a New York businessman. *So it was quite a thrill ... it was something beyond my wildest dreams ... to be playing in a Series only a year later.*

I hurt my hand in the sixth game and I couldn't swing without pain. The Cubs didn't know that, though. I came up in the first inning of the seventh game with one run in and runners on first and second. I bunted, which was quite unusual for me, and I moved the runners along. Someone was walked and then Paul Richards hit a double that cleared the bases and we had five runs in the inning. With Newhouser on the mound that was all we needed. ... There were a lot of wartime players in both lineups and the caliber of play was not as good as other years. There were a lot of errors,

Hank Greenberg hits his second homer of the Series, this one in the sixth game, tying the game, 7–7, in the eighth inning. Cubs' Peanuts Lowrey watches the ball go over the Wrigley Field vines. Roy Cullenbine reaches out to shake Greenberg's hand.

Stan Hack's grounder hops over
Greenberg's head in this sequence
from the Series movies.
Of the new commissioner, Happy
Chandler, someone wrote: "Happy
was wearing a prop smile and a tan
overcoat." Cub pitcher Ray Prim was
hit hard in two appearances. Said Ray:
"They hit me and when the ball got
out there, there wasn't nobody to get
it. They just kept hitting the ball where
there wasn't nobody..."

*but still it was a well-fought Series, going down to
the last game. . . . We lost the sixth game in the
12th inning. With a runner on first Stan Hack
slapped a ground-ball single through the hole into
leftfield. I bent down to pick up the ball and it
hit a spray head and bounced over my head. By
the time I picked up the ball the runner had
scored and the game was over. The three official
scorers ruled it an error for me, but then everyone
complained that it was a bad hop. The next morning, when I woke up, I found they had changed it
to a triple and no error. It was the first time a
scorer's decision had been changed in a Series.
The scorers were newspapermen, you know, and
they don't like to admit mistakes.*

FIRST GAME (Oct. 3, at Detroit)

CHICAGO.................403 000 200   9 13 0
DETROIT.................000 000 000   0 6 0
Borowy
Newhouser, Benton (3d), Tobin (5th), Mueller (8th)

SECOND GAME (Oct. 4, at Detroit)

CHICAGO.................000 100 000   1 7 0
DETROIT.................000 040 00x   4 7 0
Wyse, Erickson (7th)
Trucks

THIRD GAME (Oct. 5, at Detroit)

CHICAGO.................000 200 100   3 8 0
DETROIT.................000 000 000   0 1 2
Passeau
Overmire, Benton (7th)

FOURTH GAME (Oct. 6, at Chicago)

DETROIT.................000 400 000   4 7 1
CHICAGO.................000 001 000   1 5 1
Trout
Prim, Derringer (4th), Vandenberg (6th), Erickson (8th)

FIFTH GAME (Oct. 7, at Chicago)

DETROIT.................001 004 102   8 11 0
CHICAGO.................001 000 201   4 7 2
Newhouser
Borowy, Vandenberg (6th), Chipman (6th), Derringer (7th), Erickson (9th)

SIXTH GAME (Oct. 8, at Chicago)

DETROIT.................010 000 240 000   7 13 1
CHICAGO.................000 041 200 001   8 15 3
Trucks, Caster (5th), Bridges (6th), Benton (7th), Trout (8th)
Passeau, Wyse (7th), Prim (8th), Borowy (9th)

SEVENTH GAME (Oct. 10, at Chicago)

DETROIT.................510 000 120   9 9 1
CHICAGO.................100 100 010   3 10 0
Newhouser
Borowy, Derringer (1st), Vandenberg (2d), Erickson (6th), Passeau (8th), Wyse (9th)

ST. LOUIS CARDINALS —1946
BOSTON RED SOX

Here Comes Enos To Third Base— and He's Heading for Home!

"I know I've been terrible so far," Ted Williams was saying before the seventh game. "If I can hit one today, if I can help us win, I'll be a happy guy all winter."

As baseball's last .400 hitter, Williams had tapped out only five singles in 21 at-bats so far in the Series. But the hitting of Wally Moses and Bobby Doerr, plus the pitching of Joe Dobson and Boo Ferriss, had kept the Red Sox—a team that had never lost a Series—even with the Cardinals through the first six games.

Most of the 1942 Cardinals were back—Stan Musial, Whitey Kurowski, Terry Moore, Marty Marion, plus a wisecracking kid catcher, 21-year-old Joe Garagiola, who later poked fun at himself on TV about his hitting, but who would hit .316 in this Series. Gone was Mort Cooper, but new manager Eddie Dyer could put on the mound a stylish lefthander, Harry (The Cat) Brecheen. The Cat had won two games so far and was on the mound for the Cardinals in the seventh game as the two teams went into the bottom of the eighth, locked in a 3-3 tie, each pitch accompanied by the roaring of the St. Louis crowd.

Enos (Country) Slaughter opened the inning with a single. Red Sox pitcher Bob Klinger retired the next two batters, and pinch-hitter Harry (The Hat) Walker came to the plate. He slammed a low liner to left centerfield. Centerfielder Leon Culberson fumbled the ball, then picked it up and pegged it to shortstop Johnny Pesky in short center.

Second baseman Bobby Doerr saw Slaughter wheeling around third and flying for the plate. He yelled at Pesky to throw home, but Pesky didn't hear. Pesky turned, looked toward home, saw Slaughter, but didn't seem to believe what his eyes were telling him. He looked toward second,

then suddenly came alive and tossed the ball home. Slaughter slid in safely with the run that won the game, 4-3, and the championship, finishing a three-base dash that is in many minds the most spectacular play in World Series history.

Ted Williams ended up hitting .200. He gave his loser's share, $2,140, to the bat boy.

Enos Slaughter: All about that mad run for home

Enos Slaughter, after having hauled in a long drive to centerfield during an Oldtimers' Day game at Yankee Stadium, commented: *With two out and the count being three and two on Walker, I was running. I was already at second base when the ball went over the shortstop's head. I figured right then I could score. Earlier in the Series [third-base coach] Mike Gonzalez had stopped me at third and the throw went through the catcher and I could have scored. Eddie Dyer told me after that to go if I thought I had a chance and he would take the blame. So I never looked at Gonzalez and I was told later he tried to hold me up. If they hadn't taken Dom DiMaggio out of the game I wouldn't have tried to come home but Culberson didn't have the arm that DiMaggio had. They blamed Pesky for holding the ball but if someone had hollered to him and he'd heard, he could have had a chance to get me. I started to slide when I was 10 feet in front of the plate. [Catcher Roy] Partee took the ball on the first hop but I was safe easy. I had never done that, go all the way from first to home on a hit like that, ever before in my career. And I never did it after, either.*

Jubilant Cardinals lift Harry Brecheen (No. 31), Joe Garagiola (No. 18) helping on the left side, after the last out of the final game. Even an umpire reaches in to grab Harry's hand. Garagiola said before the seventh game: "I predict this will be the last game—you can quote me."

Slaughter (l.) slashes
a single. A little later
he slides home
(opposite page) on the
double by Harry Walker,
beating the throw
to Roy Partee.

196

FIRST GAME (Oct. 6, at St. Louis)

BOSTON....................010 000 001 1   3 9 2
ST. LOUIS.................000 001 010 0   2 7 0
Hughson, Johnson (9th)
Pollet

SECOND GAME (Oct. 7, at St. Louis)

BOSTON....................000 000 000   0 4 1
ST. LOUIS.................001 020 00x   3 6 0
Harris, Dobson (8th)
Brecheen

THIRD GAME (Oct. 9, at Boston)

ST. LOUIS.................000 000 000   0 6 1
BOSTON....................300 000 01x   4 8 0
Dickson, Wilks (8th)
Ferriss

FOURTH GAME (Oct. 10, at Boston)

ST. LOUIS.................033 010 104   12 20 1
BOSTON....................000 100 020   3   9 4
Munger
Hughson, Bagby (3d), Zuber (6th), Brown (8th), Ryba
  (9th), Dreisewerd (9th)

FIFTH GAME (Oct. 11, at Boston)

ST. LOUIS.................010 000 002   3   4 1
BOSTON....................110 001 30x   6 11 3
Pollet, Brazle (1st), Beazley (8th)
Dobson

SIXTH GAME (Oct. 13, at St. Louis)

BOSTON....................000 000 100   1 7 0
ST. LOUIS.................003 000 01x   4 8 0
Harris, Hughson (3d), Johnson (8th)
Brecheen

SEVENTH GAME (Oct. 15, at St. Louis)

BOSTON....................100 000 020   3 8 0
ST. LOUIS.................010 020 01x   4 9 1
Ferriss, Dobson (5th), Klinger (8th), Johnson (8th)
Dickson, Brecheen (8th)

NEW YORK YANKEES
─────────────────────
BROOKLYN DODGERS 1947

For Cookie, Bill, and Al,
It Was Here Today and Gone Tomorrow

The three names that are remembered from this 1947 Series were names dropped from big league box scores by 1948. All three were by then toiling in the minor leagues. Not forgotten, though, were the Series heroics of Cookie Lavagetto, Floyd (Bill) Bevens, and Al Gionfriddo, three unexpected and unlikely heroes.

Two other names in the 1947 box scores were rookies who would go on to the Hall of Fame. One was Brooklyn infielder Jackie Robinson, the first black major-leaguer. The other was New York's stumpy outfielder-catcher, Yogi Berra, who played rightfield in this Series, the first of a record 14 for Yogi.

Lavagetto and Bevens combined to make the fourth game, played at Ebbets Field, one of the most memorable of all time. For 8⅔ innings Bevens, 31, and a journeyman pitcher, had not yielded a hit, the closest anyone had ever come to pitching a no-hitter in the Series. He had walked nine, however, costing him a run, but the Yanks led, 2-1. There were two out in the bottom of the ninth, Carl Furillo on first base after a walk.

Dodger manager Burt Shotton sent in the speedy little Gionfriddo, a utility infielder-outfielder, to run for Furillo. Gionfriddo surprised everyone by stealing second. Yankee manager Bucky Harris then violated conventional baseball wisdom by purposely walking pinch-hitter Pete Reiser, putting the winning run on base. Eddie Miksis ran for Reiser.

Lavagetto, 34, and a part-time third baseman, batted for Eddie Stanky. He leaned into an outside pitch and smashed it on a line toward the rightfield wall. The ball hit high on the wall and bounded away from Tommy Henrich. Gionfriddo and Miksis raced home with the tying and winning runs, the Dodgers winning 3-2. Bevens trudged off the field a one-hit loser.

Two days later the biggest crowd in Series history up to then, 74,065, squeezed into Yankee Stadium to see the sixth game. With the Dodgers ahead, 8-5, in the sixth, Joe DiMaggio came to bat with two men on and two out. He hit a soaring drive toward the bullpen in leftfield. Gionfriddo raced to the bullpen railing, stuck out his glove, and snared the drive that would have tied the score. The Dodgers won the game, 8-6, but lost their fourth Series the next day, stopped by the fireballing reliefer Joe Page.

Cookie Lavagetto:
"... that's all there was to it ..."

Cookie Lavagetto, the former Dodger third baseman and big league manager, was interviewed at an Oldtimers' Day in New York. *People have asked me for years about that hit off Bevens,* he said. *To me it was like any other game. It was my last year with the club. The previous spring they had offered me a minor league managing job but I had turned it down because I thought I could play another season in the big leagues. I was used mostly as a pinch-hitter that year and I did all right as a pinch-hitter. I think I hit over .250 [.261]. So when I went up there to pinch-hit against Bevens, it was something I had been used to doing all year. The pitch was right out there and I got hold of it good. I ran down to first base and turned and saw the two runs scoring and that's all there was to it.*

Ebbets Field crowd waits as Floyd Bevens sets, then throws the final pitch of the fourth game. Cookie Lavagetto slices the pitch to right for the Dodgers' only hit of the game, two runners scoring for a Brooklyn victory. This was the first Series televised.

FIRST GAME (Sept. 30, at New York)
BROOKLYN.................100 001 100   3 6 0
NEW YORK.................000 050 00x   5 4 0
Branca, Behrman (5th), Casey (7th)
Shea, Page (6th)

SECOND GAME (Oct. 1, at New York)
BROOKLYN...............001 100 001   3 9 2
NEW YORK...............101 121 40x 10 15 1
Lombardi, Gregg (5th), Behrman (7th), Barney (7th)
Reynolds

THIRD GAME (Oct. 2, at Brooklyn)
NEW YORK.................002 221 100   8 13 0
BROOKLYN.................061 200 00x   9 13 1
Newsom, Raschi (2d), Drews (3d), Chandler (4th), Page
   (6th)
Hatten, Branca (5th), Casey (7th)

FOURTH GAME (Oct. 3, at Brooklyn)
NEW YORK.................100 100 000   2 8 1
BROOKLYN.................000 010 002   3 1 3
Bevens
Taylor, Gregg (1st), Behrman (8th), Casey (9th)

FIFTH GAME (Oct. 4, at Brooklyn)
NEW YORK.................000 110 000   2 5 0
BROOKLYN.................000 001 000   1 4 1
Shea
Barney, Hatten (5th), Behrman (7th), Casey (8th)

SIXTH GAME (Oct. 5, at New York)
BROOKLYN.................202 004 000   8 12 1
NEW YORK.................004 100 001   6 15 2
Lombardi, Branca (3d), Hatten (6th), Casey (9th)
Reynolds, Drews (3d), Page (5th), Newsom (6th),
   Raschi (7th), Wensloff (8th)

SEVENTH GAME (Oct. 6, at New York)
BROOKLYN.................020 000 000   2 7 0
NEW YORK.................010 201 10x   5 7 0
Gregg, Behrman (4th), Hatten (6th), Barney (6th),
   Casey (7th)
Shea, Bevens (2d), Page (5th)

Joe DiMaggio drives a pitch by Joe Hatten high toward the left-field bullpen some 400 feet away, where Al Gionfriddo, who had just come into the game, leans across the railing and snares it. DiMag, in a rare display of temper, kicks the dust near second base after the catch.

200

CLEVELAND INDIANS
BOSTON BRAVES
1948

For Feller the Decision
Was Not a Happy One

"I've waited all my life to win a World's Series game," Bob Feller told a reporter a few hours before the first game of the Indian-Brave Series. Since 1938 Feller had been baseball's strikeout king, possessing a dreaded fastball and a hooking curve, but this was his first appearance in a Series.

The Braves had won the pennant on the pitching of Warren Spahn and Johnny Sain, inspiring the saying that Boston's winning formula consisted of "Spahn and Sain and two days of rain." In the first game Sain opposed Feller, and for seven innings the two righthanders notched zeros on the scoreboard.

In the Braves' eighth Feller walked Bill Salkeld. Phil Masi came in to run for him. The Braves sacrificed Masi to second. All year long the Indians' shortstop-manager Lou Boudreau had polished a pick-off play with his pitchers: On a pre-arranged signal the pitcher would whirl and throw to second where Boudreau was cutting toward the bag.

The signal was flashed. Feller spun and threw to Boudreau. Masi, who had taken a long lead off base, dived for the bag. Umpire Bill Stewart threw his arms flat, indicating Masi was safe. Boudreau and Feller screamed he was out and newspaper photos the next day seemed to show they were right, but as usual the umpire's decision was the only decision.

Feller got the second out, but Tommy Holmes smacked a single to score Masi, and the Braves won, 1-0, Feller a two-hit loser.

He would never come as close to winning a Series game. He started in the fifth game in Cleveland before 86,288, the biggest Series crowd up to then, and was batted out in the seventh, the Braves winning, 11-5. The Indians, however, won three of the first five games, Bob Lemon and Gene Bearden each winning one. In the sixth game Lemon was ahead, 4-1, going into the bottom of the eighth inning. The Braves, needing this game to survive, rallied. The knuckleball-throwing Bearden came in to squelch the rally and Cleveland won its second Series in two tries.

Johnny Sain:
I saw Boudreau tag him and I
thought, "Oh, oh, he's out"

Johnny Sain, later a pitching coach for the Chicago White Sox, remembered 1948 very well. *I was very pleased about pitching that game against Feller and beating him 1-0. I was watching from the dugout when they made that pick-off play on Masi. It was a very good play they had; it was a precise-time play between Boudreau and his pitcher. When I saw Boudreau tag him with the ball, I thought at first, 'Oh, oh, he's out.' It was one of those plays where you hope your man is safe if you are on one bench and you holler loud that he is out if you are on the other bench. I thought the pictures never really showed whether he was safe or out, but he looked out from where we sat.*

Rapid Robert Feller pitching in the first game. Of umpire Bill Stewart's decision calling Masi safe at second in that first game, Feller said, "We caught two fellows napping—Masi and Stewart."

204

FIRST GAME (Oct. 6, at Boston)

CLEVELAND 000 000 000 0 4 0
BOSTON 000 000 01x 1 2 2
Feller
Sain

SECOND GAME (Oct. 7, at Boston)

CLEVELAND 000 210 001 4 8 1
BOSTON 100 000 000 1 8 3
Lemon
Spahn, Barrett (5th), Potter (8th)

THIRD GAME (Oct. 8, at Cleveland)

BOSTON 000 000 000 0 5 1
CLEVELAND 001 100 00x 2 5 0
Bickford, Voiselle (4th), Barrett (8th)
Bearden

FOURTH GAME (Oct. 9, at Cleveland)

BOSTON 000 000 100 1 7 0
CLEVELAND 101 000 00x 2 5 0
Sain
Gromek

FIFTH GAME (Oct. 10, at Cleveland)

BOSTON 301 001 600 11 12 0
CLEVELAND 100 400 000   5 6 2
Potter, Spahn (4th)
Feller, Klieman (7th), Christopher (7th), Paige (7th),
  Muncrief (8th)

SIXTH GAME (Oct. 11, at Boston)

CLEVELAND 001 002 010 4 10 0
BOSTON 000 100 020 3 9 0
Lemon, Bearden (8th)
Voiselle, Spahn (8th)

Masi dashes back toward second base
as Boudreau waits for the throw from
Feller. Watching is umpire Stewart. The
call is safe, and Boudreau (opposite
page) begins his protest.

NEW YORK YANKEES
BROOKLYN DODGERS
1949

A Wink from Casey
and an Answer from Yogi

In the first game of another Subway Series, the Dodgers' big Don Newcombe and the Yankees' Allie Reynolds pitched shutout ball for 8½ innings. In the bottom of the ninth the Yankees' Old Reliable, Tommy Henrich, drove a Newcombe fastball into the rightfield seats for a 1-0 victory. It was the first World Series victory as a manager for the Yankees' new leader, Casey Stengel.

After the game a reporter reminded Stengel about the last Series game that was won 1-0 by a homer. That game was in the 1923 Series, and the man who hit the homer for the Giants against the Yanks was Casey Stengel. But Casey's homer, a reporter pointed out, wasn't as dramatic as Henrich's, because it was hit in the seventh and not in the bottom of the ninth. "You're right," Casey growled with a wink. "You see, I'm a nervous fellow and I couldn't wait that long."

The second game was another 1-0 duel, this time won by the Dodgers behind Preacher Roe, the run scoring on a double by Jackie Robinson and a single by Gil Hodges. The Yankees won another close one, 4-3, in the third game, when Johnny Mize, a veteran slugger, came up in the ninth with the bases loaded and drove in two runs. It was the second pinch hit in two tries during this Series for Mize, who would become famous during the next few years for his Series pinch hits.

The Yankees won the next two games to win the Series, four games to one, the first of five straight championships for the Casey Stengel-model Yankees. The fifth game was the first Series game to be played under lights, which were turned on in the late innings.

During the Series the fleet Dodgers stole several bases when Yogi Berra threw poorly to second base. Yogi shrugged off the criticism he heard. "If you got them all out stealing," he said, "the game wouldn't be interesting."

Jackie Robinson:
"When I came up, he threw peas"

I never hit well in most of the Series I played in, said Jackie Robinson, later an East Coast business executive. *I don't know why except in a short Series, the pitching will tend to be good and good pitching will always stop hitting. Like Allie Reynolds. You never saw a guy pitch better against me. When I came up, he threw peas. The Yankees were a great ball club who beat you by taking advantage of every situation. If somebody made a mistake, you were just dead. And they never seemed to make a mistake in important situations. I don't think their personnel was any better than ours, but they were excellent in crisis situations. They were an opportunistic team. They made the breaks go their way. And they had confidence. It wasn't that we were nervous or afraid. But they would come out and you could sense they thought they could beat you.*

Allie Reynolds, who won seven of nine World Series decisions for the Yankees, pitching in the first game. He is tied for second in total Series victories with Red Ruffing and Bob Gibson. The leader with ten is ex-Yankee Whitey Ford.

Roy Campanella tags out Yanks' Eddie Lopat in the fourth game when Lopat tried to score from second on a single by Phil Rizzuto. Lopat, known as "the junkman" because of his assorted breaking pitches, won the game, 6–4, even though he was driven from the mound in the sixth inning when the Dodgers rapped seven singles off him, tying a Series record.

FIRST GAME (Oct. 5, at New York)

BROOKLYN.................000 000 000   0 2 0
NEW YORK.................000 000 001   1 5 1
Newcombe
Reynolds

SECOND GAME (Oct. 6, at New York)

BROOKLYN.................010 000 000   1 7 2
NEW YORK.................000 000 000   0 6 1
Roe
Raschi, Page (9th)

THIRD GAME (Oct. 7, at Brooklyn)

NEW YORK.................001 000 003   4 5 0
BROOKLYN.................000 100 002   3 5 0
Byrne, Page (4th)
Branca, Banta (9th)

FOURTH GAME (Oct. 8, at Brooklyn)

NEW YORK.................000 330 000   6 10 0
BROOKLYN.................000 004 000   4 9 1
Lopat, Reynolds (6th)
Newcombe, Hatten (4th), Erskine (6th), Banta (7th)

FIFTH GAME (Oct. 9, at Brooklyn)

NEW YORK.................203 113 000   10 11 1
BROOKLYN.................001 001 400   6 11 2
Raschi, Page (7th)
Barney, Banta (3d), Erskine (6th), Hatten (6th), Palica (7th), Minner (9th)

Casey Finds a Ford
in His Future

Winning over the Phils in four straight, the Yankees picked up their sixth sweep of a Series. (The only other team to sweep in four games up to then was the 1914 Braves.) It was the Yankees' 13th championship in 17 Series. The Philadelphia Whiz Kids almost folded in the pennant stretch, losing 8 of their last 11 and winning the pennant on the last day, when Dick Sisler hit a 10th-inning homer against the Dodgers. However, the Phils' strong pitching performed well in the Series but was weakened by several costly fielding lapses.

The Phillies' manager Eddie Sawyer surprised fans by starting his relief ace, Jim Konstanty, in the first game. It was the first start of the season for Konstanty, who was also seeing his first Series game. Konstanty allowed only four hits, but the Yanks' Vic Raschi gave up only two and won, 1-0.

Robin Roberts, a 20-game winner, was the second starter for the Phillies and lost, 2-1, to Allie Reynolds, Joe DiMaggio winning the game in the tenth inning with a home run. The Phils were winning the third game, 2-1, in the eighth inning when an error by shortstop Granny Hamner let in the tying run. In the ninth, second baseman Jimmy Bloodworth couldn't handle two infield hits, and the Yankees got another run to win, 3-2.

Stengel started a rookie, 21-year-old Ed (Whitey) Ford, in the fourth game. The cocky kid from Long Island told reporters, "I never get butterflies." He shut out the Phillies for eight innings and won, 5-2, missing a shutout when Gene Woodling dropped a flyball. It was the first

of 10 Series victories for Ford.

"I never dreamed I'd be the manager of a team that won a Series in four straight," Stengel said. For Joe DiMaggio the championship was his ninth —a record to then.

Andy Seminick:
I remember DiMaggio

Andy Seminick, the Phil catcher in the '50 Series, said: *I can still see that ball that Granny Hamner booted. He took his eyes off the ball for an instant and that's all you have to do. If he had made that play, we would still have been alive. It was a pitchers' Series. We didn't hit to our potential, but neither did the Yankees. Still, we felt embarrassed. I think most players do when they lose a Series in four straight. We told ourselves we would come back and win a Series because we were a young ball club, but then we had injuries, and it didn't happen. When I think of the Yankees, I can see DiMaggio hitting a perfect pitch from Bob Miller—it was low and outside, just where we wanted it—but DiMaggio hit it to rightfield for a single. He could handle Miller's stuff even when Bob put the ball exactly where we wanted to put it. Robin Roberts could handle DiMaggio —he could get him out with a pitch inside—but Roberts had to get the pitch in the exact spot inside. If it was a speck off, DiMaggio could put it into the seats on you.*

Gene Woodling scatters dust as he scores in the first inning of the final game, umpire Charlie Berry signaling that he's safe. Phil catcher Andy Seminick looks to nip Yogi Berra off-base, Berra having driven home the run with a single.

211

The ball (arrow) flies toward Yanks' Yogi Berra, who tags out sliding Granny Hamner. In the ninth inning of the third game, Hamner had tried to score from third on a ground ball to first. His failure to score was costly—the Yanks won with a run in the last of the ninth, 3–2. In the fourth game fans at Yankee Stadium booed Casey Stengel when he removed young Whitey Ford, making his first Series start, after Ford ran into trouble in the ninth.

212

FIRST GAME (Oct. 4, at Philadelphia)

NEW YORK.................000 100 000   1 5 0
PHILADELPHIA............000 000 000   0 2 1
Raschi
Konstanty, Meyer (9th)

SECOND GAME (Oct. 5, at Philadelphia)

NEW YORK...............010 000 000 1   2 10 0
PHILADELPHIA..........000 010 000 0   1 7 0
Reynolds
Roberts

THIRD GAME (Oct. 6, at New York)

PHILADELPHIA............000 001 100   2 10 2
NEW YORK.................001 000 011   3 7 0
Heintzelman, Konstanty (8th), Meyer (9th)
Lopat, Ferrick (9th)

FOURTH GAME (Oct. 7, at New York)

PHILADELPHIA..............000 000 002   2 7 1
NEW YORK...................200 003 00x   5 8 2
Miller, Konstanty (1st), Roberts (8th)
Ford, Reynolds (9th)

Hello To Willie and Mickey . . .
and Where Have You Gone, Joe DiMaggio?

Shouting "Let 'er rip," their season-long battle cry, the Giants rode into this Subway Series still exuberant over Bobby Thomson's climactic play-off home run against the Dodgers. Two rookie outfielders played against each other in this, their first World Series: Willie Mays for the Giants and Mickey Mantle for the Yankees.

In the second game Mantle was chasing a fly-ball when he suddenly crumpled to the grass and lay motionless. He was taken to a hospital where doctors diagnosed the injury as a weakened knee and Mantle played no more in the Series. It was the first of many knee injuries that would hobble Mantle throughout his career. Mays, who had been hitting poorly in the Giants' stretch run for the pennant, hit only .182 in the Series.

The Giants won two of the first three games without the help of their two aces, Sal Maglie and Larry Jansen, both of whom were arm-weary after the Giants' exhausting dash from 13½ games behind to catch the Dodgers. Neither won a game in the Series. The Yankees, with Phil Rizzuto and Joe DiMaggio doing most of the hitting, won the next two games to pull ahead, three games to two, Allie Reynolds and Eddie Lopat the victors.

In the sixth inning of the sixth game Hank Bauer drove a bases-loaded triple over Monte Irvin's head in leftfield, and the Yankees went into the ninth ahead, 4-1. But these Giants tried to stage one more miracle finish. They scored twice and had the tying run on base with two out. Stengel relieved with lefty Bob Kuzava, who would become a Stengel favorite in getting the last outs in hairy World Series situations. Kuzava threw to pinch-hitter Sal Yvars, who hit a twisting liner to rightfield. Hank Bauer lost the ball, then saw it, and grabbed it with a skidding catch inches off the ground, ending the Series.

In the bottom of the eighth of that game Joe DiMaggio had smacked a double and a little later was retired at third base. He trotted off the field, a crescendo of applause rising in Yankee Stadium, the crowd sensing this would be Joe DiMaggio's last game. It was his 51st Series game, a record. A few weeks later he announced his retirement, his No. 5 never to be worn again by a Yankee.

Eddie Lopat:
What Branca threw to Thomson

Eddie Lopat, the former Yankee pitcher, now lives in New Jersey. He said: *A lot of the Yankees, we went to the three games of the playoffs between the Dodgers and the Giants that year. Most of us were rooting for the Giants because we had played the Dodgers before and the Giants played in a bigger park [so there would be a bigger player pool]. Also it was closer to home than Ebbets Field. I saw Bobby Thomson hit that home run off [Ralph] Branca. I thought Branca pitched to Thomson just the way he should have, from everything our scouts had told us about Thomson. Branca pitched the fastball in, he kept it tight. I pitched Thomson tight all during that Series and I don't think he got a hit off me. . . . It was a sad affair for us, that Series, because we knew DiMaggio was retiring. It's always sad; you hate to lose a big guy like that.*

Joe DiMaggio connects for his last hit —a double in the final game off Larry Jansen. The catcher is Ray Noble. Giant scouting reports said DiMag couldn't get around quick enough any longer on fastballs, but he hit .261 and a homer in his last Series.

216

Opposite page: Giants' Eddie Stanky races toward second, but a throw from Yogi Berra is waiting in Phil Rizzuto's glove as Stanky slides. Stanky (l.) kicks the ball out of Phil's glove and goes on to third. Phil later claimed Stanky never touched second.

FIRST GAME (Oct. 4, at Yankee Stadium)
GIANTS.....................200 003 000 5 10 1
YANKEES...................010 000 000 1 7 1
Koslo
Reynolds, Hogue (7th), Morgan (8th)

SECOND GAME (Oct. 5, at Yankee Stadium)
GIANTS.....................000 000 100 1 5 1
YANKEES...................110 000 01x 3 6 0
Jansen, Spencer (7th)
Lopat

THIRD GAME (Oct. 6, at Polo Grounds)
YANKEES...................000 000 011 2 5 2
GIANTS.....................010 050 00x 6 7 2
Raschi, Hogue (5th), Ostrowski (7th)
Hearn, Jones (8th)

FOURTH GAME (Oct. 8, at Polo Grounds)
YANKEES...................010 120 200 6 12 0
GIANTS.....................100 000 001 2 8 2
Reynolds
Maglie, Jones (6th), Kennedy (9th)

FIFTH GAME (Oct. 9, at Polo Grounds)
YANKEES...................005 202 400 13 12 1
GIANTS.....................100 000 000   1 5 3
Lopat
Jansen, Kennedy (4th), Spencer (6th), Corwin (7th),
  Konikowski (9th)

SIXTH GAME (Oct. 10, at Yankee Stadium)
GIANTS.....................000 010 002 3 11 1
YANKEES...................100 003 00x 4 7 0
Koslo, Hearn (7th), Jansen (8th)
Raschi, Sain (7th), Kuzava (9th)

NEW YORK YANKEES
BROOKLYN DODGERS
1952

And Here Comes Billy from a Long Way Off

Brooklyn and the Bronx squared off again, the Dodgers hoping to win their first Series against the Joe DiMaggio-less Yankees. This was the Dodger team close to its peak, the Dodgers of Pee Wee Reese, Gil Hodges, Billy Cox, Andy Pafko, Roy Campanella, Jackie Robinson, Duke Snider, Carl Furillo, and of pitchers Carl Erskine and Joe Black.

To win this Series in seven games, Stengel needed all his guile. He got surprising help from the 39-year-old Johnny Mize, used mostly as a pinch-hitter that season for the Yankees. Mize slashed six hits, three of them home runs. He played the entire fourth game at first base, and hit a home run that helped win the game, 2-0. And Casey got a vital catch from a rookie who would be a perennial Series star for him—second baseman Billy Martin.

The Yankees, down three games to two, seemed on the edge of losing their first Series since 1942. But Mickey Mantle hit an eighth-inning homer to win the sixth game, 3-2, and to even the Series at three games apiece.

In the seventh game Mantle hit a home run in the sixth to put the Yankees ahead, 3-2, and a single in the seventh to put New York ahead, 4-2. In their half of the seventh the Dodgers loaded the bases with one out. Stengel brought in Bob Kuzava. He threw a high curve to Duke Snider on a three-and-two count and Snider popped out. Again the count went to three-and-two, this time on Jackie Robinson, who hit a towering fly over the infield. First baseman Joe Collins and Kuzava stared at the ball, not moving. As the ball dropped toward the mound second baseman Billy Martin dashed from what seemed like a mile away to catch the ball at his shoe tops and retire the side, the Yankees preserving the lead and winning their fourth straight Series. "The Yankees don't miss DiMaggio," Jackie Robinson said ruefully.

Billy Martin:
Squeeze it in the bare hand

Billy Martin, when he was the Detroit Tigers' manager, recalled: *It was a three and two count on Robinson and I played him to pull a little, moving closer to second and I was almost on the outfield grass. When the ball went up in the air I looked at Collins and I saw he had lost it in the sun. We'd been having trouble with the sun all day. I took off. I was worried about the wind because the prevailing wind at Ebbets Field blew the ball toward home plate. Also I was thinking about Yogi. I was afraid he'd be coming out for the ball and sometimes when he did he kept his mask on. I heard nothing, no one yelling, no one calling me off the ball. But I knew I might knock into sombody. So when I reached down and grabbed the ball with my glove, I pulled it out and held it in my bare hand. If you get knocked out, you'll squeeze the ball with your bare hand, while you won't squeeze the ball in your glove, for some reason. But I didn't run into anybody and I didn't think the play was so much until I got to the dugout and they were all slapping me on the back and saying great play. I was really surprised. But then, when I saw the films of the play, I realized how far I had come.*

Fans surround Yankee shortstop Phil Rizzuto, at the wheel of his vintage car, as he leaves Ebbets Field after the New York victory in the seventh game. Behind Phil's car is a bus carrying the Yankees.

219

FIRST GAME (Oct. 1, at Brooklyn)

NEW YORK.................001 000 010 2 6 2
BROOKLYN................010 002 01x 4 6 0
Reynolds, Scarborough (8th)
Black

SECOND GAME (Oct. 2, at Brooklyn)

NEW YORK.................000 115 000 7 10 0
BROOKLYN................001 000 000 1 3 1
Raschi
Erskine, Loes (6th), Lehman (8th)

THIRD GAME (Oct. 3, at New York)

BROOKLYN................001 010 012 5 11 0
NEW YORK.................010 000 011 3 6 2
Roe
Lopat, Gorman (9th)

FOURTH GAME (Oct. 4, at New York)

BROOKLYN................000 000 000 0 4 1
NEW YORK.................000 100 01x 2 4 1
Black, Rutherford (8th)
Reynolds

FIFTH GAME (Oct. 5, at New York)

BROOKLYN.............010 030 100 01 6 10 0
NEW YORK.............000 050 000 00 5 5 1
Erskine
Blackwell, Sain (6th)

SIXTH GAME (Oct. 6, at Brooklyn)

NEW YORK.................000 000 210 3 9 0
BROOKLYN................000 001 010 2 8 1
Raschi, Reynolds (8th)
Loes, Roe (9th)

SEVENTH GAME (Oct. 7, at Brooklyn)

NEW YORK.................000 111 100 4 10 4
BROOKLYN................000 110 000 2 8 1
Lopat, Reynolds (4th), Raschi (7th), Kuzava (7th)
Black, Roe (6th), Erskine (8th)

A hatless Billy Martin, shown here in a sequence from the Series movie, makes the long dash to pluck Jackie Robinson's pop fly off the grass, squeezing the ball with his bare hand. In this Series Brooklyn fans—noted for their toughness—stood and applauded their beloved "nice guy," Gil Hodges, even though he went hitless in 21 at-bats—then a record for seven games.

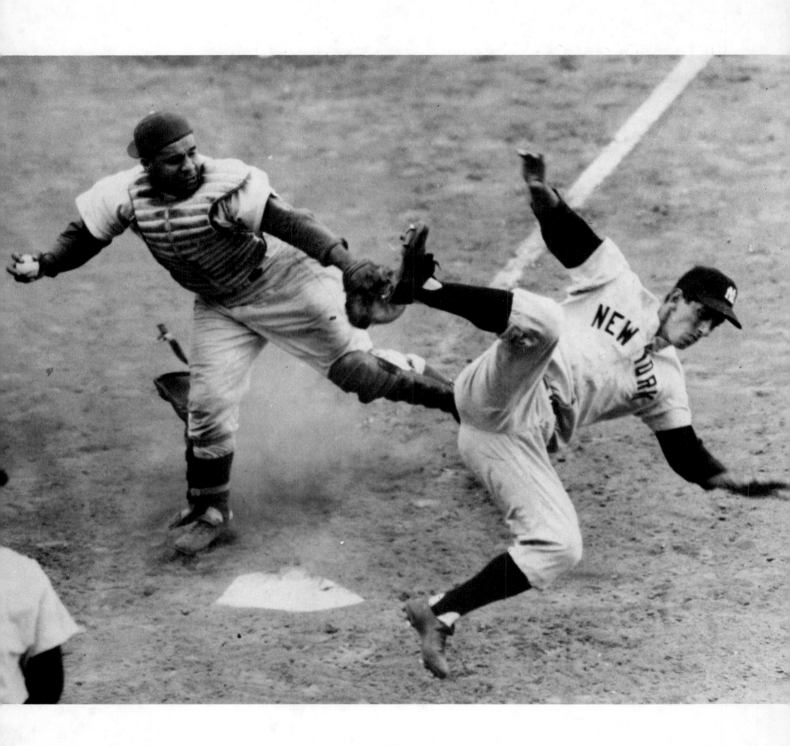

NEW YORK YANKEES
BROOKLYN DODGERS
1953

The Preacher Tells It the Way It Is

Sitting in box seats for this 50th anniversary of the World Series were six players who had played or watched from the bench in the first World Series in 1903—Bill Dinneen, Fred Parent, Fred Clarke, Tommy Leach, Otto Krueger, and Cy Young. The 86-year-old Young, who had thrown the first pitch in that 1903 Series between Pittsburgh and Boston, threw out the first pitch of the first game to Yogi Berra.

Billy Martin was again a Series hero with 12 hits, a record for a six-game Series. Mickey Mantle struck out five times in a row but hit two home runs, one of them a grand slam. The Dodgers' usually impeccable defense committed seven errors, and their strong pitching did not distinguish itself. The exception was Carl Erskine, known to the habitués of Ebbets Field as "Oisk."

With the Dodgers trailing two games to none, manager Charley Dressen started "Oisk," although he had started the first game two days earlier and had been batted out of the box in the first inning. Carl won, 3-2, striking out 14 Yankees and breaking Howard Ehmke's record of 13 set in 1929. Ehmke listened to the game on a car radio in Philadelphia. When the game ended he told his downcast wife, "Records are made to be broken." He paid for that bromide when he tried to start the car. The battery had run down.

The Dodgers also won the fourth game to tie the Series at two games apiece, but the Yankees won the next two. In the sixth and last game the Yankees broke out with a quick three runs against Erskine, but the Dodgers tied the game, 3-3, when Carl Furillo hit a two-run homer in the ninth.

In the bottom of the ninth Hank Bauer walked, and Mantle hit a single to send him to second base. Billy Martin cracked his record-setting 12th hit, a single to centerfield, and Bauer galloped home with the winning run for Casey Stengel's fifth straight championship—a record. The Yankees now had won 15 Series in their last 16 attempts. Someone asked the Dodgers' Preacher Roe if the Yanks were hard to pitch to. "No," said the laconic Preacher, "but they're hard to beat."

Roy Campanella: "What a coincidence!"

Roy Campanella, the catcher for the Dodgers and later a Manhattan businessman: *It was in that third game that Erskine struck out all the men, what was it? Fourteen, yeah. I recall that for a funny reason. I did the first Person to Person TV show that Edward R. Murrow ever did with him that night after the game. It was a live telecast from our home. They set up the cameras in the house and we talked with Murrow who was in a studio, you know. Well, a couple of weeks before the show Murrow said to me, 'The show is going to be on the night after the World Series game. So all you have to do is hit a home run in the bottom of the ninth to win the game.' Well, I came up in the bottom of the eighth and the score was tied, 2-2. I hit a home run and we won the game, 3-2. That night, on the first Person to Person show that Murrow ever did, he reminded me that he'd asked me to hit a home run in the bottom of the ninth to win the game. 'Instead you hit it in the bottom of the eighth,' he said. 'What a coincidence!'*

Roy Campanella tags out Billy Martin to end the fourth game. Martin had tried to score from second on a single. The Dodgers accused Yanks' Vic Raschi of throwing at their heads on orders from Stengel. Said Casey: "The Dodgers are crybabies even when they win."

223

"Oisk," throwing in the third game, strikes out pinch-hitter Johnny Mize for his 14th strikeout to break Howard Ehmke's 1929 record. Striking out four times in the game was Mickey Mantle. The 35,270 jammed into little Ebbets Field paid an all-time high to see Erskine break the record, box seats priced at $10, grandstand reserved seats costing $7.

FIRST GAME (Sept. 30, at New York)

BROOKLYN..................000 013 100	5 12 2
NEW YORK..................400 010 13x	9 12 0

Erskine, Hughes (2d), Labine (6th), Wade (7th)
Reynolds, Sain (6th)

SECOND GAME (Oct. 1, at New York)

BROOKLYN..................000 200 000	2 9 1
NEW YORK..................100 000 12x	4 5 0

Roe
Lopat

THIRD GAME (Oct. 2, at Brooklyn)

NEW YORK..................000 010 010	2 6 0
BROOKLYN..................000 011 01x	3 9 0

Raschi
Erskine

FOURTH GAME (Oct. 3, at Brooklyn)

NEW YORK..................000 020 001	3 9 0
BROOKLYN..................300 102 10x	7 12 0

Ford, Gorman (2d), Sain (5th), Schallock (7th)
Loes, Labine (9th)

FIFTH GAME (Oct. 4, at Brooklyn)

NEW YORK..................105 000 311	11 11 1
BROOKLYN..................010 010 041	7 14 1

McDonald, Kuzava (8th), Reynolds (9th)
Podres, Meyer (3d), Wade (8th), Black (9th)

SIXTH GAME (Oct. 5, at New York)

BROOKLYN..................000 001 002	3 8 3
NEW YORK..................210 000 001	4 13 0

Erskine, Milliken (5th), Labine (7th)
Ford, Reynolds (8th)

NEW YORK GIANTS
CLEVELAND INDIANS ━━1954

"Now Pinch-Hitting for the Giants . . . Dusty Rhodes"

Only the 1906 Cubs had won more games, 116, than the 1954 Indians, who won 111. With a pitching staff of imposing strength—Mike Garcia, Bob Lemon, and Early Wynn each won 19 or more games that year—the Indians had mastered the Yankees by eight games in the pennant race. They were heavy favorites over Leo Durocher's Giants, despite the presence in the New Yorkers' dugout of Willie Mays, at .345 the National League batting champion, and of 21-game winner Johnny Antonelli.

It was a bench warmer, however, who came out of the dugout to shine in this Series. He was James Lamar (Dusty) Rhodes, a 27-year-old outfielder who had been Durocher's "lucky-card" pinch-hitter all during the season, delivering a number of game-winning hits.

In the first game the teams were tied, 2-2, in the eighth. With two Indians on base Vic Wertz slammed a high drive far into centerfield. Willie Mays, his back to the plate, ran to the bleacher wall and snared the ball over his head at the 460-foot mark, one of the half-dozen great catches of Series history.

The teams went into the bottom of the tenth still tied at 2-2. With two Giants on base, the lefthanded Rhodes pinch-hit for Monte Irvin. He tapped a pitch on a low line toward the lower rightfield seats only 260 feet away. The ball looped over the wall for a homer, perhaps the cheapest in Series history, but it won the game, 5-2.

In the second game, with Wynn ahead in the fifth, 1-0, Durocher again put up Rhodes to pinch-hit. Rhodes popped a soft fly that fell into centerfield for a single to drive in the tying run. Rhodes stayed in the game. In the seventh he slammed a solid home run over the rightfield roof, and the Giants were 3-1 victors.

In the third inning of the third game Durocher called on Rhodes to pinch-hit for Irvin for the third time. Dusty smacked a single to drive in two runs and, with the help of Hoyt Wilhelm's relief hurling, the Giants won, 6-2.

The Giants, by winning the fourth game, became the first team, except for the Yanks, to sweep a Series in four games since the 1914 Braves. Each Giant received $11,147, each Indian massaged his sunken pride with $6,712—both record sums up to that time.

Willie Mays: The longest run

After 21 years in a Giants' uniform, Willie Mays joined the Mets. *Oh, I think I made a lot better catches than the one against Cleveland. I couldn't name them for you, but I knew I had that ball all the way from the time it left Wertz' bat. I could see the ball as soon as it left the bat, I got a good jump on it. But what a lot of people forget about that catch was that I had to make a throw on it because there were two men on base who could have moved up after I caught it. That was the toughest part of that play. When I caught the ball I had to spin around and that's when I lost my cap. It was hit a long way, I'll say that for that ball, and I don't think I ever caught any ball any deeper than I caught that one.*

Chris Durocher, Leo's adopted son (his mother was actress Laraine Day), comes out to shake hands with Dusty Rhodes after Dusty's home run in the second game. Near the bat rack in the rear is a grinning Willie Mays. No. 2 is Leo Durocher.

Vic Wertz lashes into a pitch from
the Giants' Don Liddle, who has just
relieved Sal Maglie, in the first game.
Wertz connected, socking a 460-foot
drive to the centerfield bleacher wall
in the Polo Grounds, where Willie
Mays gathers in the ball like a football
pass receiver for what is probably the
most famous Series catch in history.

FIRST GAME (Sept. 29, at New York)

CLEVELAND..............200 000 000 0 2 8 0
NEW YORK...............002 000 000 3 5 9 3
Lemon
Maglie, Liddle (8th), Grissom (8th)

SECOND GAME (Sept. 30, at New York)

CLEVELAND................100 000 000 1 8 0
NEW YORK.................000 020 10x 3 4 0
Wynn, Mossi (8th)
Antonelli

THIRD GAME (Oct. 1, at Cleveland)

NEW YORK.................103 011 000 6 10 1
CLEVELAND...............000 000 110 2 4 2
Gomez, Wilhelm (8th)
Garcia, Houtteman (4th), Narleski (6th), Mossi (9th)

FOURTH GAME (Oct. 2, at Cleveland)

NEW YORK.................021 040 000 7 10 3
CLEVELAND...............000 030 100 4 6 2
Liddle, Wilhelm (7th), Antonelli (8th)
Lemon, Newhouser (5th), Narleski (5th), Mossi (6th),
   Garcia (8th)

BROOKLYN DODGERS
NEW YORK YANKEES
1955

"Next Year" Finally Came To Brooklyn

The Dodgers lost the first two games, and on Brooklyn's Flatbush Avenue you heard the first mutterings: "Wait till next year." The Faithful, as Dodger fans were called with sympathy by the New York press, were already accepting another Series defeat, the seventh without a victory by the Dodgers. And certainly there was reason for resignation; no team in World Series history had lost the first two games and gone on to win a seven-game Series.

Brooklyn did come back to win the next two games, helped by the pitching of young Johnny Podres and the home runs of Roy Campanella, Gil Hodges, and Duke Snider. Brooklyn went ahead in the Series, three games to two, when Snider hit a pair of homers in the fifth game, his eighth and ninth Series homers, the most by a National Leaguer. But Whitey Ford won the sixth game, his second of the Series, and the two teams went into a seventh game. Before the game Hank Bauer said what players have said before dozens of seventh games: "There's no tomorrow."

The Yanks started Tommy Byrne against the 23-year-old Podres. With the Dodgers leading, 2-0, in the bottom of the sixth, Walter Alston moved Junior Gilliam from leftfield to second base, and Sandy Amoros to left. With two Yankees on base Yogi Berra lofted a fly along the leftfield foul line. Amoros raced from left center and speared the ball with his right, or glove, hand. A righthanded thrower like Gilliam could never have made the catch. Amoros threw to Pee Wee Reese, who threw to first to double a Yankee runner and kill the rally. From then on Podres fooled the Yankees with his breaking pitches, winning his second Series game, 2-0. The game ended on a roller to Reese, who threw to Gil Hodges, and the Brooklyn Dodgers, for this one and only time, were world champions.

Pee Wee Reese:
A $20 call to Gil Hodges

That last out, I'll never forget it, said Pee Wee Reese, former Dodger shortstop and later a TV sportscaster. *Elston Howard hit a ground ball to me. Don Hoak, God rest his soul, was playing third base, and he always said I threw the ball into the dirt and Gil [Hodges] scooped it up. I remember one year, when I was broadcasting, Don and I had a few beers and we bet twenty dollars I threw the ball into the dirt. I knew I hadn't because I had seen the movies. Anyway we called Gil long distance—I don't know where we were—and I asked him on the telephone, 'Gil, was it in the dirt?' Right away he said, 'Yes, it was.' I said, 'Gil, come on, this is for twenty dollars.' And then he admitted, 'No, it wasn't.' It's funny, though, I think more about it afterwards, what might have happened if I had booted the ball. At the time I wasn't thinking about what would have happened.*

Brooklyn's Pee Wee Reese hops over the sliding Billy Martin to throw to first, but his throw was too late to double up Yogi Berra. Pee Wee shares with Elston Howard the record for being on the most losing Series teams —six.

FIRST GAME (Sept. 28, at New York)

BROOKLYN................021 000 020   5 10 0
NEW YORK................021 102 00x   6 9 1
Newcombe, Bessent (6th), Labine (8th)
Ford, Grim (9th)

SECOND GAME (Sept. 29, at New York)

BROOKLYN................000 110 000   2 5 2
NEW YORK................000 400 00x   4 8 0
Loes, Bessent (4th), Spooner (5th), Labine (8th)
Byrne

THIRD GAME (Sept. 30, at Brooklyn)

NEW YORK................020 000 100   3 7 0
BROOKLYN................220 200 20x   8 11 1
Turley, Morgan (2d), Kucks (5th), Sturdivant (7th)
Podres

FOURTH GAME (Oct. 1, at Brooklyn)

NEW YORK................110 102 000   5 9 0
BROOKLYN................001 330 10x   8 14 0
Larsen, Kucks (5th), R. Coleman (6th), Morgan (7th),
     Sturdivant (8th)
Erskine, Bessent (4th), Labine (5th)

FIFTH GAME (Oct. 2, at Brooklyn)

NEW YORK................000 100 110   3 6 0
BROOKLYN................021 010 01x   5 9 2
Grim, Turley (7th)
Craig, Labine (7th)

SIXTH GAME (Oct. 3, at New York)

BROOKLYN................000 100 000   1 4 1
NEW YORK................500 000 00x   5 8 0
Spooner, Meyer (1st), Roebuck (7th)
Ford

SEVENTH GAME (Oct. 4, at New York)

BROOKLYN................000 101 000   2 5 0
NEW YORK................000 000 000   0 8 1
Podres
Byrne, Grim (6th), Turley (8th)

Sandy Amoros dashes toward the leftfield foul line, watched by two umpires, and spears the ball hit by Yogi Berra. The catch was especially difficult because in October the sun glares almost directly into leftfielders' eyes at Yankee Stadium. Note the slant of the shadows.

NEW YORK YANKEES
BROOKLYN DODGERS 1956

Get Rid of the Windup and Have a Few Beers

Don Larsen looked at his watch. It was near midnight. He finished the beer, one of several he'd put away this night, and went off to bed. Tomorrow, he knew, he would be starting the fifth game of the Series which was deadlocked at two games apiece, the Dodgers and Yankees battling for the sixth time in 10 years.

Don Larsen was no All Star. He'd labored for several years with the basement St. Louis Browns, who once thought of making him into an outfielder. With the Yankees this season he had struggled through a 9-2 record, completing only five of 13 starts. Late in the season he had adopted a no-windup delivery after discovering that opposing teams could tell whether he was throwing a curve or a fastball by the way he wound up. Yankee manager Casey Stengel thought Larsen could be a top pitcher if he would stay away from the Broadway lights and get more sleep. But Don, even before a Series start, liked a few nightcaps with friends.

The next afternoon, at nearly 3:30 p.m., Larsen stood on the mound as the Dodgers came to bat in the ninth. So far he had not yielded a walk or a hit to 24 batters, and none had reached base because of an error. He was within three outs of pitching the first Series no-hitter, the first Series perfect game, and only the sixth perfect game in the modern era of big league baseball.

Earlier, in the second inning, Jackie Robinson had hit a drive that ricocheted off third baseman Andy Carey's glove, but shortstop Gil McDougald scooped up the ball and threw Robinson out. Mickey Mantle had sped to left center in

the fifth inning and backhanded a drive by Gil Hodges. And the Dodgers' Sandy Amoros had hit a towering drive that hooked foul into the seats, said Yankee rightfielder Hank Bauer later, "by inches." They were the closest the Dodgers had come to a hit.

Now, here in the ninth, the Yanks ahead, 2-0, Larsen threw to Carl Furillo, who flied out. Roy Campanella tapped a roller to second baseman Billy Martin, who threw him out. Pinch-hitter Dale Mitchell came to bat. The count went to a ball and two strikes. Larsen leaned back and muscled homeward an outside fastball. Umpire Babe Pinelli's arm jerked upward for the third strike and the third out, and a jubilant Larsen leaped into Yogi Berra's arms and into the record books.

Two days later the Series winner was decided in a seventh game. The Dodgers started Don Newcombe, never effective in a Series since his heartbreaking 1-0 loss to the Yankees in 1949. The Yankees rammed three home runs out of Ebbets Field, driving Newcombe off the mound and into despair—his wife didn't see him for 24 hours—and the Dodgers' one-year reign as world champions had ended, the Yankees again the best in baseball.

Yogi Berra:
"I just remember Larsen"

Suppose you're in a game that can become a no-hitter. What does a catcher do? What does he think? Yogi Berra, the former Yankee catcher

Dodgers' Pee Wee Reese leaps for a blooper off Hank Bauer's bat, but the ball drops for a hit in the final game. From 1956 to 1958 Bauer hit safely in 17 straight World Series games.

Don Larsen, shown in
the World Series film,
goes through his
no-windup delivery
and, at right, releases
the ball for the game's
final pitch, striking out
Dale Mitchell. Behind
Larsen is second
baseman Billy Martin
and a scoreboard that
tells its own story. His
knees, Larsen said later,
were buckling with
nervousness in the
ninth inning.

236

and manager of the Mets, said: *I can still remember that last pitch to Mitchell that Larsen threw. I called for a fastball. He didn't shake me off during the whole game. It was high, the pitch, and I dunno whether it was a strike or not. I just ran out there to the mound. I jumped on Larsen and I said something like, 'Great game, Don!' In the dugout you sometimes talk about a no-hitter when a guy has one going, and we might have if the score had been 8-0 or something like that. But a walk and a home run could've tied the game in the ninth and we could've lost it so nobody said nothing. People have asked me what I did in that game. I had to look it up because I couldn't remember. I don't remember what any of us did. I just remember Larsen.*

237

Don Larsen (top) talks to reporters after his perfect game. Bottom: Casey clowns for the photographers. Opposite page, top: Larsen and his manager. Bottom: Winning pitcher Whitey Ford and outfielder Enos Slaughter. Slaughter is telling the world he batted in three runs during the Yankees' 5–3 victory in the third game.

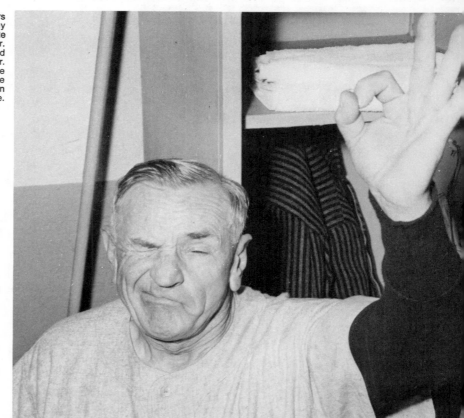

FIRST GAME (Oct. 3, at Brooklyn)

NEW YORK 200 100 000   3 9 1
BROOKLYN 023 100 00x   6 9 0
Ford, Kucks (4th), Morgan (6th), Turley (8th)
Maglie

SECOND GAME (Oct. 5, at Brooklyn)

NEW YORK 150 100 001   8 12 2
BROOKLYN 061 220 02x 13 12 0
Larsen, Kucks (2d), Byrne (2d), Sturdivant (3d), Mor-
   gan (3d), Turley (5th), McDermott (6th)
Newcombe, Roebuck (2d), Bessent (3d)

THIRD GAME (Oct. 6, at New York)

BROOKLYN 010 001 100 3 8 1
NEW YORK 010 003 01x 5 8 1
Craig, Labine (7th)
Ford

FOURTH GAME (Oct. 7, at New York)

BROOKLYN 000 100 001 2 6 0
NEW YORK 100 201 20x 6 7 2
Erskine, Roebuck (5th), Drysdale (7th)
Sturdivant

FIFTH GAME (Oct. 8, at New York)

BROOKLYN 000 000 000 0 0 0
NEW YORK 000 101 00x 2 5 0
Maglie
Larsen

SIXTH GAME (Oct. 9, at Brooklyn)

NEW YORK 000 000 000 0 0 7 0
BROOKLYN 000 000 000 1 1 4 0
Turley
Labine

SEVENTH GAME (Oct. 10, at Brooklyn)

NEW YORK 202 100 400 9 10 0
BROOKLYN 000 000 000 0 3 1
Kucks
Newcombe, Bessent (4th), Craig (7th), Roebuck (7th),
   Erskine (9th)

MILWAUKEE BRAVES
NEW YORK YANKEES **1957**

The Best Shoeshine Nippy Ever Bought

With a little bit of help from a smudged baseball and a lot of help from a towering righthander named Lou Burdette, the Milwaukee Braves—the transplanted Boston Braves—won their first Series in their first try.

The smudged baseball helped in the fourth game, when the Braves seemed headed for a defeat that would have left them behind the Yankees, three games to one. They were losing, 5-4, going into the bottom of the tenth. Vernal (Nippy) Jones batted for Warren Spahn. Tommy Byrne threw a low pitch that umpire Augie Donatelli called a ball. Jones claimed the pitch had hit him in the foot. He showed Donatelli a smudge of shoe polish on the ball, and Donatelli waved him to first. That set off a Brave rally and a 7-5 victory that evened the Series at two games each.

For the third straight year the Series came down to a seventh game. Burdette, often accused of throwing illegal spitballs but always found innocent by the umpires, had already won two complete games. With Spahn ill with the flu Burdette started after only two days of rest. He shut out the Yankees, 5-0, pitching his second successive shutout of the Series, blanking the ex-champions for 24 straight innings. The Yankees' Yogi Berra went home with a consolation prize. He had played in a record 53 World Series games.

Eddie Mathews:
At the end everything broke wild

Eddie Mathews, the Milwaukee Braves' third baseman, was later the Atlanta Braves' manager. *In the ninth inning of that last game,* he remembered, *there were two out and the bases were loaded. I knew a sinkerball pitcher like Burdette would be keeping the ball down and [Bill] Skowron was a good pull hitter so I got closer to the line. I know Skowron said later I was playing too close to the line, but I don't think I was. He hit it to my right. I reached out with my glove and made a good play on it. I didn't have to look in my glove, I knew I had it. I stepped on third base and everything broke wild around me. Burdette ran over, we jumped on each other. None of us, except Spahn, had ever been in a Series before, and it was exciting for us.*

241

Yogi Berra stretches for a high throw that arrives too late for Berra to tag out Johnny Logan in the final game. Signaling his teammate to slide is No. 44—Hank Aaron. The Braves' jet, returning to Milwaukee after the victory, couldn't land until crowds were cleared from runways.

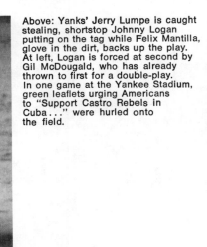

Above: Yanks' Jerry Lumpe is caught stealing, shortstop Johnny Logan putting on the tag while Felix Mantilla, glove in the dirt, backs up the play. At left, Logan is forced at second by Gil McDougald, who has already thrown to first for a double-play. In one game at the Yankee Stadium, green leaflets urging Americans to "Support Castro Rebels in Cuba..." were hurled onto the field.

FIRST GAME (Oct. 2, at New York)

MILWAUKEE.................000 000 100   1 5 0
NEW YORK.................000 012 00x   3 9 1
Spahn, Johnson (6th), McMahon (7th)
Ford

SECOND GAME (Oct. 3, at New York)

MILWAUKEE.................011 200 000   4 8 0
NEW YORK.................011 000 000   2 7 2
Burdette
Shantz, Ditmar (4th), Grim (8th)

THIRD GAME (Oct. 5, at Milwaukee)

NEW YORK.................302 200 500   12 9 0
MILWAUKEE.................010 020 000   3 8 1
Turley, Larsen (2d)
Buhl, Pizarro (1st), Conley (3d), Johnson (5th), Trow-
   bridge (7th), McMahon (8th)

FOURTH GAME (Oct. 6, at Milwaukee)

NEW YORK...............100 000 003 1 5 11 0
MILWAUKEE.............000 400 000 3 7 7 0
Sturdivant, Shantz (5th), Kucks (8th), Byrne (8th),
   Grim (10th)
Spahn

FIFTH GAME (Oct. 7, at Milwaukee)

NEW YORK.................000 000 000   0 7 0
MILWAUKEE.................000 001 00x   1 6 1
Ford, Turley (8th)
Burdette

SIXTH GAME (Oct. 9, at New York)

MILWAUKEE.................000 010 100   2 4 0
NEW YORK.................002 000 10x   3 7 0
Buhl, Johnson (3d), McMahon (8th)
Turley

SEVENTH GAME (Oct. 10, at New York)

MILWAUKEE.................004 000 010   5 9 1
NEW YORK.................000 000 000   0 7 3
Burdette
Larsen, Shantz (3d), Ditmar (4th), Sturdivant (6th),
   Byrne (8th)

Joy Flies Back
To New York in Blackface

A few hours before the start of the fifth game, with the Yankees losing three games to one, a Brooklyn fan who had been betting on the Yankees said to a friend, "How am I going to make up all I'm going to lose when the Yankees get beat?"

"What more have you got to lose?" said his friend. "Look, the Braves are now favored to win the Series at odds like eight to one. When again will you be able to bet on the Yankees and get odds of eight to one? So bet more money on the Yankees. If they win you'll more than make up for what you have lost. Even if they lose, you can always tell people years later you bet on the Yankees when they were underdogs."

The Brooklyn fan went out and put another $25 on the Yankees, and a few days later he was some $200 richer. He could be thankful for a great catch by Elston Howard and for the pitching of Bob Turley. In the fifth game, the Yankees ahead, 1-0, the Braves put a runner on first base. Red Schoendienst looped a soft liner that seemed likely to drop in and score a run, but Howard dove across the grass, caught the ball, then threw to first to double the runner. Eddie Mathews followed with a single that would have put the Braves ahead if Howard had not caught Schoendienst's drive. Instead, Mathews was stranded, and the Yankees blasted Lou Burdette off the mound. Turley shut out the Braves the rest of the way to win, 7-0. The Yanks now trailed, three games to two.

The Yankees tied the Series at three games each by winning the sixth game in the tenth, 4-3, Turley stalking in from the bullpen to get the last out with the winning run on base. Don Larsen started the seventh game against Burdette,

but Turley, pitching in his third straight game, relieved him in the third inning. He yielded only one run, but the game was tied, 2-2, as the Yankees came to bat in the eighth. With two out Yogi Berra doubled; it was his 61st Series hit in his 61st Series game, two of a dozen Series records for Yogi, who was setting a new one each time he batted. That hit seemed to exhaust Burdette, who could no longer keep his pitches low. The Yankees drove four runs across to win, 6-2, and regain their world championship.

The Yankees flew home in boisterous spirits, their faces blackened by burned champagne corks. They were the first team since the 1925 Pirates to come from behind and win after being down three games to one. And now they had beaten every National League team in World Series play.

Elston Howard:
"I wasn't a good outfielder"

Elston Howard is now a Yankee coach, but he formerly was a Yankee catcher-outfielder. And he said, *You know, I wasn't a good outfielder. I was quick behind the plate but I was never quick on the jump for the fly ball when I played the outfield. Some guys, the ball is hit and they are moving but I was never that way. But for some reason, on that line drive that Schoendienst hit, I got a good jump. I was running in and I caught the ball at the grass. Some people thought I trapped it but I didn't. To tell you the truth, I thought it was going to fall in, and so did Billy Bruton, the runner. He was already around second when I caught it and it was easy to double him.*

Yanks' Norm Siebern is safe at third, beating a throw to Eddie Mathews as coach Frank Crosetti watches. Crosetti shared in the pots of 23 Series as a player and coach. Siebern, playing left—the "sunfield" at the stadium— lost two flyballs in the glare during the fourth game.

FIRST GAME (Oct. 1, at Milwaukee)

NEW YORK 000 120 000 0 3 8 1
MILWAUKEE 000 200 010 1 4 10 0
Ford, Duren (8th)
Spahn

SECOND GAME (Oct. 2, at Milwaukee)

NEW YORK 100 100 003 5 7 0
MILWAUKEE 710 000 23x 13 15 1
Turley, Maas (1st), Kucks (1st), Dickson (5th), Monroe
  (8th)
Burdette

THIRD GAME (Oct. 4, at New York)

MILWAUKEE 000 000 000 0 6 0
NEW YORK 000 020 20x 4 4 0
Rush, McMahon (7th)
Larsen, Duren (8th)

FOURTH GAME (Oct. 5, at New York)

MILWAUKEE 000 001 110 3 9 0
NEW YORK 000 000 000 0 2 1
Spahn
Ford, Kucks (8th), Dickson (9th)

FIFTH GAME (Oct. 6, at New York)

MILWAUKEE 000 000 000 0 5 0
NEW YORK 001 006 00x 7 10 0
Burdette, Pizarro (6th), Willey (8th)
Turley

SIXTH GAME (Oct. 8, at Milwaukee)

NEW YORK 100 001 000 2 4 10 1
MILWAUKEE 110 000 000 1 3 10 4
Ford, Ditmar (2d), Duren (6th), Turley (10th)
Spahn, McMahon (10th)

SEVENTH GAME (Oct. 9, at Milwaukee)

NEW YORK 020 000 040 6 8 0
MILWAUKEE 100 001 000 2 5 2
Larsen, Turley (3d)
Burdette, McMahon (9th)

Photographers and
reporters encircle two
New York heroes of the
fifth game: Gil Mc-
Dougald (l.) and Elston
Howard. They are
seated on a table in the
middle of the Yankee
clubhouse. New York
writers Jack Lang and
Milton Gross (in cap)
are on Howard's left.
Louis Effrat is between
the players. Gil hit a
homer and knocked in
three runs in the 7–0
victory over that old
Yankee nemesis Lou
Burdette. Howard, the
leftfielder, dived to
snare a low liner hit
by Red Schoendienst
and turned the catch
into a double-play. The
play preserved a thin
1–0 Yankee lead.

247

LOS ANGELES DODGERS 1959
CHICAGO WHITE SOX

The Crowds Came
and Not for Football

In the first Series ever played west of St. Louis, the Dodgers won in six games, three of which were played in a stadium that held more than 100,000 people. As a result, this was, until 1970, the best-attended Series ever. A total of 420,784 watched, more than the combined attendance for all the Series played from 1903 through 1907. The third, fourth, and fifth games, played in the Los Angeles Memorial Coliseum—where the transplanted Dodgers played while awaiting the building of Dodger Stadium—drew successive crowds of 92,394, 92,650, and 92,706. The games were played on an oval field designed for football. The leftfield line ran only 251 feet to the seats, but a screen 42 feet high made home runs more difficult. Righthanded batters—left-handed batters too—tried to punch the ball into the screen for a double or knock it over the screen into the seats. But often they tried too hard and popped up; only two homers were hit over the screen in the Series.

A young Dodger relief pitcher, Larry Sherry, drew attention away from the screen. In all four Dodger victories it was the 24-year-old Sherry who came out of the bullpen to nip White Sox rallies. The White Sox, called the Go-Go-Sox by their fans because of the speed on the bases of Luis Aparicio and other whippets, had no power except for the hulking Ted Kluszewski. But the Go-Go-Sox surprised the nation with their power in the first game, Big Klu hitting two homers, and the Sox winning, 11-0.

Sherry stopped the White Sox in the next three games. He was helped by one of the few Brooklyn Dodgers still on the team, Gil Hodges, who hit an eighth-inning homer for a 5-4 Dodger victory in the fourth game, putting Los Angeles ahead, three games to one.

Walter Alston sent a wild young lefty, Sandy Koufax, to the mound to end the Series, but Sandy lost his first Series start, 1-0. The two teams went back to Chicago, where Sherry came in to relieve Johnny Podres in the fourth inning, blanking the Sox the rest of the way in a 9-3 Dodger victory. Each losing Sox received $7,257, each winning Dodger, $11,231—the heaviest pots yet. The surprise of the Series was Sox manager Al Lopez' failure to start Billy Pierce, long a Chicago ace. Pierce pitched only in relief and didn't allow a run in four innings.

Ted Kluszewski:
"This was the *only* game"

It was the ultimate for me, playing in that Series, said Ted Kluszewski, the former first baseman for the Reds and the White Sox and now a Cincinnati coach. *It wasn't like I was a kid with stars in my eyes. I had been 13 years in the big leagues. But I had never been in a Series and it was hard to be blasé about it. I remember when we went out for that first game in Chicago, when I ran onto the field, I thought, this is the only game, absolutely the only baseball game, being played today. It's not like during the season when there are ten or so games being played in both leagues. This was the* only *game, and fifty million people are watching. It was something special. I think it's what every ballplayer looks forward to and what made it better for me, I had a good Series.*

Ted Kluszewski, an ex-National Leaguer, hits a home run in the third inning of the first game. He socked another in the fourth inning. In this Series Big Klu knocked in 10 runs, a record for a six-game Series.

Larry Sherry, who wore a "football number"—51—pitching for the Dodgers. One of the "reporters" at the Series, covering the games for *Life* magazine, was Casey Stengel. Another hero for the Dodgers was one of the last of the Brooklyn Dodgers—"The Boys of Summer"—Gil Hodges. In the fourth game Gil hit a home run in the bottom of the eighth to break a tie and give Los Angeles a 5–4 victory.

FIRST GAME (Oct. 1, at Chicago)

```
LOS ANGELES............000 000 000    0  8  3
CHICAGO................207 200 00x   11 11  0
```
Craig, Churn (3d), Labine (4th), Koufax (5th), Klippstein (7th)
Wynn, Staley (8th)

SECOND GAME (Oct. 2, at Chicago)

```
LOS ANGELES............000 010 300    4  9  1
CHICAGO................200 000 010    3  8  0
```
Podres, Sherry (7th)
Shaw, Lown (7th)

THIRD GAME (Oct. 4, at Los Angeles)

```
CHICAGO................000 000 010    1 12  0
LOS ANGELES............000 000 21x    3  5  0
```
Donovan, Staley (7th)
Drysdale, Sherry (8th)

FOURTH GAME (Oct. 5, at Los Angeles)

```
CHICAGO................000 000 400    4 10  3
LOS ANGELES............004 000 01x    5  9  0
```
Wynn, Lown (3d), Pierce (4th), Staley (7th)
Craig, Sherry (8th)

FIFTH GAME (Oct. 6, at Los Angeles)

```
CHICAGO................000 100 000    1  5  0
LOS ANGELES............000 000 000    0  9  0
```
Shaw, Pierce (8th), Donovan (8th)
Koufax, Williams (8th)

SIXTH GAME (Oct. 8, at Chicago)

```
LOS ANGELES............002 600 001    9 13  0
CHICAGO................000 300 000    3  6  1
```
Podres, Sherry (4th)
Wynn, Donovan (4th), Lown (4th), Staley (5th), Pierce (8th), Moore (9th)

251

PITTSBURGH PIRATES
NEW YORK YANKEES
1960

The Spoiler for Casey Was a Bad Hop

The Yankees hit .338—a record for one Series. The Yankees belted out 91 hits—a record. The Yankees scored 55 runs—a record. The Yankees won three games by scores of 16-3, 10-0, and 12-0, the last two victories the most lopsided shutouts in Series history. The Pirates hit only .256 and four home runs. But the Pirates sent out little Elroy Face to save 6-4, 3-2, and 5-2 victories for them. And in the seventh game they had a little bit of luck and one very big home run to end what is often called the weirdest of all Series.

The seventh game will always be among the most memorable of Series games. Bob Turley started against Vernon Law, but neither went the distance. Even Face could not stem a four-run Yankee attack in the sixth inning as the Yankees took a 5-4 lead. They scored two more in the eighth off Face and seemed on the way to winning Casey Stengel's eighth world championship in 10 World Series. But a bad hop would lead to Casey's third loss in his last World Series.

With a runner on first base in the bottom of the eighth, Bill Virdon hit a hopping ball right at shortstop Tony Kubek. "Oh, ———," thought Virdon as he ran to first, figuring he had hit into a double play. But the ball hopped up and hit Kubek in the throat, sending him to a hospital. Dick Groat singled in a run, and Roberto Clemente beat out a hit to score another. Then reserve catcher Hal Smith belted a homer to put the Pirates ahead, 9-7. Forbes Field became a caldron of noise.

The Yankees fought back with two runs in the ninth, tying the score. The first batter for the Pirates in the bottom of the ninth was second baseman Bill Mazeroski. The Yanks' Ralph Terry threw an inside pitch to the muscular Maz, who whipped it over the leftfield wall to win the game, 10-9. While Pirate fans danced in the Golden Triangle to celebrate their first championship since 1925, someone asked Terry what kind of pitch he had thrown to Mazeroski. "The wrong one," said Terry.

Bill Skowron:
Mickey asked, "How's Tony?"

The conversation was about the Series and, of course, talk soon centered on Mickey Mantle. Bill Skowron, the former Yankee first baseman and now a Chicago businessman, remembered the excitement and the hitting. *Mickey had a great Series. He hit some balls that were among the hardest drives he's ever hit. He hit one drive over the centerfield wall that was close to 500 feet and I read later where some of the Pirates, like Bill Virdon, said they'd never seen a ball hit farther in Forbes Field. He'd lost a Series before, but Mickey figured the Yankees had lost because the other team played better. But we beat the Pirates so bad in those games [in 1960] and then, also, there was some things being said by some of the Pirate players that none of us liked. Anyway, after that seventh game, Mickey sat in front of his locker and he couldn't stop crying. It was almost embarrassing, he felt so bad. They'd taken Tony [Kubek] to the hospital, and when Mickey stopped crying, the first thing he asked was, 'How's Tony?'*

Yanks' Bobby Richardson toes home plate a split second before the tag by catcher Hal Smith in the sixth game. Bobby scored from third base on a surprise bunt by Whitey Ford. In the Yankee clubhouse after the final game, Mickey Mantle sobbed uncontrollably.

253

Bobby Richardson touches home after hitting a grand-slam home run in the third game. He is congratulated by Bill Skowron (14), Elston Howard (32), and Gil McDougald (12). Hal Smith is the Pirate catcher. Richardson set Series records by driving in six runs in the game, 12 in the Series. Opposite page: Smith tags out Roger Maris in the third game. Maris, his chest injured on the play, had to leave the game and was replaced in rightfield by Yogi Berra. Watching the play is Gil McDougald.

FIRST GAME (Oct. 5, at Pittsburgh)

NEW YORK.................100 100 002 4 13 2
PITTSBURGH 300 201 00x 6 8 0
Ditmar, Coates (1st), Maas (5th), Duren (7th)
Law, Face (8th)

SECOND GAME (Oct. 6, at Pittsburgh)

NEW YORK.................002 127 301 16 19 1
PITTSBURGH...............000 100 002   3 13 1
Turley, Shantz (9th)
Friend, Green (5th), Labine (6th), Witt (6th), Gibbon
  (7th), Cheney (9th)

THIRD GAME (Oct. 8, at New York)

PITTSBURGH...............000 000 000   0 4 0
NEW YORK.................600 400 00x 10 16 1
Mizell, Labine (1st), Green (1st), Witt (4th), Cheney
  (6th), Gibbon (8th)
Ford

FOURTH GAME (Oct. 9, at New York)

PITTSBURGH................000 030 000 3 7 0
NEW YORK.................000 100 100 2 8 0
Law, Face (7th)
Terry, Shantz (7th), Coates (8th)

FIFTH GAME (Oct. 10, at New York)

PITTSBURGH...............031 000 001 5 10 2
NEW YORK.................011 000 000 2 5 2
Haddix, Face (7th)
Ditmar, Arroyo (2d), Stafford (3d), Duren (8th)

SIXTH GAME (Oct. 12, at Pittsburgh)

NEW YORK.................015 002 220 12 17 1
PITTSBURGH...............000 000 000   0 7 1
Ford
Friend, Cheney (3d), Mizell (4th), Green (6th), Labine
  (6th), Witt (9th)

SEVENTH GAME (Oct. 13, at Pittsburgh)

NEW YORK.................000 014 022   9 13 1
PITTSBURGH...............220 000 051 10 11 0
Turley, Stafford (2d), Shantz (3d), Coates (8th), Terry
  (9th)
Law, Face (6th), Friend (9th), Haddix (9th)

Ralph Terry pitches and Bill Mazeroski
swings, the ball rocketing toward the
leftfield corner, where Yogi Berra
watches it sail out of sight. A smiling
Maz strides toward home (r.) and at
the plate is mobbed by ecstatic fans
and players. The game was marked by
a rarity that made its way into what
has become a 80-odd-page list of
World Series records. In this game
there were the fewest strikeouts by
two teams: none.

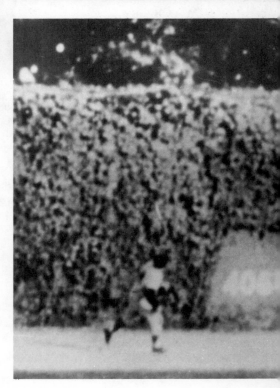

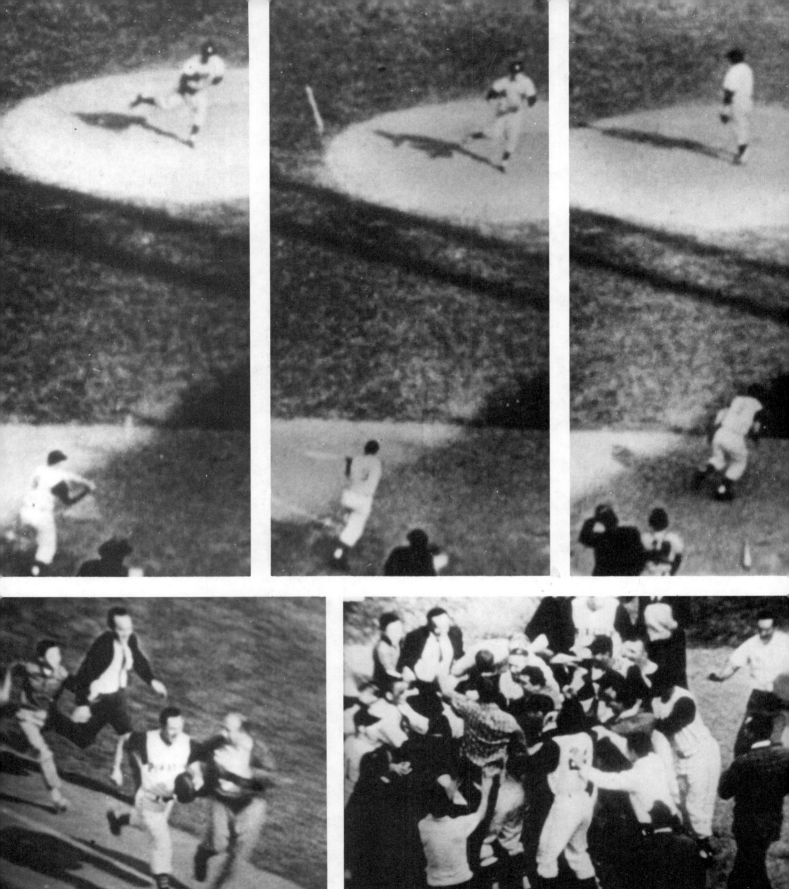

NEW YORK YANKEES
CINCINNATI REDS
1961

Whitey Ford
Is the New Babe Ruth

"Maybe I'll go after some of the Babe's batting records," Whitey Ford announced in his wise-cracking, cock-of-the-walk way. This was after the fourth game, in which he had shut out the Reds for the first five innings to extend to 32 innings his string of shutout World Series pitching, breaking Babe Ruth's record of 29⅔ innings. Whitey had shut out the Pirates in his two appearances in 1960, then blanked the Reds, 2-0, in the first game of the '61 Series. Pitching in the fourth game, he could go only five innings because of an injured ankle, but the Reds could not score on him, and he left the field in the sixth after breaking a record that Ruth had said was the one he cherished the most.

In this Series Mickey Mantle tried to come back after surgery on an abscessed hip. But in the fourth game he limped to first base after hitting a long drive, blood spurting from the hip and splotching his pants, and he was finished for the Series. But the other "M" of what was called the Dial-M-for-Murder Yankees—Roger Maris, hitter of 61 homers that season—smashed a ninth-inning homer in the third game to beat Bob Purkey, 3-2. That loss seemed to deflate the Reds, and with strong hitting from Johnny Blanchard, coming off the bench to pinch-hit and replace Mantle in the outfield, the Yankees swept by the Reds in five games. The Reds used eight pitchers in the final contest, a record number for a Series game. (That game consumed a little more than three hours, more than an hour longer than it took to finish any game in the '03 Series.)

Whitey Ford:
I remember the record and see the blood

The Series to Whitey Ford, the ex-Yankee pitcher and later a part-time Yankee coach, was especially vivid. *In that fourth game, when I broke Ruth's record, I got hit in the foot and I had to leave the game. I came into the clubhouse and I saw Mickey. His pants were all bloody. The abscess was wide open and you could see the tendon and muscles in it. It was wide enough to put a golf ball into it. I was watching from the dugout earlier in the game when he hit a ball off the wall in right field. He ran for first and he was halfway to first when he pulled up and you could see the blood on the pants. I can still see it. Now, when I think about that game, I remember Ruth's record . . . breaking Ruth's record . . . but what I see is Mickey trying to run to first and the blood running down his pants leg.*

Top: Reds' Elio Chacon scores on a passed ball by catcher Elston Howard, who pins the ball on Chacon too late. Watching is Ralph Terry. Bottom: Reds' Gordon Coleman sticks out a mitt to tag Bobby Richardson on a pick-off attempt, but Richardson skidded back ahead of the tag.

259

The Yankees (in the foreground) and the Reds line up for the playing of the "Star Spangled Banner" before the first game. Maris is No. 9, Mantle No. 7. No. 35 is Ralph Houk in his first Series as a manager. Behind the two groundskeepers is starting pitcher Whitey Ford. On the third-base side of home plate is Red starter Jim O'Toole.

FIRST GAME (Oct. 4, at New York)

CINCINNATI 000 000 000   0 2 0
NEW YORK 000 101 00x   2 6 0
O'Toole, Brosnan (8th)
Ford

SECOND GAME (Oct. 5, at New York)

CINCINNATI 000 211 020   6 9 0
NEW YORK 000 200 000   2 4 3
Jay
Terry, Arroyo (8th)

THIRD GAME (Oct. 7, at Cincinnati)

NEW YORK 000 000 111   3 6 1
CINCINNATI 001 000 100   2 8 0
Stafford, Daley (7th), Arroyo (8th)
Purkey

FOURTH GAME (Oct. 8, at Cincinnati)

NEW YORK 000 112 300   7 11 0
CINCINNATI 000 000 000   0 5 1
Ford, Coates (6th)
O'Toole, Brosnan (6th), Henry (9th)

FIFTH GAME (Oct. 9, at Cincinnati)

NEW YORK 510 502 000   13 15 1
CINCINNATI 003 020 000   5 11 3
Terry, Daley (3d)
Jay, Maloney (1st), Johnson (2d), Henry (3d), Jones (4th), Purkey (5th), Brosnan (7th), Hunt (9th)

NEW YORK YANKEES
SAN FRANCISCO GIANTS 1962

It Was a Case of
You Do or You Don't

It all came down, after seven games and almost two weeks of rain-interrupted play, to one line drive. If the Yankees caught that line drive, they were winners; if it fell safely the Giants were winners in this first coast-to-coast renewal of a feud that had begun 42 years earlier on the bank of the Harlem River—even before Yankee Stadium was built. Now, instead of a nickel subway ride between Yankee Stadium and the Polo Grounds, the two teams had to fly over 3,000 miles to meet each other.

The pitchers lorded it over the hitters throughout the Series, the Yankees hitting only .199, the Giants only a little higher at .226. Neither team could gain a lead in the first six games; first one team would go ahead by a game, then the other. The only batting of note was in the fourth game when the Giants' Chuck Hiller hit a grand-slam homer, the first ever made in a Series by a National Leaguer.

Ralph Terry started against Jack Sanford in the seventh game. The Yankees established a 1-0 lead in the fifth when Bill Skowron scored as Tony Kubek hit into a double play. The Yankees still led, 1-0, as the Giants came to bat in the bottom of the ninth. With Matty Alou on first base and two out, Willie Mays cracked a drive that skidded along the grass down the rightfield line. Roger Maris swept up the ball on the run, knowing a bobble would cost the tying score. He fielded the ball flawlessly and threw to the infield, holding Alou at third base. Mays reached second, from where he could score the winning run on a base hit.

Big Willie (Stretch) McCovey was the next batter. Yankee manager Ralph Houk came to the mound and asked Terry if he wanted to walk McCovey, who was a home run threat, but Terry said no. With millions of TV viewers recalling his home run pitch to Mazeroski two years earlier, Terry threw to McCovey. The big slugger swung at a fastball and hit it on a low line toward rightfield. It flew straight at second baseman Bobby Richardson, who grabbed it at eye level for the last out. Said McCovey later, "If it had been a foot higher or two feet either left or right, I would have been a hero."

Willie Mays:
"I was thinking of going all the way"

Willie Mays finished his career where it began —in New York, but with the Mets. *That was a base hit that McCovey hit. Richardson never would have caught that ball except he was playing out of position. He was playing on the outfield grass in short rightfield. If he'd been where a second baseman should have been, it would have gone through for a hit. Would I have scored? Shoot. I was thinking of going all the way around the bases to score on that ball I hit to Maris, except he stopped it and I had to stop with a double. If it had gotten by him, I was sure I could have scored so, shoot, you know I would have scored from second base on a line-drive single into right field. I was running toward third when I turned and I saw Richardson catching that ball and I thought, 'Oh, geez, there goes three-four thousand dollars.'*

Tony Kubek hammers a pitch in the first game. The Giant catcher is Ed Bailey. President John F. Kennedy watched one of the games on TV in Air Force One, some 30,000 feet in the air.

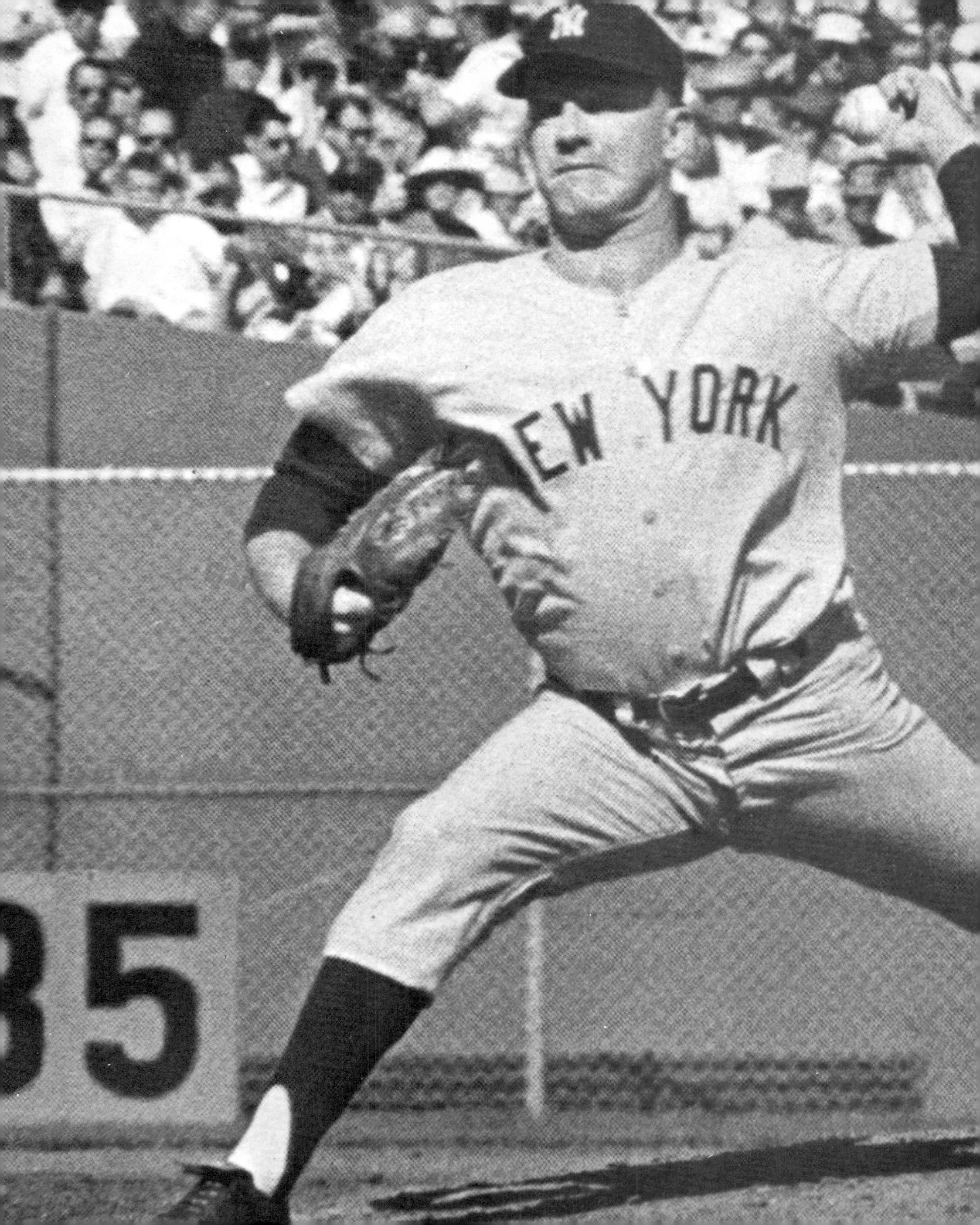

NY
EW YORK
35

Whitey Ford pitching his way to a 6–2 victory over the Giants at Candlestick Park in the first game. When Willie Mays scored in the second inning of this game, the run snapped Ford's scoreless streak at 33 innings. The sixth game in San Francisco was delayed three days by rainstorms. The Yanks, stuck in hotels, complained: "We're going stir crazy." On the third day the teams were bussed to Modesto, 94 miles away, to work out.

FIRST GAME (Oct. 4, at San Francisco)

NEW YORK 200 000 121   6 11 0
SAN FRANCISCO 011 000 000   2 10 0
Ford
O'Dell, Larsen (8th), Miller (9th)

SECOND GAME (Oct. 5, at San Francisco)

NEW YORK 000 000 000   0 3 1
SAN FRANCISCO 100 000 10x   2 6 0
Terry, Daley (8th)
Sanford

THIRD GAME (Oct. 7, at New York)

SAN FRANCISCO 000 000 002   2 4 3
NEW YORK 000 000 30x   3 5 1
Pierce, Larsen (7th), Bolin (8th)
Stafford

FOURTH GAME (Oct. 8, at New York)

SAN FRANCISCO 020 000 401   7 9 1
NEW YORK 000 002 001   3 9 1
Marichal, Bolin (5th), Larsen (6th), O'Dell (7th)
Ford, Coates (7th), Bridges (7th)

FIFTH GAME (Oct. 10, at New York)

SAN FRANCISCO 001 010 001   3 8 2
NEW YORK 000 101 03x   5 6 0
Sanford, Miller (8th)
Terry

SIXTH GAME (Oct. 15, at San Francisco)

NEW YORK 000 010 010   2 3 2
SAN FRANCISCO 000 320 00x   5 10 1
Ford, Coates (5th), Bridges (8th)
Pierce

SEVENTH GAME (Oct. 16, at San Francisco)

NEW YORK 000 010 000   1 7 0
SAN FRANCISCO 000 000 000   0 4 1
Terry
Sanford, O'Dell (8th)

LOS ANGELES DODGERS —1963
NEW YORK YANKEES

To Make Matters Worse, a Little League Play

"There are only two ways you can come out of a Series," Mickey Mantle was saying in the clubhouse after the fourth game. "You can come out of it feeling great or feeling like we are."

The Yankees were feeling mighty low, enduring the humiliation they had pinned on other teams: a loss in a four-game sweep. In losing to their old foes, the Dodgers, the Yankees hit only .171, a record low in a four-game Series. From the first game they seemed to be in trouble as Sandy Koufax, in his first Series triumph, struck out the first five batters he faced. He struck out 15 altogether, breaking Carl Erskine's record, to win over Whitey Ford, 5-2.

Next came Johnny Podres, who had won that seventh game in 1955 for the Dodgers' first Series triumph. He blanked the Yankees until the ninth and won, 4-1. The teams went off to Los Angeles to play in the new Dodger Stadium, and Don Drysdale outdueled and outlucked Jim Bouton, who gave up a run in the first when he put a runner in scoring position with a wild pitch. The Yanks lost, 1-0. Back came Koufax, to finish off the Yankees in the fourth and final game with a 2-1 triumph over Whitey Ford. In that game the Yankees endured the further humiliation of yielding the second and winning run on a Little League kind of error in the seventh inning. Junior Gilliam tapped a hopping ball to third baseman Clete Boyer, who threw to Joe Pepitone at first. Joe lost the ball in the glare of white shirts behind third base, and the ball flew out into right-field while Gilliam scurried around to third base. He scored on a flyball, and two innings later the Yankees walked off losers. The teams took home the richest player pot up to then—$12,794 for

each Dodger, $7,874 for each Yankee. The Dodgers became only the third team—apart from the Yankees—to win a Series in four games.

Jim Bouton:
"Kid, you're throwing nervous fast"

I'll never forget that game I pitched, said Jim Bouton, later a TV sportscaster in New York City. *It was the first World Series I was in and it was an experience hard to describe. You try to get your normal concentration before the game but then you get to the ball park, there are sportswriters from all over the world, you see all the flags, it's a festive occasion, the politicians in the box seats . . . it's big. I was incredibly nervous. All we'd heard was, 'Don't let Maury Wills get on base.' That was the year he stole all those bases. All I could think of was, 'I'll walk him, he'll steal second, third and home and I'll look like an ass in front of millions of people.' He was the first batter. The first pitch I threw was high but he leaped up and bunted it right back at me. I threw him out. I was so relieved. If he had stood there I would have walked him and everyone in the house. After the inning Whitey Ford said to me, 'Kid you're throwing what we call nervous fast.' I had a chance to win the game. I came up in the sixth or seventh with the bases loaded. Drysdale was throwing really hard. Later I thought I should have tried to tip the catcher's mitt with my bat and get first base on interference. I should have known I couldn't hit him. He struck me out on three pitches and I lost, 1-0.*

Dodger fans, some camped here for five days, wait to buy tickets two days before the first game in Los Angeles. For many the long wait was a waste of time: They bought tickets for the fifth game, which was never played.

A hit and a miss: Dodgers glad-hand
Bill Skowron after he hit a home run
in Yankee Stadium off the team that
had traded him away the previous
winter. Walter Alston is at far left.
Opposite page (l. to r.): Maury Wills,
Willie Davis, and Dick Tracewski watch
a Texas leaguer hit by Bobby
Richardson drop between them for a
single in the final game.

FIRST GAME (Oct. 2, at New York)

LOS ANGELES 041 000 000   5 9 0
NEW YORK 000 000 020   2 6 0
Koufax
Ford, Williams (6th), Hamilton (9th)

SECOND GAME (Oct. 3, at New York)

LOS ANGELES 200 100 010   4 10 1
NEW YORK 000 000 001   1 7 0
Podres, Perranoski (9th)
Downing, Terry (6th), Reniff (9th)

THIRD GAME (Oct. 5, at Los Angeles)

NEW YORK 000 000 000   0 3 0
LOS ANGELES 100 000 00x   1 4 1
Bouton, Reniff (8th)
Drysdale

FOURTH GAME (Oct. 6, at Los Angeles)

NEW YORK 000 000 100   1 6 1
LOS ANGELES 000 010 10x   2 2 1
Ford, Reniff (8th)
Koufax

ST. LOUIS CARDINALS ——1964
NEW YORK YANKEES

And the Records, They Came Falling Down

In Philadelphia's Franklin Institute a group of technicians fed data on the Yanks and Cardinals into a computer called Big Magic and then asked the computer to pick the winner. Big Magic picked the Yankees.

Big Magic's choice was proof again of the difficulty of picking the winner in a World Series. The favored Yankees went down to defeat in seven games, keeping intact the Cardinal record of never having lost a Series that went to seven games. For the Yankees these were the first back-to-back Series losses since 1922. Since 1921 the Yankees had won 29 pennants in 44 years, and as of 1964, 20 of 29 Series. In this Series their four-decade dominance of baseball would end.

The end, perhaps, was symbolized in the first game. Whitey Ford started his 22d Series game—a record—and led going into the bottom of the sixth, 4-2. The Cardinals blasted him out with four runs to win, 9-5, and Ford, his arm aching with assorted ailments that would end his career, did not pitch again in the Series.

But for another Yankee there was one last hurrah. As usual Mantle was playing in a Series on aching legs, but he hit .333 in his last Series. In the third game he came up in the ninth with the score tied, 1-1, and slammed a pitch by the veteran Barney Schultz into the seats for the game-winning homer—his 16th Series homer, breaking Babe Ruth's record of 15.

Mantle clubbed two more homers in the Series. The Cardinals, meanwhile, were sparked by the .478 hitting of catcher Tim McCarver and by the nine base hits and the running of Lou Brock. For the 19th time the championship was awarded in the seventh game. Bob Gibson opposed rookie Mel Stottlemyre, each pitching with only two days of rest. The Cardinals built a 6-0 lead. The Yan-

kees tried to surge back on a three-run homer by Mantle, but the tiring Gibson, on his way to a strikeout record of 31 in 27 innings of pitching in this Series, went into the ninth ahead, 7-3. He gave up two home runs, and Bobby Richardson, with a record 13 hits, came to bat with two out. On deck was home run hitter Roger Maris. Gibson slipped an inside pitch to Bobby, who popped it up, and the Cardinals were 7-5 winners, their seventh championship in ten World Series.

Mickey Mantle:
Like the Babe, he called it

That homer off Barney Schultz, it broke Babe Ruth's record, said Mickey Mantle, the former Yankee star and now a Dallas businessman. *It made 16 for me. As Schultz came in from the bullpen, I walked back to talk to Elston Howard, who was the next batter up after me. I said, 'What should I do against this son of a bitch? Drag one?' Ellie didn't say anything. I looked out at Schultz as he warmed up and I knew his first pitch would be his best pitch, the knuckler. Usually the first knuckler they throw isn't a real good knuckler so I decided I'd be swinging at the first pitch. I said to Ellie, 'Ellie, I'm going to hit the first one out.' Ellie kind of grinned and said, 'Yeah, you hit it out, Mick, and I won't have to bat.' Sure enough, in came that knuckler, and I caught it good. I sent it halfway back into the right field seats, it was a homer all the way. I hardly remember running the bases or running into the crowd of players at the plate. I think it was the only time in my career that I ever called a home run. And it won the game and broke Ruth's record.*

Cards' Ken Boyer sprints toward the third-base boxes for a pop foul off the bat of Roger Maris with two out in the 10th inning of the fifth game. Boyer leans on the rail and snares the ball above the bald head of National League President Warren Giles, ending the game, the Cards 5–2 victors.

Jim Bouton snaps off the first pitch of the third game. Curt Flood is the hitter, Elston Howard the catcher. In this Series, as in 1921 when the Meusel brothers opposed each other, two brothers were playing the same position: Ken Boyer at third base for the Cardinals, Clete Boyer at third for the Yanks. The Yankee loss in the first game was their fifth straight Series loss—their longest losing streak in Series competition.

FIRST GAME (Oct. 7, at St. Louis)

NEW YORK 030 010 010   5 12 2
ST. LOUIS 110 004 03x   9 12 0
Ford, Downing (6th), Sheldon (8th), Mikkelsen (8th)
Sadecki, Schultz (7th)

SECOND GAME (Oct. 8, at St. Louis)

NEW YORK 000 101 204   8 12 0
ST. LOUIS 001 000 011   3 7 0
Stottlemyre
Gibson, Schultz (9th), G. Richardson (9th), Craig (9th)

THIRD GAME (Oct. 10, at New York)

ST. LOUIS 000 010 000   1 6 0
NEW YORK 010 000 001   2 5 2
Simmons, Schultz (9th)
Bouton

FOURTH GAME (Oct. 11, at New York)

ST. LOUIS 000 004 000   4 6 1
NEW YORK 300 000 000   3 6 1
Sadecki, Craig (1st), Taylor (6th)
Downing, Mikkelsen (7th), Terry (8th)

FIFTH GAME (Oct. 12, at New York)

ST. LOUIS 000 020 000 3   5 10 1
NEW YORK 000 000 002 0   2 6 2
Gibson
Stottlemyre, Reniff (8th), Mikkelsen (8th)

SIXTH GAME (Oct. 14, at St. Louis)

NEW YORK 000 012 050   8 10 0
ST. LOUIS 100 000 011   3 10 1
Bouton, Hamilton (9th)
Simmons, Taylor (7th), Schultz (8th), G. Richardson
  (8th), Humphreys (9th)

SEVENTH GAME (Oct. 15, at St. Louis)

NEW YORK 000 003 002   5 9 2
ST. LOUIS 000 330 10x   7 10 1
Stottlemyre, Downing (5th), Sheldon (5th), Hamilton
  (7th), Mikkelsen (8th)
Gibson

LOS ANGELES DODGERS
MINNESOTA TWINS
1965

Luck Was Having a Handy Guy Named Sandy

Junior Gilliam puffed nervously on a cigarette, snuffed it out, lit another. He was sitting on a table in the Dodger dressing room at Minnesota's Metropolitan Stadium, listening to the radio. "Sandy's pitching on instinct," Gilliam said to a clubhouse man. Outside, Minnesota Twin fans were roaring as the Twins came to bat in the bottom of the ninth of the seventh game, the Twins losing 2-0.

Sandy Koufax stood on the mound, pitching with only two days of rest, his arthritic left elbow aching. So far he had allowed only two hits, but Gilliam—who had later been removed for a pinch-runner—had saved him at least one run. In the fifth, with Twin runners on first and second, Zoilo Versalles slammed a skipping grounder that looked like a sure double. The veteran Gilliam, playing third, threw his glove across his body, snared the ball, and stepped on third for the third out.

Later Versalles called the Dodgers "lucky," but "tenacious" might have been a better word. They had lost the first two games, their aces—Don Drysdale and Sandy Koufax—mauled by the big Twin sluggers: Harmon Killebrew, Don Mincher, Tony Oliva. But the highly praised Dodger pitching seemed to numb the Twin bats in the third, fourth, and fifth games, Claude Osteen, Drysdale, and Koufax each winning to put the Dodgers ahead, three games to two.

The teams flew back to the Twin Cities, where the pattern of this Series—the home team hadn't lost—continued. The Twins beat Osteen, and now, in the seventh game, Koufax opposed Jim Kaat, the Dodgers hoping to upset the home-field jinx. In the fourth inning a veteran outfielder, Lou Johnson, brought up from the minors when a Dodger outfielder had broken his leg earlier in the year, hit a home run, and the Dodgers added another run to lead, 2-0.

Koufax, arm-sore, could not control his curve. By the ninth he was leaning back and throwing his fastball, a pitch most hitters liked to see because he rarely threw close to batters. With one out Killebrew rammed one of those fastballs for a single, but Koufax challenged the next two batters with his hopping fastballs and struck them out, winning his second straight shutout of the Series. For the first time since 1909, the National League had won three straight world championships. And for Dodger manager Walt Alston, this was his fourth World Series triumph, a record for National League managers.

Sandy Koufax:
Take him out before someone gets killed

Sandy Koufax, who was enjoying a quiet life in Maine, recalled stormier days. *What sticks out in my mind—what sticks out in the mind of all the ballplayers on that ball club—was one writer in Minnesota who went through the stands after the first or second game, I don't remember which one, and belittled and belabored the Dodger wives sitting there. He told them what the Twins were going to do to the Dodgers and he put a few things in the paper that were a little bit out of line and possibly in bad taste. It sort of lifted up*

In the third game Twin catcher Earl Battey, followed by first baseman Don Mincher, chases a pop foul to the Dodger dugout, where Battey (middle photo) catches his Adam's apple on a rail and is knocked to his knees. He had to leave the game.

The magnificent Koufax throwing the hard one that may have been the best ever. After yielding only three hits and striking out 10 in that final game, Koufax said: "This was not one of my better games." He meant it, pointing out that he couldn't control his curve. Some 306 TV stations in the U.S., Canada, Mexico, and Puerto Rico broadcast the games, along with 558 radio stations— both the most up to this time. A potentate in Saudi Arabia requested a kinescope of the TV broadcast— and got it.

the team. There's a good chance you are going to be down after losing the first two and I think this writer may have helped. A team doesn't ordinarily need a lift in a World Series . . . a World Series itself is enough usually . . . but I think this may have helped a little bit. Sometimes this can happen. . . . My memory of that last game is struggling through the first half of it. I guess there was a little doubt in Walt's mind whether he was going to leave me in or take me out. He had a pretty good bullpen ready, he had Drysdale and Perranoski. He was sort of playing it by ear. I think once or twice [catcher John] *Roseboro said to him, 'Get him out of there before someone gets killed.'* [Laughs]. *But after the first half I thought I had pretty good stuff. I never did get a good curveball in the game but I had a good fastball and good control.*

276

FIRST GAME (Oct. 6, at Minnesota)

LOS ANGELES..............010 000 001 2 10 1
MINNESOTA...............016 001 00x 8 10 0
Drysdale, Reed (3d), Brewer (5th), Perranoski (7th)
Grant

SECOND GAME (Oct. 7, at Minnesota)

LOS ANGELES...............000 000 100 1 7 3
MINNESOTA...............000 002 12x 5 9 0
Koufax, Perranoski (7th), Miller (8th)
Kaat

THIRD GAME (Oct. 9, at Los Angeles)

MINNESOTA................000 000 000 0 5 0
LOS ANGELES.............000 211 00x 4 10 1
Pascual, Merritt (6th), Klippstein (8th)
Osteen

FOURTH GAME (Oct. 10, at Los Angeles)

MINNESOTA................000 101 000 2 5 2
LOS ANGELES.............110 103 01x 7 10 0
Grant, Worthington (6th), Pleis (8th)
Drysdale

FIFTH GAME (Oct. 11, at Los Angeles)

MINNESOTA................000 000 000 0 4 1
LOS ANGELES..............202 100 20x 7 14 0
Kaat, Boswell (3d), Perry (6th)
Koufax

SIXTH GAME (Oct. 13, at Minnesota)

LOS ANGELES...............000 000 100 1 6 1
MINNESOTA...............000 203 00x 5 6 1
Osteen, Reed (6th), Miller (8th)
Grant

SEVENTH GAME (Oct. 14, at Minnesota)

LOS ANGELES...............000 200 000 2 7 0
MINNESOTA................000 000 000 0 3 1
Koufax

Kaat, Worthington (4th), Klippstein (6th), Merritt
  (7th), Perry (9th)

BALTIMORE ORIOLES
LOS ANGELES DODGERS ——1966

Did Moe Unnerve the Dodgers?

Again the Dodgers lost the first two games of the Series. After the second game Walter Alston shook his head and said, "It seems like we're always having to come back."

The Dodgers would not come back in the Series that might well be called The Powderpuff Series. The winning Orioles hit only .200, the lowest average ever for a team winning a Series in four straight. The losing Dodgers could tap out only 17 hits in four games, bat only .142, and score only two runs in the 36 innings of the four games—all records for impotency. In the last three games they failed to produce even one run.

Oriole manager Hank Bauer said later that the relief pitching of Moe Drabowsky in the first game might have psyched out the Dodgers. In the third inning the weak-hitting but speedy Dodgers mounted a typical offense: three bases on balls. Drabowsky, whom the Dodgers knew well from his days as a mediocre National League pitcher, came on to relieve Dave McNally. Drabowsky allowed one run but then hurled 6⅔ innings of one-hit shutout pitching. He struck out 11 Dodgers, the most for any Series reliever, and at one point fanned six in a row, to tie another record.

From that third inning of the first game, the Dodgers failed to score for the next 33 innings of the Series, getting only 14 hits off the next three Oriole starters: Jim Palmer, a Series starter a few days before his 21st birthday, Wally Bunker, and Dave McNally. In the second game the Orioles beat Sandy Koufax, who was making his last Series appearance, by a score of 6-0. Sandy was not helped by centerfielder Willie Davis, who muffed two flyballs and threw wild to third base,

the first Series player to commit three errors in one inning. In the fourth and final game Frank Robinson—the Series Most Valuable Player—hit a homer, and McNally had a 1-0 victory over Don Drysdale. The Orioles celebrated with beer. "Too many of our guys get sick on champagne," Frank Robinson said.

Frank Robinson:
Bad news for the Dodgers

Granted there may be no school spirit or rah-rah stuff with the ball teams. But what about being in a World Series? What about pride? Frank Robinson, the outfielder for the champion Orioles, had an answer. *When we got to Los Angeles for the first game, all the papers were writing about how the National League was so much stronger than the American. It got us all up. A lot of people forget that pros have pride. . . . People have always argued which league is better—the National or the American. In recent years there is no doubt in my mind that overall the National League is stronger, but if you take the top three or four teams from each league and let them play among themselves, no one team is going to come out that much ahead. Anyway, I know I got a greater feeling of satisfaction over what we had accomplished in the Series because of the things that were written about us by the Los Angeles writers. When you hear people bad-mouthing a World Series team—any team—you should remember that if one team can lead all the rest over 162 games, that team is no fluke.*

Atoning in part for his Series muffs, the Dodgers' Willie Davis skirts the centerfield fence in Baltimore in the fourth inning of the fourth game, lining up a towering drive from the bat of Boog Powell, then leaps and plucks the ball off the top of the fence.

279

Strip of film from the Series movie, in sequence here from top to bottom, shows Drabowsky (top l.) striking out one of the 11 Dodgers he fanned— this time with a breaking ball low and away. In this Series Baltimore pitcher Jim Palmer, only 20 years old, became the youngest pitcher in Series history to pitch a shutout. In 1913 the A's Bullet Joe Bush, also only 20, pitched and won a complete game. Palmer would be 21 nine days after his shutout while Bush was six weeks from his 21st birthday, so Bullet Joe is still the youngest ever to win a complete Series game.

281

Orioles' Curt Blefary rolls into
shortstop Maury Wills on a force
play at second base, but Maury leaps
over Blefary to throw to first and
complete a double-play. The losing
Dodgers were consoled with $8,189,
the most ever up to that time for
Series losers.

282

FIRST GAME (Oct. 5, at Los Angeles)

BALTIMORE..................310 100 000 5 9 0
LOS ANGELES..............011 000 000 2 3 0
McNally, Drabowsky (3d)
Drysdale, Moeller (3d), R. Miller (5th), Perranoski (8th)

SECOND GAME (Oct. 6, at Los Angeles)

BALTIMORE..................000 031 020 6 8 0
LOS ANGELES..............000 000 000 0 4 6
Palmer
Koufax, Perranoski (7th), Regan (8th), Brewer (9th)

THIRD GAME (Oct. 8, at Baltimore)

LOS ANGELES...............000 000 000 0 6 0
BALTIMORE..................000 010 00x 1 3 0
Osteen, Regan (8th)
Bunker

FOURTH GAME (Oct. 9, at Baltimore)

LOS ANGELES...............000 000 000 0 4 0
BALTIMORE..................000 100 00x 1 4 0
Drysdale
McNally

ST. LOUIS CARDINALS
BOSTON RED SOX
1967

It Was Yaz and Jim, Bob and Lou

In the second game Jim Lonborg pitched what some called "the second-best World Series game ever pitched," the best being Don Larsen's perfect game. For six innings Lonborg pitched a perfect game, retiring every Cardinal who came to bat. He walked Curt Flood with one out in the seventh but did not give up a hit until two were out in the eighth. Then Julian Javier plopped a double down the leftfield line. That was the only Cardinal hit. Lonborg won, 5-0, the fourth one-hit game of Series history.

That victory tied the Series at one game apiece. A 100-1 shot to win the pennant after finishing ninth the year before, the "Cinderella" Sox had won it on the last day of the season, mainly on the clutch hitting and fielding of leftfielder Carl Yastrzemski. Yaz would hit .400 in this Series, and Lonborg, by winning two games, helped to offset the .414 hitting of Lou Brock and the two excellent pitching victories by Bob Gibson.

For the sixth time in their history, the Cardinals entered the seventh game of a Series, still not having lost a showdown battle. For the first time in the Series, Lonborg opposed Gibson, but Lonborg was pitching with only two days of rest.

"He doesn't have it," the Cardinal pitchers told each other, watching Lonborg warm up. They were right. The Cardinals scored four runs off him in the first five innings, Gibson himself hitting a homer. But Red Sox manager Dick Williams stubbornly stuck with his ace even as the Cardinals bashed across three more runs in the sixth to take a 7-1 lead. That was a lead enough for Gibson, who was on his way to his third victory of the Series, this time by a 7-2 score. *Sport* magazine gave him a car as the Series' Most Valuable Player, but St. Louis radio station KMOX awarded another car to Brock, who had stolen a record seven bases and collected 12 hits.

Lou Brock: Up there with Ruth and Cobb

Lou Brock, still a Cardinal batting and base-running star, recalled: *That seventh game was especially exciting because it was the last day, you know, the last straw in the hat and you had to dig down and get it. But what I remember the most was all the excitement of the Series, everyone talking about it, all the fuss of the hundreds of reporters and the TV cameras. I got 12 hits in that 1967 Series and I got 13 in 1968, which tied the World Series record. I don't know what it is exactly [.391], but I have the highest batting average for World Series games of anyone. I think I've tied or own seven or eight World Series records for batting and base-stealing. People are always reminding me of them. Honest, most of the records don't mean that much to me. I figure, though, that if you break a record set by Babe Ruth or Ty Cobb or one of those guys, that's something special. I got on base five times in a row in one of those games in 1967 and that tied a record set by Ruth. And I stole two bases in one inning in 1967, tying a record owned by both Ruth and Cobb. Those records will always have a special place in my memory because baseball is measured by the things that Ruth and Cobb did.*

Lou Brock steals a base in the seventh inning of the first game. As Brock dives headfirst for second base, Rico Petrocelli sets to tag him, but the umpire calls Brock safe, the decision hotly debated by Rico. Brock then scored on two infield outs to put the Cards ahead 2–1— the final score.

Lonborg mowing down
Cardinals in the second
game. "Gentleman Jim"
won 22 games in 1967,
including a 5-3 victory
on the last day of the
season that lifted the
Red Sox into the Series.
A few months later he
was injured in a skiing
accident, won only six
games in 1968, and in
succeeding years was
not the overpowering
pitcher he'd been
in 1967.

286

FIRST GAME (Oct. 4, at Boston)

```
ST. LOUIS..................001 000 100   2 10 0
BOSTON....................001 000 000   1  6 0
```
R. Gibson
Santiago, Wyatt (8th)

SECOND GAME (Oct. 5, at Boston)

```
ST. LOUIS..................000 000 000   0  1 1
BOSTON....................000 101 30x   5  9 0
```
Hughes, Willis (6th), Hoerner (7th), Lamabe (7th)
Lonborg

THIRD GAME (Oct. 7, at St. Louis)

```
BOSTON....................000 001 100   2  7 1
ST. LOUIS..................120 001 01x   5 10 0
```
Bell, Waslewski (3d), Stange (6th), Osinski (8th)
Briles

FOURTH GAME (Oct. 8, at St. Louis)

```
BOSTON....................000 000 000   0  5 0
ST. LOUIS..................402 000 00x   6  9 0
```
Santiago, Bell (1st), Stephenson (3d), Morehead (5th),
   Brett (8th)
R. Gibson

FIFTH GAME (Oct. 9, at St. Louis)

```
BOSTON....................001 000 002   3  6 1
ST. LOUIS..................000 000 001   1  3 2
```
Lonborg
Carlton, Washburn (7th), Willis (9th), Lamabe (9th)

SIXTH GAME (Oct. 11, at Boston)

```
ST. LOUIS..................002 000 200   4  8 0
BOSTON....................010 300 40x   8 12 1
```
Hughes, Willis (4th), Briles (5th), Lamabe (7th), Hoer-
   ner (7th), Jaster (7th), Washburn (7th), Woodeshick
   (8th)
Waslewski, Wyatt (6th), Bell (8th)

SEVENTH GAME (Oct. 12, at Boston)

```
ST. LOUIS..................002 023 000   7 10 1
BOSTON....................000 010 010   2  3 1
```
R. Gibson
Lonborg, Santiago (7th), Morehead (9th), Osinski (9th),
   Brett (9th)

In this movie sequence, Lou Brock soars high against the leftfield wall at Fenway Park to catch a drive by Jerry Adair. After the seventh game in Boston, the winning Cardinals were invited to come to the White House by President Lyndon Johnson, but the Cardinals elected to return to St. Louis, where some attended a rock 'n' roll dance at Stan Musial's restaurant.

DETROIT TIGERS
ST. LOUIS CARDINALS ———1968

As Mickey Would Find, Every Dog Has Its Day

As the Series began baseball fans were looking forward to the match-up in the first game between the Tigers' Denny McLain, winner of 31 games, and Bob Gibson, the winner of five straight complete Series games. Newspapers called it The Duel of the Century. McLain added spice to the duel with his Dizzy-Dean-like talk—"I want to humiliate the Cardinals." The night before the game he entertained fans in a St. Louis hotel lounge by sitting at an organ and playing "Stardust." But the next day the Cardinals drummed McLain from the mound in five innings while Gibson was striking out 17 Tigers—a record—on his way to a 4-0 victory.

It passed relatively unnoticed, compared with all the hullabaloo about McLain, but a soft-spoken lefty, Mickey Lolich, beat the Cardinals in the second game, 8-1. All season long Lolich, a 17-game winner, had been "that other Tiger pitcher," while McLain "got the ink," as the players say. Another "ink-getter," Bob Gibson, won the fourth game, his seventh straight complete-game victory—a record. The Cardinals now led, three games to one. They seemed on their way to a second straight championship when they took a 3-0 lead over Lolich in the first inning of the fifth game. But the Tigers, with veteran Al Kaline punching out a key two-run hit in the seventh, won, 5-3, to stay alive.

The disappointing McLain, helped by a 10-run Tiger outburst in the third inning (that tied the record for runs scored in an inning set by Connie Mack's A's in 1929), won the sixth game, 13-1,

and the Cardinals again put on the line their record of never having lost a seventh Series game. Gibson opposed Lolich. For six innings the two hurled shutout baseball. With two out in the seventh and two men on base, the Tigers' Jim Northrup hoisted a high drive toward center. The sure-handed Curt Flood lost the ball for a moment, then turned to run back. He slipped, the ball flying over his head, and two runs scored. The Tigers got two more runs, and Lolich held on to win, 4-1. As confetti poured down on Detroit streets, Lolich sat in the clubhouse and said, "All my life somebody has been a big star and Lolich was No. 2. I figured my day would come and this was it." In this Series the Cardinals' Lou Brock tied Bobby Richardson's Series record of 13 hits and his own record of 7 stolen bases.

Mickey Lolich:
It began with a boil

Talking about his three victories in the Series, the Tigers' Mickey Lolich said: *I got a boil on my penis a few days before the Series started. The doctors loaded me up with antibiotics and that made me pretty groggy when I went out to pitch the first time. All my life I'd reared back and thrown as hard as I could and as a result I never really had good control. I'd been an all-brawn pitcher. But that day I didn't have the brawn. I had to use my head. I had to pitch to spots. I had to nick the corners. And I won. The next time I pitched I had my full strength and I was rearing*

Grimacing Tiger second baseman Dick McAuliffe steps over sliding Orlando Cepeda as he watches his throw to first beat Mike Shannon for a double-play. Lou Brock came out of this Series with the highest batting average for anyone who had played in 20 or more games—.391.

back and throwing as hard as I could. Well, right away, in the first inning, I was behind 3-0 when [Orlando] Cepeda hit a home run off me. After that inning, in the dugout, I said to myself, 'Hey, you did pretty good pitching to the corners the first time. Why don't you go back to throwing that way?' I did and we won. When I went out to pitch the seventh game, I had only two days' rest and was too arm-weary to throw real hard, so again I used my head and pitched to spots. After I won I realized I could be a control pitcher and I could pitch within myself. I didn't have to be throwing as hard as I could on every pitch. When I needed to, then I could rear back and throw aspirins. Winning those three games also helped my pride. I used to be the kind who would give up on himself when things were going bad. I'd say, 'Hey, you can't get this guy out. He always gets a hit off you.' Naturally, he'd get a hit off me when I'd have that attitude. But after winning those three games I felt I had to prove it was no fluke, that I was a good pitcher.

The scoreboards tell the story as Bob Gibson strikes out Al Kaline in the first game to tie Koufax's record, then strikes out Norm Cash (center) for his 16th strikeout to set a new record. Opposite page: He strikes out Willie Horton for his 17th strikeout, breaking his own record. Gibson set another Series record when he hit a home run, his second in Series competition, the most ever by a pitcher.

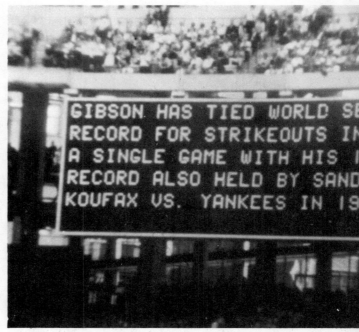

GIBSON HAS TIED WORLD SE
RECORD FOR STRIKEOUTS IN
A SINGLE GAME WITH HIS
RECORD ALSO HELD BY SAND
KOUFAX VS. YANKEES IN 19

AND A NEW RECORD----16

FIRST GAME (Oct. 2, at St. Louis)

DETROIT.....................000 000 000 0 5 3
ST. LOUIS...................000 300 10x 4 6 0
McLain, Dobson (6th), McMahon (8th)
Gibson

SECOND GAME (Oct. 3, at St. Louis)

DETROIT.....................011 003 102 8 13 1
ST. LOUIS...................000 001 000 1 6 1
Lolich
Briles, Carlton (6th), Willis (7th), Hoerner (9th)

THIRD GAME (Oct. 5, at Detroit)

ST. LOUIS...................000 040 300 7 13 0
DETROIT.....................002 010 000 3 4 0
Washburn, Hoerner (6th)
Wilson, Dobson (5th), McMahon (6th), Patterson (7th),
   Hiller (8th)

FOURTH GAME (Oct. 6, at Detroit)

ST. LOUIS...................202 200 040 10 13 0
DETROIT.....................000 100 000 1 5 4
Gibson
McLain, Sparma (3d), Patterson (4th), Lasher (6th),
   Hiller (8th), Dobson (8th)

FIFTH GAME (Oct. 7, at Detroit)

ST. LOUIS...................300 000 000 3 9 0
DETROIT.....................000 200 30x 5 9 1
Briles, Hoerner (7th), Willis (7th)
Lolich

SIXTH GAME (Oct. 9, at St. Louis)

DETROIT.................02 10 010 000 13 12 1
ST. LOUIS...............00 0 000 001 1 9 1
McLain
Washburn, Jaster (3d), Willis (3d), Hughes (3d), Carl-
   ton (4th), Granger (7th), Nelson (9th)

SEVENTH GAME (Oct. 10, at St. Louis)

DETROIT.....................000 000 301 4 8 1
ST. LOUIS...................000 000 001 1 5 0
Lolich
Gibson

The champion Tigers—Front row: Don Wert, John Wyatt, coach Tony Cuccinello, coach Wally Moses, manager Mayo Smith, coach Hal Naragon, coach Johnny Sain, Wayne Comer, Willie Horton, Mickey Lolich. Second row: equipment man John Hand, trainer Bill Behm, batting-practice pitcher Julio Moreno, Jim Northrup, Ray Oyler, Earl Wilson, Fred Lasher, Don McMahon, Al Kaline, traveling secretary Charles Creedon. Third row: Dick Tracewski, Norm Cash, Eddie Mathews, Jim Price, Jon Warden, Denny McLain, Gates Brown, John Hiller, Dick McAuliffe. Back row: Roy Face, Bob Christian, Mickey Stanley, Joe Sparma, Daryl Patterson, Pat Dobson, Tom Matchick, Bill Freehan. Wyatt and Christian did not play in this Series.

NEW YORK METS

—————————————

BALTIMORE ORIOLES

1969

And Then Mrs. Payson Covered Her Eyes

Call it The Impossible Dream. Call it That Old Met Magic. It was called that and other things by fans, but the New York Mets' upset of the Baltimore Orioles was not only one of the most surprising of upsets, it came about through circumstances that were almost eerie. In one game the Mets won with a bunt, the sun's glare, and an illegal play. In another game a Met fan (named John Devaney) bemoaned the fact that Jerry Koosman, who was pitching well, would have to be removed in the next inning for a pinch-hitter. "No," said another Met fan, "he won't have to come out for a pinch-hitter because Al Weis, who's batting in front of him, will hit a home run to tie the score." Minutes later Al Weis hit a home run to tie the score.

As the Series opened, the Orioles seemed as menacing as the old Yankees. They had Brooks and Frank Robinson, Boog Powell, and a tested pitching staff: Dave McNally, Jim Palmer, Mike Cuellar. The Mets owned two strong pitchers, Jerry Koosman and Tom Seaver, but several of the team's best players were other teams' rejects, notably Tommie Agee and Donn Clendenon.

This was the first Series in which the teams had to win a division playoff for the pennant, the Mets beating the Braves, the Orioles beating the Twins. The Orioles were no surprise, but the appearance of the Mets in a Series was a shocker, for this had been baseball's joke team, never finishing higher than ninth. The Orioles looked like sure winners after the first game, Cuellar defeating the Mets, 4-1. And then strange things began to happen.

Jerry Koosman pitched a no-hitter for six innings in the second game and went into the ninth ahead, 2-1. The Orioles put two men on with two out. Brooks Robinson came to bat, and Met owner Mrs. Joan Payson covered her eyes with a scarf. Robinson rolled out and the Series was tied.

In the third game Agee hit a homer and made two acrobatic catches, preventing at least five Oriole runs. The Mets won, 5-0. The score was tied, 1-1, in the tenth inning of the fourth game when the Orioles' Don Buford lost a flyball in the sun, and it dropped for a double. Then J. C. Martin bunted. Pitcher Pete Richert threw the ball to first, but the ball glanced off Martin's wrist and bounced away, a Met scoring with the winning run. Pictures later showed Martin had been running in illegal territory.

The Orioles led, 3-0, in the fifth game when Cleon Jones claimed he was hit in the foot by a pitch. Met manager Gil Hodges showed the umpires a smudge of polish on the ball and Jones was waved to first, setting off a rally. Little Al Weis, who had hit three homers in two years, poled a homer to tie the score. The unhinged Orioles committed a pair of errors, and the Mets won, 5-3, their "impossible dream" suddenly come true.

Tom Seaver:
Seeing the dream come true

Tom Seaver was the Mets' pitcher who won the fourth game when J. C. Martin bunted and pinch-runner Rod Gaspar raced home with the winning run. *I was in the batter's circle when I saw Gaspar coming home. It was a sudden shock. I hadn't thought about winning a World Series game all that much up until then. I hadn't thought about*

Met fans turn thumbs down on Orioles' Frank Robinson after he struck out in the final game. Robinson had claimed he was hit on the leg by a pitch, but the umpire disagreed. Robinson delayed the game while being treated for a bruise on the leg that earned him only hoots.

Plate umpire Shag Crawford advances toward the Orioles' dugout (r.) to hush some carping of his calls. Oriole manager Earl Weaver comes out of the dugout, tailing Crawford, to speak a few words of his own and is told where to go—out of the ball game. Weaver became only the third manager in Series history to be thrown out of a game by an umpire.

losing it, either, and then there was that sudden shock of seeing a dream come true. I had always had this boyhood dream of winning a World Series game and now I was standing there and seeing it happen right in front of me as Gaspar crossed the plate. The enormity of it really hit me at that moment . . . boom! . . . it flashed in front of my eyes . . . a World Series winner.

FIRST GAME (Oct. 11, at Baltimore)

NEW YORK 000 000 100   1 6 1
BALTIMORE 100 300 00x   4 6 0
Seaver, Cardwell (6th), Taylor (7th)
Cuellar

SECOND GAME (Oct. 12, at Baltimore)

NEW YORK 000 100 001   2 6 0
BALTIMORE 000 000 100   1 2 0
Koosman, Taylor (9th)
McNally

THIRD GAME (Oct. 14, at New York)

BALTIMORE 000 000 000   0 4 1
NEW YORK 120 001 01x   5 6 0
Palmer, Leonhard (7th)
Gentry, Ryan (7th)

FOURTH GAME (Oct. 15, at New York)

BALTIMORE 000 000 001 0   1 6 1
NEW YORK 010 000 000 1   2 10 1
Cuellar, Watt (8th), Hall (10th), Richert (10th)
Seaver

FIFTH GAME (Oct. 16, at New York)

BALTIMORE 003 000 000   3 5 2
NEW YORK 000 002 12x   5 7 0
McNally, Watt (8th)
Koosman

299

Another bit of Met Magic: Tommie Agee, having one of the great days of Series history, dives to pluck a drive by Paul Blair off the grass with two out and the bases loaded in the seventh inning of the third game. Agee made another leaping catch earlier and also hit a home run.

300

Ed Charles dances to
his own tune as Jerry
Koosman leaps into the
arms of catcher Jerry
Grote after the final out
that made the Mets
World Champions.
While Grote and the
other Mets flee from
their admirers, one
fan's banner sums up
the Met Miracle.

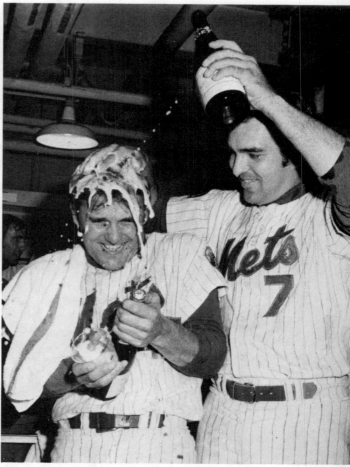

Casey Stengel smooches a jubilant Gil Hodges as Ed Kranepool douses a teammate with champagne. Manhattan office workers celebrate while Tom Seaver, an hour after the final game, surveys the pitching mound at Shea Stadium, the turf ripped up and carted away by souvenir-wild fans. Before the Series began, Seaver agreed to sign an ad stating: IF THE METS CAN WIN THE PENNANT, WE CAN GET OUT OF VIETNAM. Although he never did sign the ad, some fans and writers criticized him.

BALTIMORE ORIOLES
CINCINNATI REDS
1970

A Car for Brooks,
a Glove for the Hall of Fame

Before one of the games an Oriole was late for the bus carrying the team to the ball park. "My watch had the wrong time," he explained. "It was the one they gave us after we lost to the Mets so that explains it."

The Orioles made up for that embarrassing loss to the Mets by winning this Series against the Reds, a slugging bunch that had been labeled the Big Red Machine. The star of the Orioles—and the Series' Most Valuable Player—was third baseman Brooks Robinson, who hit .429 and two home runs. But it was his glove, later shipped to the Hall of Fame, that made Brooks the star of this Series and the winner of *Sport* magazine's Dodge Charger. "If I'd known he wanted a car so badly," Cincinnati's Pete Rose said during the Series, "we would have given him one."

Time after time Brooks dived to his left and right to snare smashes and throw out runners at first base. After Brooks knocked down one of his drives, the Reds' Johnny Bench hollered at him, "I'll hit the next one over your head." In the final game Bench hit a drive. Brooks leaped and grabbed that one, too.

The Orioles demolished the pitching of the Big Red Machine, the Cincinnati staff weakened by injuries. The most memorable play, apart from Brooks' acrobatics, was a play at home plate in the first game. With the Reds' Bernie Carbo on third, Ty Cline hit a high chopper in front of the plate. Umpire Ken Burkhart ran out to see if the ball was fair or foul as it came down into catcher Elrod Hendricks' mitt. Burkhart's side was toward third as Carbo charged down the line. Carbo slid around Burkhart. Hendricks lunged at Carbo, tagging him with his mitt, but the ball was in his other hand. Although his back was to the play, Burkhart called Carbo out, later insisting he saw Hendricks tag the runner. "The umpires didn't beat us," Red manager Sparky Anderson said after the Series, "the Orioles did."

Brooks Robinson:
Under the circumstances, appropriate

Before the Series I thought I would get a lot of ground balls, said Brooks Robinson, the veteran third baseman of the Orioles. *I knew that Bench and Tony Perez would be pulling a lot of pitches down the line no matter how good our pitching was. They are too good a pair of hitters to stop all the time. I felt it was going to happen. But this is the odd thing: In baseball what you expect to happen often doesn't happen. But it did happen. I don't think it will ever happen to me again— that I will get that many opportunities to make plays like that, not day after day, the way it was. It was amazing, so many chances. I laughed when I read what Rose said about him giving me a car. I thought it was pretty appropriate considering the circumstances.*

Boog Powell (l.) and Elrod Hendricks cavort in the clubhouse after Baltimore won the Series. Hendricks' head is crowned with netting and shaving cream, while Boog grips the neck of a bottle of champagne.

In the first Series game to be played on artificial turf, Oriole catcher Elrod Hendricks (below) reaches for a high chopper in front of the plate. Oriole pitcher Jim Palmer is pointing toward third, from where Bernie Carbo (1) is dashing homeward. Umpire Ken Burkhart, forgetting about Carbo, is busy signaling the ball is fair, blocking the plate as Carbo slides around him. Hendricks tags Carbo with his mitt, the ball in his bare hand (2), but Burkhart's back is to the play. Carbo (3) slides wide of the plate as Hendricks bowls over Burkhart, who calls Carbo out (4). While he was protesting the call, Carbo did touch home.

310

Johnny Bench (at bat, l.) rams a pitch thrown by the Orioles' Mike Cuellar down the third-base line in the final game. The ball is snared by the diving Brooks Robinson, who skids across the foul line, gets up, and throws out Bench. It was the last of at least a half-dozen brilliant plays by Brooks in the Series.

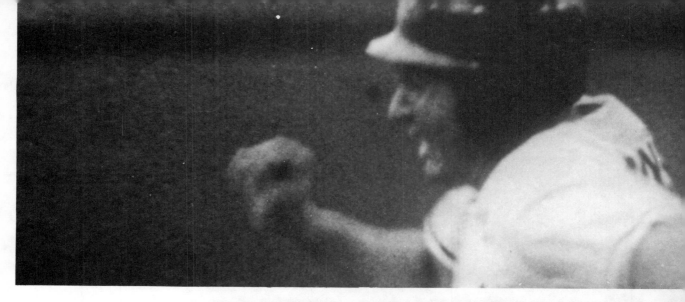

Closeup photos taken from the motion-picture film show the agonized face of 33-year-old Brooks Robinson, never a fast runner, as he tries to go from first to third on a base hit in the fourth game. A throw from the Reds' Pete Rose to third base skipped into the dugout and Brooks was waved home to put the Orioles ahead 5–3. The Reds won, 6–5, but still had failed to stop Brooks: In this game he had four hits in four at-bats.

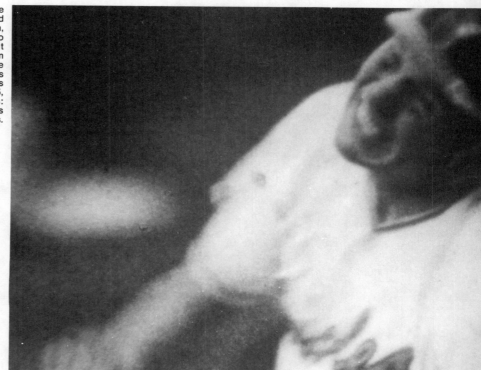

FIRST GAME (Oct. 10, at Cincinnati)

BALTIMORE.................000 210 100   4 7 2
CINCINNATI................102 000 000   3 5 0

Palmer, Richert (9th)
Nolan, Carroll (7th)

SECOND GAME (Oct. 11, at Cincinnati)

BALTIMORE...............000 150 000   6 10 2
CINCINNATI...............301 001 000   5 7 0

Cuellar, Phoebus (3d), Drabowsky (5th), Lopez (7th),
   Hall (7th)
McGlothlin, Wilcox (5th), Carroll (5th), Gullett (8th)

THIRD GAME (Oct. 13, at Baltimore)

CINCINNATI...............010 000 200   3 9 0
BALTIMORE...............201 014 10x   9 10 1

Cloninger, Granger (6th), Gullett (7th)
McNally

FOURTH GAME (Oct. 14, at Baltimore)

CINCINNATI................011 010 030   6 8 3
BALTIMORE.................013 001 000   5 8 0

Nolan, Gullett (3d), Carroll (6th)
Palmer, Watt (8th), Drabowsky (9th)

FIFTH GAME (Oct. 15, at Baltimore)

CINCINNATI................300 000 000   3 6 0
BALTIMORE.................222 010 02x   9 15 0

Merritt, Granger (2d), Wilcox (3d), Cloninger (5th),
   Washburn (7th), Carroll (8th)
Cuellar

PITTSBURGH PIRATES
BALTIMORE ORIOLES
1971

Proved One More Time:
In a Series, Anything Can Happen

As the Pirates flew home to Pittsburgh after losing the first two games to the Orioles in Baltimore, Pirate outfielder Roberto Clemente stood up in the plane and told two other Pirates, "We will win this in six games. I'm only sorry we didn't win a game in Baltimore. Then we could win the next three in Pittsburgh and we wouldn't have to go back to their lousy ball park."

The Pirates became the first club since the Dodgers of 1965 to lose the first two games and come back to tie the Series and force a seventh game. They did it against an Oriole team thought to be so superior to the Pirates that one National League executive, the Dodgers' Al Campanis, said before the Series, "If the Orioles had a top catcher, there wouldn't be any need for a World Series." The Orioles had a sound infield, power hitters in Frank Robinson, Boog Powell, Brooks Robinson, and Merv Rettenmund, and four 20-game winners. But in this Series—the first in which one game (the fourth) was played at night—the Pirates again proved that the unexpected often happens in a World Series. With Clemente making two marvelous throws to check Oriole runners on the bases and hitting .414 and two homers, the Pirates showed they were, as Clemente said, "not the Little League team they were saying we were." They won three straight games: a three-hitter by Steve Blass, a one-hit relief performance over six innings by young Bruce Kison, and a two-hit shutout by Nelson Briles.

Back in friendly Baltimore, though, the Orioles won the sixth game, 3-2, when aging Frank Robinson raced home from third on a flyball in the tenth inning, sliding under catcher Manny Sanguillen with the winning run. Steve Blass started the seventh game for the Pirates, so nervous he'd heaved his breakfast. He swallowed Cokes during the game and threw them up, too. A homer by Clemente, and a double by José Pagan brought Blass and the Pirates into the ninth ahead, 2-1, with the muscle of the Oriole batting order coming to the plate: Powell, Robinson, Rettenmund. Blass put all three down with eight pitches and leaped off the mound to hug his straw-hatted dad, who rushed out of the stands. The Pirates were world champions for the fourth time in the 68 years since another Pittsburgh team had lost that first World Series way back in 1903.

Roberto Clemente:
"Don't read the newspapers"

Roberto Clemente, speaking during the spring of 1972 (he died in December of the same year), talked about the Series and about pressures in particular. *This happened before the second game in Baltimore. I was taking the cab to the ball park and the cab driver said to me, 'There is no way you guys can win.' I said to him, 'You must have been reading the Baltimore newspapers because they are saying we can't beat the American League.' I told all the young players on our team: 'Don't read the newspapers.' They can propaganda you and young players will believe what they read. Newspapers can build up a ballplayer until a young ballplayer will be afraid of him. I won't name the players but a lot of players have big images built up by the newspapers. I see these big image players come down to Puerto Rico to play in winter ball and they are not so great. I kept telling the Pirates, especially after those first two games, 'Do not read the newspapers and you will see, we will win.' And we did, just as I told them.*

Pirates' Nelson Briles powders a pitch by Frank Robinson for a swinging strike, the momentum of his follow-through toppling him off the mound. The beaten Orioles visited Japan after the Series. "Maybe we should have gone before the Series," said one Oriole.

Roberto Clemente (below) waits for a pitch from Jim Palmer, then cracks the outside pitch for a triple to right in the first inning of the sixth game, won 3–2 by Baltimore. Clemente complained that Baltimore's Memorial Stadium, shown here, was "the worst field I've ever played on." He said there were holes in the outfield. "You can't charge a ball," he said. "You have to watch the ditches."

AT BAT BALL STRIKE OUT SCORING
21 2 2
CLEMENTE 341 AVG 13 HR 86 RBI

0 0 0
0 0 0
AT BAT BALL STRIKE OUT SCORING
21 2 2
CLEMENTE 341 AVG 13 HR 86 RBI

CLEMENTE 341 AVG 13 HR 86 RBI

Pirates' Roberto Clemente
shows why he was voted the Series'
Most Valuable Player as he races
toward the rightfield foul line to glove
a ball that came close to dropping
for a two-base hit. The turmoil of the
time was reflected during this Series:
Dock Ellis, a young black pitcher for
the Pirates, labeled the Pirate
ownership "The Establishment" and
claimed it exploited the Pirate players.

FIRST GAME (Oct. 9, at Baltimore)

PITTSBURGH................030 000 000   3   3 0
BALTIMORE.................013 010 00x   5 10 3
Ellis, Moose (3d), Miller (7th)
McNally

SECOND GAME (Oct. 11, at Baltimore)

PITTSBURGH..............000 000 030   3   8 1
BALTIMORE...............010 361 00x 11 14 1
R. Johnson, Kison (4th), Moose (4th), Veale (5th),
   Miller (6th), Giusti (8th)
Palmer, Hall (9th)

THIRD GAME (Oct. 12, at Pittsburgh)

BALTIMORE.................000 000 100   1   3 3
PITTSBURGH................100 001 30x   5   7 0
Cuellar, Dukes (7th), Watt (8th)
Blass

FOURTH GAME (Oct. 13, at Pittsburgh)

BALTIMORE.................300 000 000   3   4 1
PITTSBURGH................201 000 10x   4 14 0
Dobson, Jackson (6th), Watt (7th), Richert (8th)
Walker, Kison (1st), Giusti (8th)

FIFTH GAME (Oct. 14, at Pittsburgh)

BALTIMORE.................000 000 000   0   2 1
PITTSBURGH................021 010 00x   4   9 0
McNally, Leonhard (5th), Dukes (6th)
Briles

SIXTH GAME (Oct. 16, at Baltimore)

PITTSBURGH..............011 000 000 0   2   9 1
BALTIMORE...............000 001 100 1   3   8 0
Moose, R. Johnson (6th), Giusti (7th), Miller (10th)
Palmer, Dobson (10th), McNally (10th)

SEVENTH GAME (Oct. 17, at Baltimore)

PITTSBURGH................000 100 010   2   6 1
BALTIMORE.................000 000 010   1   4 0
Blass
Cuellar, Dobson (9th), McNally (9th)

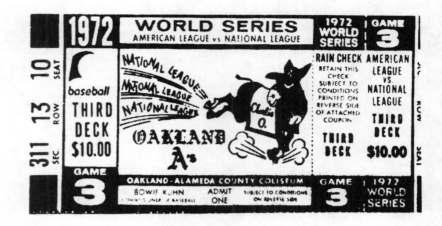

OAKLAND ATHLETICS
CINCINNATI REDS
1972

Charlie O. Nips the Big Red Machine at the Wire

The losing Reds' manager, Sparky Anderson, called this the best-played and most exciting Series in his memory, and one would have to strain to fault him. Six of the seven games were decided by a single run, a Series record. Despite the tenseness of one close game after another, both teams fielded with almost nonchalant grace. In the second game, the A's leftfielder Joe Rudi speared a liner off the wall that probably saved the victory for Oakland, a catch some called the equal of Al Gionfriddo's in 1947 and Willie Mays' in 1954.

The Series hero was catcher-infielder Fury Gene Tenace, the A's bullpen catcher for most of the season. In the regular season, he hit only five home runs; in the Series, he hit four, tying a record held by Babe Ruth and Lou Gehrig, among others. Of the 16 runs scored by the A's in the Series, Tenace drove in 9.

For the first time, both pennant winners were decided on the final day of the season. The Reds beat the Pirates and the A's defeated the Tigers in the fifth and final games of the playoffs.

After toppling the World Champion Pirates, Sparky Anderson was one of several Reds who said: "You just saw the World Series—these are the two best teams in baseball." A number of sportswriters agreed. With the A's home-run slugger Reggie Jackson out of the Series with an injury, the Reds were heavy favorites. The A's retorted that they could have won the pennant in the National League. Then they captured the first two games in Cincinnati and flew to Oakland laughing at the Reds' embarrassment.

Sparks of controversy continued to fly. On the plane, A's first baseman Mike Epstein exchanged words with manager Dick Williams about being taken out of a game. In Oakland, the A's owner Charlie Finley, who put his name on the club's mule mascot Charlie O., berated his players for ducking away from a welcoming celebration. Meanwhile, a debate familiar to the times began when Sparky Anderson said his clean-shaven Reds were a better example to American youth than the shaggy-haired A's, most of whom had grown moustaches during the season and now looked like the Temple Cup finalists of the 1890s. A West Coast writer called Anderson "a short-haired creep," but Finley stood up for conservative values: during a seventh-inning stretch, he led the A's customers in the singing of "God Bless America."

The A's went ahead three games to one, then lost a 5-4 game. The Big Red Machine, with its lineup of strong hitters—Pete Rose, Johnny Bench, Tony Perez—finally clanked into action, powering five runs home in one inning to win the sixth game, 8-1, and even the Series.

In the first inning of the seventh game, the Reds' centerfielder Bob Tolan misjudged a drive by Angel Mangual for a three-base error. Tenace drove in Mangual with a bad-hop single over third base. In the sixth, Tenace doubled home another run. Sal Bando then hit a long drive to center. Tolan in pursuit suddenly slowed down, a hamstring pulled in his leg. The liner dropped for a double, driving home the run that won the game, 3-2, and the championship.

For the A's, once of Philadelphia and later of Kansas City, this was the first Series victory since Connie Mack's A's won in 1930. Of Tenace's surprise hitting Sparky Anderson said: "It can hap-

The A's Joe Rudi picks off Denis Menke's drive against the leftfield wall in the ninth inning of the second game. A's manager Dick Williams called it the greatest Series catch because "this one was for me." Said Rudi: "It was not my greatest catch, but it certainly was the most important one I have ever made." Earlier in the game, won 2-1 by the A's, he had hit a homer to put the A's ahead 2-0.

pen anytime when the adrenalin starts to flow in the excitement of a World Series."

Johnny Bench:
It's easier on the road

How does a baseball star feel on the eve of a World Series? Johnny Bench told about the way it was for him: *The pressure of the World Series seems to come more at home games than at road games. I wish we had opened up this Series on the road. At home the phones never stop ringing, everyone wants to visit you, friends and your family all want to see you before the game. Everybody means well, but it is just a little too much and that creates a lot of extra stress. There's also some nervousness before the game because you realize how important everything is. But I've been there before so I know what to expect from both the fans and the press. I guess the pressure also comes from psyching yourself up to get ready for the biggest effort of the season. The big thing is to try to relax and play baseball the way you know you can play . . .*

Above: One of Charlie O's hostesses serves coffee to the umpires between innings. Opposite page: Johnny Bench (top) blocks home and tags out Blue Moon Odom, who tried to score from third—with two out in the bottom of the ninth of the fifth game—on a short pop to Joe Morgan. The tag ended the game, the Reds 5-4 victors. The enraged Odom (bottom) argues with the umpire, but even the A's said he was clearly out.

324

326

Opposite page: Red pitcher Gary Nolan pounds his glove in disgust after Gene Tenace, trotting the bases in the background, hit his second homer in the first game. Tenace, whose two homers drove in all three runs in the 3-2 A's victory, became the first to hit home runs in his first two at-bats in a Series. Opposite page (r.): Pete Rose waits for the first pitch of the fifth game from Catfish Hunter. Pete socked it for a homer. Top: Charlie O. and his manager, Dick Williams, kiss their wives atop the dugout after the last out of the final game. Mrs. Williams weeps. Mrs. Finley said Charlie O. gave her "the biggest kiss since we were married."

FIRST GAME (Oct. 14, at Cincinnati)

OAKLAND.................020 010 000   3 4 0
CINCINNATI.............010 100 000   2 7 0
Holtzman, Fingers (6th), Blue (7th)
Nolan, Borbon (7th), Carroll (8th)

SECOND GAME (Oct. 15, at Cincinnati)

OAKLAND.................011 000 000   2 9 2
CINCINNATI.............000 000 001   1 6 0
Hunter, Fingers (9th)
Grimsley, Borbon (6th), Hall (8th)

THIRD GAME (Oct. 18, at Oakland)

CINCINNATI.............000 000 100   1 4 2
OAKLAND.................000 000 000   0 3 2
Billingham, Carroll (9th)
Odom, Blue (8th), Fingers (8th)

FOURTH GAME (Oct. 19, at Oakland)

CINCINNATI.............000 000 020   2 7 1
OAKLAND.................000 010 002   3 10 1
Gullett, Borbon (8th), Carroll (9th)
Holtzman, Blue (8th), Fingers (9th)

FIFTH GAME (Oct. 20, at Oakland)

CINCINNATI.............100 110 011   5 8 0
OAKLAND.................030 100 000   4 7 2
McGlothlin, Borbon (4th), Hall (5th), Carroll (7th),
  Grimsley (8th), Billingham (9th)
Hunter, Fingers (5th), Hamilton (9th)

SIXTH GAME (Oct. 21, at Cincinnati)

OAKLAND.................000 010 000   1 7 1
CINCINNATI.............000 111 50x   8 10 0
Blue, Locker (6th), Hamilton (7th), Horlen (7th)
Nolan, Grimsley (5th), Borbon (6th), Hall (7th)

SEVENTH GAME (Oct. 22, at Cincinnati)

OAKLAND.................100 002 000   3 6 1
CINCINNATI.............000 010 010   2 4 2
Odom, Hunter (5th), Holtzman (8th), Fingers (8th)
Billingham, Borbon (6th), Carroll (6th), Grimsley
  (7th), Hall (8th)

328

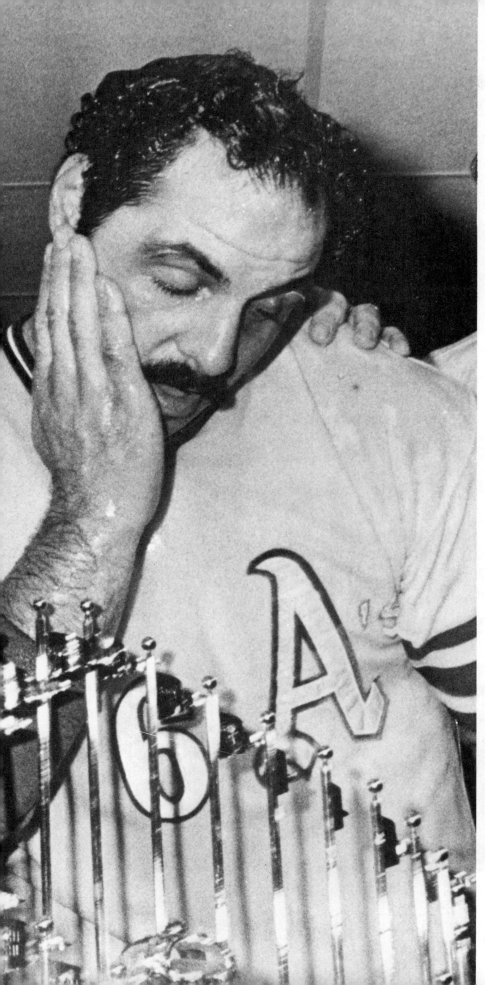

In a classic scene that is repeated year after year after the final game of a World Series—only the faces change—the champagne-soaked winners accept the World Championship trophy. Charlie Finley (center) insisted his players, Blue Moon Odom (l.) and captain Sal Bando, accept the trophy and while they do, a hand at top pours more champagne on the owner of the newest of the long line of World Series winners.

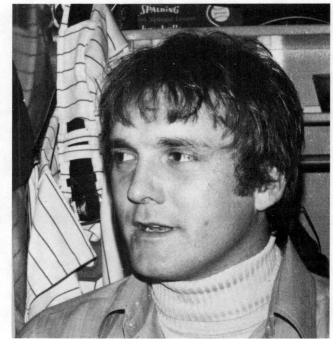

John Devaney

United Press International

OAKLAND ATHLETICS
NEW YORK METS
1973

"Ya Gotta Believe!" Cried the Mets. But True Believers the A's Were Not.

It was a time of scandal in high places: Vice-President Spiro Agnew had resigned just before the Series began. At this 70th World Series the attention of fans was drawn to the box seat of the A's owner, Charlie Finley, the perpetrator of baseball's own Watergate: The Andrews Affair. The boyish-faced Mike Andrews, a utility second baseman, made two errors during the 12th inning of the second game that leaked in the decisive run for a 10-7 New York victory. After the game the dynamic Finley harangued Andrews into signing a letter—"for the good of the team"—stating falsely that he was physically unable to play. Angry Oakland players told reporters that Finley had fired Andrews so he could replace him with a better fielder. In protest the players taped Andrews' No. 17 onto their sleeves. Commissioner Bowie Kuhn reprimanded Finley for "embarrassing" Andrews and ordered him reinstated. Andrews came back to rejoin the team in New York for the fourth game.

Late in the game, Manager Dick Williams sent in Andrews to pinch-hit. "They'll probably give you a standing ovation," Williams told Andrews. Both laughed, but as Andrews strode to the plate, nearly 50,000 New York fans rose and thundered an emotional greeting, the salute from every guy who has been fired and dreams one day of punching the boss in the nose. During the ovation, Finley sat frozen, finally twirling an Oakland banner. Andrews hit into an easy putout. As he trotted back to the dugout, the fans stood and poured down more applause.

The Andrews Affair was another incident in a long series of feuds between the A's players and Finley. "We have had years of this crap," growled outfielder Reggie Jackson. "This is supposed to be the fall classic," said catcher-first baseman Gene Tenace, "and look what that man has done to mess it up."

When the A's came to New York for the third game, they discovered that their wives had been assigned to seats near the roof, half a skyscraper above their husbands. The wives feared they might be assaulted by Met fans, who had mussed the hairdos of Cincinnati wives during the playoffs. Tenace said Finley had assured him the wives would be seated near the dugout, close by the muscle of their menfolk. Instead, Tenace said, friends of Finley were seated near the dugout.

"A mixup," claimed an Oakland official. By the next game the wives were secure in an enclosure near the dugout. But the A's claimed the damage had been done to their psyches. "Half my thoughts are on the mucking up that Finley has done and half my thoughts are on Tom Seaver," Reggie Jackson said before the third game. Seaver struck him out three times.

At a clubhouse meeting before the third game, Dick Williams told his players that he was going to quit after the Series, "win or lose." And only minutes after the Series ended, with TV cameras showing the scene to millions, Williams looked into Finley's face and told him he was quitting.

As to the baseball: The A's and Mets were evenly matched rivals despite their disparate season records. The A's had won a second straight American League pennant by winning their division with a .580 record, then beating the Orioles in a five-game playoff. The Mets languished last

Mayor John Lindsay flaunts a banner that proclaims the Met war cry, first uttered by Tug McGraw (top). "My arm was tired after the second game," said the impish Tug. "Then I visited a friend and now it's OK." The friend's name? "John Jameson," Tug said.

331

in the weak National League East for most of the season, playing as sickly as 13 games under .500 in mid-August. Suddenly relief pitcher Tug McGraw's arm, dead all summer, began to crackle fastballs and screwballs. Shouting a cry coined by McGraw—"Ya gotta believe"—the Mets made believers of the city's millions by winning 20 of 28 down the stretch, capturing the Eastern division title with a .509 record. The Reds had won the Western title with a .611 record, best in baseball, but the Mets won the playoff in five games that were punctuated by fistfights between the players and bottle throwing at Red players by Met fans. And so, with a .509 record, the worst ever to be taken into a Series, the Mets squared off against the World Champion A's.

The Reds' Johnny Bench counseled the A's not to take the Mets lightly. He said the Mets had "the best starting four in baseball—Tom Seaver, Jerry Koosman, Jon Matlack, and George Stone." The A's could match that quartet with three 20-game winners—Jim (Catfish) Hunter, Vida Blue, and Ken Holtzman—and the A's boasted sluggers that made the Met hitters look puny. The A's ranked ninth among the 24 big-league teams in hitting, the Mets 23d.

What equalized the teams in many minds were two old baseball theorems: pitching is 75 percent of baseball and good pitching stops good hitting. Met pitching figured to keep the New York hitters close enough so that only three or four runs would be needed to win.

Before the Series the A's players confessed to knowing little about a Met team that few had thought would rise all the way to the Series. "If you had told me in August we would be in the Series," Tom Seaver said, "I would have said you were crazy." But Dick Williams warned his A's: "We're not playing the below-.500 Mets of June. We are playing the above-.600 Mets of September."

As events unreeled, the Met hitters surprised people by outhitting the A's (.253 to .212, four homers to two), but what decided the Series were (1) the loose fielding on both sides—three mistakes (two errors and a passed ball) led to the winning run in three of the seven games; (2) the

road-blocking relief pitching of the A's Darold Knowles and Rollie Fingers who together saved all four of the A's victories, the Mets leaving a Series record of 72 runners on base; (3) the opportunistic hitting of A's shortstop Bert Campaneris and the explosive hitting of Reggie Jackson in the final two games when the A's had their backs to the abyss.

The A's won the first game, 2-1, Holtzman besting Matlack. The winning run scored after Campaneris hit a two-out groundball that skittered through the legs of Met second baseman Felix Millan. The Mets tied the Series by winning the second game in 12 innings, 10-7; the game consumed 4 hours and 13 minutes, longer by 45 minutes than any Series game ever played.

In New York, the next three games were played in the 50 degrees of chilly October nights. In game No. 3, the teams were tied, 2-2, in the 11th inning. With a runner on first, Met reliefer Harry Parker threw a third strike by Angel Mangual. But the ball shot by catcher Jerry Grote for a passed ball, the runner dashing to second. Campaneris singled him home and the A's won, 3-2.

Carrot-topped Rusty Staub, the Met rightfielder, whacked a three-run homer in the first inning of the fourth game, then drove in two more runs for a 6-1 Met victory that evened the Series at two victories apiece. In the fifth game, Koosman and McGraw stopped the A's as cold as the night air, 2-0. "We've come all the way from underneath everybody to one game from the top," exulted Seaver in the clubhouse.

Seaver and Catfish Hunter went at each other in a sixth game that the A's had to win. Seaver had won the last game of the season and the Eastern division title, then went on to beat the Reds in the fifth game of the playoffs to capture the pennant. In the third game of the Series, he struck out 12 A's before leaving after eight innings with the score 2-2. But some Met fans still grumbled that "Seaver doesn't win the big ones."

He didn't win this big one, his right arm obviously tender after 300 innings of pitching in 1973. "He was not the real Tom Seaver," Reggie Jackson said after the game, "but he showed me the gutsy Tom Seaver." Seaver allowed only two runs in eight innings, but Catfish Hunter was even stingier, winning 3-1.

For the 25th time in 70 World Series, it all came down to that Armageddon in October: a winner-take-all seventh game. Holtzman opposed Matlack. In the third inning, with a man on base, Campaneris poked a hanging curve into the right-field seats for a 2-0 Oakland lead. Moments later Reggie Jackson drove another hanging curve into those same seats for a 4-0 lead. When Holtzman ran into a Met uprising, Fingers came on to suppress it. In the ninth inning—with the tying run at the plate—Knowles strode in to pitch in his seventh game (a Series record) and saved the 5-2 victory. The A's pummeled each other and ran to the clubhouse through grabbing fans with their second World Championship in two years: the first back-to-back Series triumph since Yankee victories of 1961 and 1962.

A footnote of this Series: For the first time the two leagues had played a season with a major difference in the rules. The American League had allowed a designated hitter to bat in place of the pitcher. As a result, few of the Oakland pitchers had batted during the 1973 season. Ken Holtzman had come to the plate only once. But in the Series, with the designated hitter not allowed, Holtzman came to the plate three times and smacked two doubles. So much for practice.

McGraw, Jones, and Harrelson: Remembrances of things past

Three New York Mets, before the start of the Mets' second World Series, talk about the impact of the Series on a ballplayer.

Relief pitcher Tug McGraw: *When I was a little boy, I thought the Series was exciting, but now that I am a part of it, I realize there is so much more to being here than I could ever have dreamed of as a boy. No outsider can know what it's like—the six months of ups and downs before you get here. And then there are the playoffs. In some ways the playoffs are taking some of the excitement away from the Series. There is a lot of tension in the playoffs because if you don't win, then you don't get in the Series. You can't make that $15,000 or $20,000 a man, win or lose, in the Series if you don't get by the playoffs. And yet there is a special excitement about the Series because you have a chance to be more than a league champion; you can be the world champion. That's why you really can't compare the playoffs and the Series. Each has its own unique type of excitement. And the World Series has all that history.*

Outfielder Cleon Jones: *I don't think I really ever knew how much the World Series meant to a player until one day—this was in 1969—Ernie Banks came into our clubhouse before a Series game. He was dancing and singing and fooling around the way he does, you know. He started to sing, 'Hey, I wanna be a Met, gimme a Met uniform, I wanna be a Met, I wanna play in the World Series.' I looked at him and I thought, 'Hey, here's this man who has been in the big leagues—what, 18 years?—and done all the things he has done, hit all the home runs he has hit, and he has never been in what I am in right now. Look at all he has accomplished, but he is begging to be in a World Series.'*

Shortstop Bud Harrelson: *In a Series you can lose the first game, like we did in 1969, and come back to win. What lingers in my mind—it always will—is the first inning of that first game. Don Buford was the first man up for Baltimore, and he hit the first or second pitch for a home run. Right away we were behind, 1-0. He ran around the bases yelling, 'Hey, you guys ain't seen nothing yet.' I wouldn't ever do a thing like that. In a World Series, and this you should never forget, those guys playing for the other side, they're all pretty good, too.*

Henry Aaron throws out the first ball at the first game—the first active player so honored. For Met manager Yogi Berra this was his 17th Series as a player, coach, and manager; in 11 of those Series he was a winner. For Dick Williams this was a hectic third year under Finley. Pointing to the gaudy green-and-gold A's uniforms, Williams said, "This team is more colorful than our uniforms."

THE METS ARE FLYIN' HIGH; and SO AM I

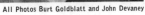

GIVE UJA ISRAEL EMERGENCY FUND

All Photos Burt Goldblatt and John Devaney

Fans (top) huddle against the chill
during night game in New York.
Games were played at night to draw a
large TV audience. But shivering
fans asked if TV were ruining "the
summer game." Thousands fled before
the end of the exciting 11-inning third
game. Left: Raising funds outside
the park. Right, top to bottom: Met
banner; prodigal son Mike Andrews;
A's wives Sharon Rudi (l.) and Jill
Fingers safe at last.

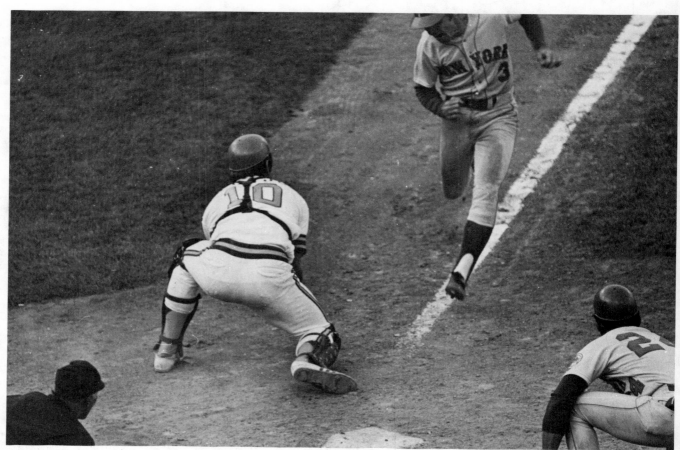

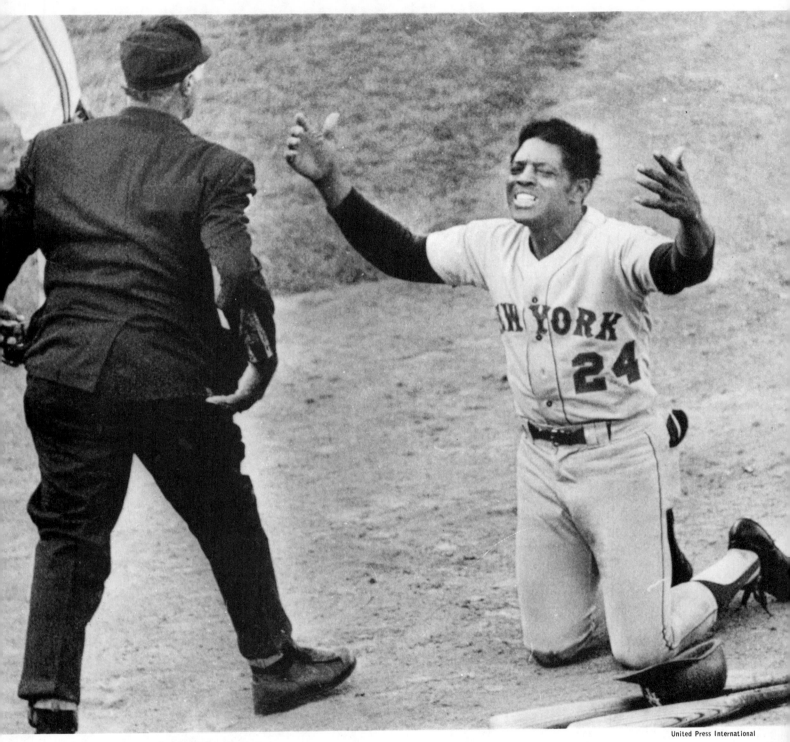

In the 10th inning of the longest Series
game ever played, the Mets' Bud
Harrelson tries to score from third on
a fly ball. Joe Rudi's throw to catcher
Ray Fosse arrives ahead of Harrelson
(top, opposite page). But Harrelson
seems to snake around the tag (bottom).
Umpire Augie Donatelli says you're
out. Willie Mays (above) pleads in vain.
"The tag brushed him on the hip,"
Augie said. "I brushed him on the arm,"
Fosse said. In a game of ups and
downs for both sides, the Mets
won in 12 innings, 10-7.

337

Sloppy play abounds. Top: Jerry Grote chases passed ball that cost Mets third game. Center: Ball hops through Mike Andrews as winning run scores in second game. Bottom: Willie Mays, in the last hours of his career, flops groping for a liner he lost in a glaring sun that blinded outfielders during all the games in Oakland.

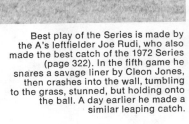

Best play of the Series is made by the A's leftfielder Joe Rudi, who also made the best catch of the 1972 Series (page 322). In the fifth game he snares a savage liner by Cleon Jones, then crashes into the wall, tumbling to the grass, stunned, but holding onto the ball. A day earlier he made a similar leaping catch.

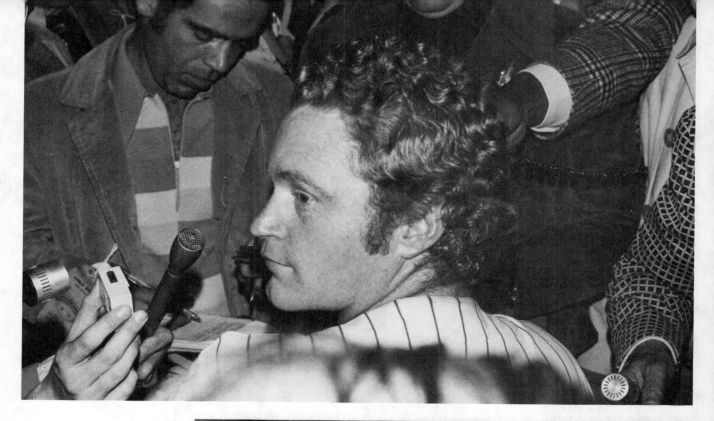

Scenes showing the madness of a club-house after a winning game as media people descend on the newest heroes. Center: A mass of cameramen focus on half-hidden Rusty Staub, who (top) answers questions after getting four hits in game four. Bottom: Bert Campaneris is swamped by questioners after batting in winning run in game three.

All Photos John Devaney

340

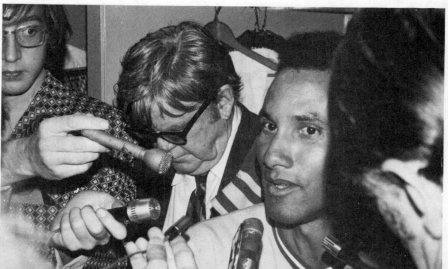

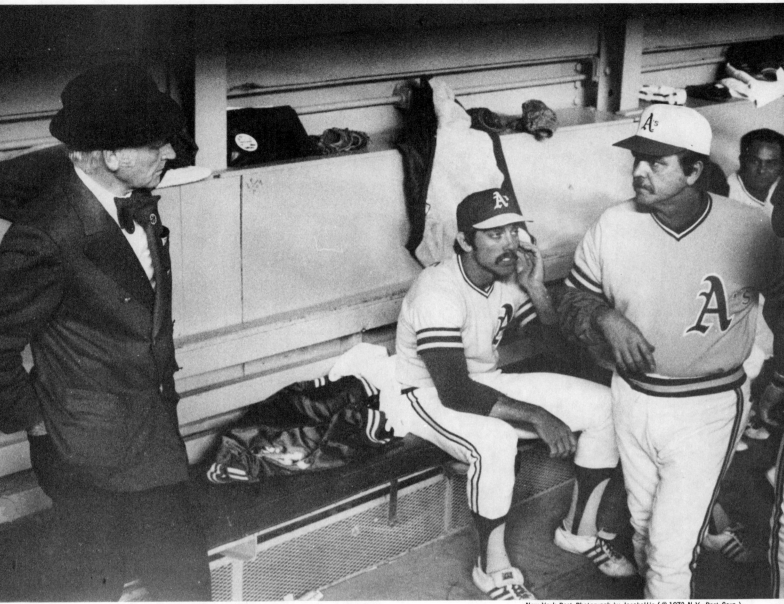

New York Post Photograph by Jacobellis (© 1973 N.Y. Post Corp.)

Dick Williams trades wary glances with
his boss, Charlie Finley, in the dugout
before the third game while outfielder
Billy Conigliaro stays in the middle.
The A's kept their shaggy-haired,
moustached look for the 1973 Series,
Catfish Hunter and Ken Holtzman
wearing their hair shoulder length.
Finley had lost weight after a heart
attack during the summer.

341

Top (l.): Yogi Berra clowns with the 84-year-old first Met manager, Casey Stengel. Top (r.): Gene Tenace pops a bubble. In 1972 Series he hit four home runs to tie a record co-held by Babe Ruth. In 1973 he tied another Ruth record with 11 walks. Left: Bert Campaneris hits his homer in final game.

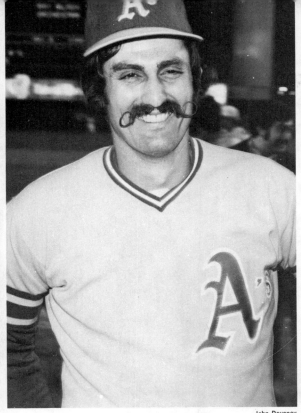

A's heroes were Rollie Fingers (top l.), Darold Knowles (top r.), and .310-hitting star Reggie Jackson (l.), who was named the Series' Most Valuable Player. The FBI guarded Jackson during the Series after a threat was made to kill him.

FIRST GAME (Oct. 13, at Oakland)
NEW YORK.................000 100 000   1 7 2
OAKLAND..................002 000 00x   2 4 0
Matlack, McGraw (7th)
Holtzman, Fingers (6th), Knowles (9th)

SECOND GAME (Oct. 14, at Oakland)
NEW YORK...........011 004 000 004   10 15 1
OAKLAND............210 000 102 001   7 13 5
Koosman, Sadecki (3d), Parker (5th), McGraw (6th),
    Stone (12th)
Blue, Pina (6th), Knowles (6th), Odom (8th), Fingers
    (10th), Lindblad (12th)

THIRD GAME (Oct. 16, at New York)
OAKLAND.............000 001 010 01   3 10 1
NEW YORK............200 000 000 00   2 10 2
Hunter, Knowles (7th), Lindblad (9th), Fingers (11th)
Seaver, Sadecki (9th), McGraw (9th), Parker (11th)

FOURTH GAME (Oct. 17, at New York)
OAKLAND.................000 100 000   1 5 1
NEW YORK................300 300 00x   6 13 1
Holtzman, Odom (1st), Knowles (4th), Pina (5th),
    Lindblad (8th)
Matlack, Sadecki (9th)

FIFTH GAME (Oct. 18, at New York)
OAKLAND.................000 000 000   0 3 1
NEW YORK................010 001 00x   2 7 1
Blue, Knowles (6th), Fingers (7th)
Koosman, McGraw (7th)

SIXTH GAME (Oct. 20, at Oakland)
NEW YORK.............:...000 000 010   1 6 2
OAKLAND..................101 000 01x   3 7 0
Seaver, McGraw (8th)
Hunter, Knowles (8th), Fingers (8th)

SEVENTH GAME (Oct. 21, at Oakland)
NEW YORK.................000 001 001   2 8 1
OAKLAND..................004 010 00x   5 9 1
Matlack, Parker (3d), Sadecki (5th), Stone (7th)
Holtzman, Fingers (6th), Knowles (9th)

344

Moments after winning the World
Championship (opposite page), Oakland
catcher Ray Fosse (at the bottom)
and first baseman Gene Tenace (at the
top) leap on pitcher Darold Knowles.
Above: Teammates pour out to rush
Tenace (far r.) and other A's to the clubhouse. Oakland's captain, Sal Bando,
visited the Met clubhouse after the game
and said, "You guys are the best I've
seen," and no World Series winner ever
paid a more fitting tribute to a
World Series loser.

OAKLAND ATHLETICS
LOS ANGELES DODGERS
1974

Rollie Sticks His Fingers into the Oakland Dike

For the first time, all the World Series games were played west of the Grand Canyon. And the Oakland A's were hoping to win a third straight world championship, a string of crowns no team had put together since the Yankees of 1951. These were the conversation pieces among fans as this Series began between the veteran A's, who had flung punches at each other during the season, and the young, speedy, and hard-hitting Los Angeles Dodgers. With the teams based only 400 miles apart, one reporter compared this all-California battle to the old "Subway Series" between the Yanks and Giants and called it "the commuter-airline Series."

The A's new manager was Alvin Dark, who had managed the Giants in the 1962 World Series. Dark had been hired by A's owner Charles O. Finley three days before the start of spring training to replace Dick Williams, who had quit after the '73 Series. This was much the same Oakland Gashouse Gang that had cussed at Finley, brawled with each other, and won the American League's Western division title in 1971, 1972, and 1973. It had a lineup laden with home-run hitters: Reggie Jackson, Gene Tenace, Joe Rudi, and Sal Bando. It had speed: Centerfielder Bill North stole 54 bases to lead the league, and shortstop Bert Campaneris stole 34. It had three *cordon bleu* starters: Jim (Catfish) Hunter, Ken Holtzman, and Vida Blue. And they were backed up in the

bullpen by Rollie Fingers and John (Blue Moon) Odom.

Though the team didn't hit for a high average, the A's cracked a disproportionate number of hits when there were runners poised to fly homeward. With 121 hits, for example, third baseman Bando drove in 103 runs. Supported by such opportunism—and 132 homers, second highest in the league—Catfish Hunter won 25 games, Holtzman 19, and Blue 17. The staff hero, though, was reliefer Rollie Fingers, who arrived in the latter portions of 76 games and saved 18 of them while winning 9 others. He and Catfish Hunter put their arms in more than half of the A's 90 victories. After a sluggish start, during which the A's growled about Dark ("He couldn't manage a meat market," Bando snapped), Oakland had seized the lead in late May and coasted to a fourth straight Western division title.

For the fifth time in the six years since the divisions were created in 1969, the Baltimore Orioles won in the East, closing with a rush—28 victories in their last 34 games—to collar the Yanks and Red Sox. The Orioles barreled right on into the playoffs, knocking Catfish Hunter out of their way with three homers in the first five innings of the first game to win, 6-3.

Enough! cried Ken Holtzman, who halted the Orioles by throwing a five-hit, 5-0 shutout into their faces. The next day Vida Blue slammed an-

Fans swarm onto the field and rockets burst as Oakland celebrates a third straight championship. But the electric sign was a false prophet.

other gate with a two-hit, 1-0 triumph. Ahead two games to one, the A's stood only one game away from their third straight pennant. In that fourth game Catfish pitched seven innings of three-hit ball before being replaced by Fingers in the eighth, and the A's crept into the ninth inning with a 2-0 lead. Coming to bat, the Orioles had seen 30 straight goose eggs posted after their name. Their bats suddenly sprang to life, knocking in one run to make the score 2-1 and stationing the tying and winning runs on base. But Rollie Fingers whistled a fastball by Don Baylor for a third strike, and the A's had their third straight pennant.

For the Los Angeles Dodgers the summer of 1974 had seemed like a nightmare revisited. In the summer of 1973 they had watched in horror as their 11-game lead was whittled away by the Cincinnati Reds, who shot by them to win in the National League West. In the summer of '74 the Dodgers' 10½-game lead was shortened to 1½ by the very same Reds. "But this is a different

Dodgers' Joe Ferguson (below) skips in front of Jimmy Wynn in eighth inning of first game, after snatching a flyball. He throws to catcher Steve Yeager (opposite page) and Yeager jams the ball into sliding Sal Bando, who tried to score from third after the catch. As Bando looks, Yeager shows he held onto the ball.

Dodger team," insisted Los Angeles pitcher Don Sutton. "The difference is centerfield and the relief pitcher."

In centerfield was stumpy Jimmy Wynn, obtained from Houston, and he was hitting more homers in a season than any other Dodger ever— 32. The relief pitcher was Mike Marshall, a Michigan State physiologist who claimed any well-conditioned right arm could do what his would do this season: pitch in 106 games, 13 of them in a row—both big league records.

Walter Alston, in his 21st season as Dodger manager, had to call even more often on Marshall after his best pitcher, Tommy John, snapped a tendon and was lost for the season. But Don Sutton, a loser up to then, inexplicably became a winner. He won 19 games, Andy Messersmith 20, and young Doug Rau 13.

What helped the pitchers were home runs. The Dodgers poled more balls into the seats than any other team in the league. Almost everybody in the lineup made his hits count. First baseman Steve

Garvey, with a .312 average, led the team in runs batted in with 111. Bill Russell drove in 65 runs, the most ever for a Dodger shortstop. Third baseman Ron Cey accounted for 97. Leftfielder Bill Buckner (.314) and second baseman Davey Lopes (.266) were among the league's best base-stealers.

"Our strength is that we are well-balanced," Walter Alston said. "If we have any weakness, it's on defense."

In September the Dodgers fended off the Reds' drive and won in the West. In the East the Pirates slipped in first a hair ahead of the Cardinals. The Pirates came to the playoffs bearing heavy weapons—Al Oliver (.321), Richie Zisk (.313), Willie Stargell (.301), Rennie Stennett (.291), Richie Hebner (.291)—and they had blown the Dodgers out of the water in every game at Pittsburgh's Three Rivers Stadium during the regular season. But in the first game Don Sutton whisked pills by the Pirate bats for a 3-0 Dodger victory. The next day the Pittsburgh hitters waved weakly at more smoke thrown by Andy Messersmith and Mike

Marshall, and the Dodgers won, 5-2. In Los Angeles for the third game the young Dodgers seemed shaken at the prospect of being only one game away from winning what, for most, would be their first pennant. They bumbled away five balls and the Pirates won, 7-0. But the next day Steve Garvey's bat exploded for two home runs as the Dodgers ran up the most lopsided score of any playoff game, a 12-1 triumph that put the Dodgers in their first Series since 1966.

The day before this first all-California Series began, Rollie Fingers and Blue Moon Odom swapped implications about their private lives in the Oakland clubhouse. Words escalated to punches. Fingers gashed his head on a locker, Odom twisted an ankle. "Nothing unusual," shrugged the A's. Earlier in the season, Reggie Jackson had slugged toe to toe with fellow outfielder Bill North. Caught in the middle was catcher Ray Fosse, who limped out of that battle with a crushed neck disc. But this latest fracas caused only five stitches in Fingers' skull, and the next day, when the Series opened at Dodger Stadium, he and Odom sat together peaceably in the A's bullpen.

The A's Holtzman opposed the Dodgers' Messersmith in the first game. Reggie Jackson began the scoring with a home run in the second inning. In the fifth Holtzman, who hadn't batted all season because of the American League's designated-hitter rule, slammed a double, reviving memories of the two doubles he'd hit in the 1973 Series. Holtzman was moved to third. He streaked for home as the batter, Bert Campaneris, neatly dropped a two-strike, suicide-squeeze bunt, and the A's led 2-0.

With Fingers now pitching, the A's led 2-1 as they came to bat in the eighth. Campaneris—a pesky Series player—singled, moved to second on a sacrifice, then scooted home when Ron Cey picked up a hopper near third base and flung it by the first baseman. That put Oakland ahead 3-1 and proved to be the decisive run. In the ninth Jimmy Wynn smacked a homer to bring the Dodgers to within a run, 3-2, and haul a surprise —Catfish Hunter—out of the A's bullpen. Catfish took the ball from Fingers and wafted it by catcher-outfielder Joe Ferguson to save the 3-2 Oakland victory.

The Dodgers came out for the second game at Dodger Stadium well aware (they'd been educated by innumerable reporters) that no team ever had lost the first two games at home and survived to win a Series. A crowd of 55,989, biggest ever in Dodger Stadium, watched in the soft Sunday sunshine as Don Sutton stymied the A's with only four hits over eight innings while the Dodgers clipped away at Vida Blue for a 3-0 lead. But in the ninth, Sutton put runners on second and third, and Marshall came in to relieve him. Joe Rudi singled, knocking in two runs. With one out, the A's had the tying run at first base.

At that point Al Dark called on his "designated runner," Herb Washington, a former college sprinter with Olympic speed. Washington had been hired at the direction of the imaginative Finley, even though the sprinter couldn't hit nor field and had no pro baseball experience. But as a pinch-runner during the season Washington had stolen 29 bases in 45 attempts. Now Dark put him into the game to try to steal second, from where he could hurry home on a base hit and tie the game.

Iron Mike, as the indefatigable Marshall was called, stood on the mound for Los Angeles. As Washington edged off the bag, Iron Mike suddenly wheeled and threw to first. Washington was caught frozen as Steve Garvey slapped the ball on him for the second out. Moments later Iron Mike struck out Angel Mangual to preserve the 3-2 Dodger victory. Later he revealed he had taught a course in child development at Michigan State and Washington had been one of his students. "Today," someone said, "the professor taught the student about the pickoff."

The teams flew to Oakland for game No. 3. Starting for the A's would be Catfish Hunter. Catfish's lawyers had demanded that Commissioner Bowie Kuhn declare Catfish a free agent because Finley had defaulted on payment of $50,000 of his $100,000 salary. "Nonsense!" snorted Finley, but Catfish's lawyers said that after the Series Catfish would be free to offer his good right arm to the highest bidder.

Apparently unruffled by the wrangle, Catfish stroked his mustache between pitches as he mowed down the Dodgers over seven innings. The A's led, 3-0, in the eighth. But then Dodger leftfielder Bill Buckner cuffed a home run, and

Dark waved for Fingers. Rollie gave up another home run—to Willie Crawford in the ninth—but that was all, and Oakland fans left the Coliseum pleased with a 3-2 victory. The first three Series games had all ended in 3-2 scores.

With the A's leading two games to one, Charles O. Finley resorted to a motivational tactic that even Knute Rockne might have thought too obvious. He assembled the A's players and read to them a newspaper interview in which Bill Buckner claimed the Dodgers would beat the A's in 100 of 162 regular-season games. At the game that night, the A's didn't appear all that mad as they meekly dipped their bats at Andy Messersmith curves and fastballs and went into the sixth trailing 2-1. But then they made connections and banged in four runs to assume a 5-2 lead. In the eighth the Dodgers began to make contact with Ken Holtzman's serves. But the ubiquitous Fingers ran in from the bullpen to strike out Joe Ferguson, stop the Dodgers in the ninth, and save the 5-2 victory.

Needing only one more victory for their third straight championship, the A's sent Vida Blue into the Coliseum to win it. In five Series starts, Vida had yet to win a game, his record 0-3. The A's went ahead 1-0 in the first inning, helped by catcher Steve Yeager's wild throw ("Defense *is* our big weakness," Alston conceded later). Catcher Ray Fosse's homer put the A's ahead 2-0 after two innings. In the sixth, however, the Dodgers caught up, and the teams went into the seventh tied, 2-2.

Iron Mike was now pitching for the Dodgers. Just as he finished his warmups, time was called to clear away debris thrown by Oakland partisans at Bill Buckner, whose words had irritated the fans as well as Charles Finley. During the six-minute delay, Iron Mike—an independent thinker with a disdain for the conventional wisdoms of baseball—did not keep his arm loose by tossing to his catcher, as other pitchers would have done. Nor did he choose to toss some practice pitches when the first A's hitter, Joe Rudi, finally stepped up to hit.

"I sort of expected an inside fastball," Rudi said later, "and that was what I got."

Rudi jerked the fastball into the arms of the Oakland rooters in those leftfield seats, obviously brightening their mood, for they quickly forgot about throwing rotten apples at Buckner now that the A's led, 3-2. Blue Moon Odom had replaced the still victory-less Vida Blue, and in the eighth he was replaced by his sparring partner, the always-available Rollie Fingers, who put down the Dodgers in the eighth and ninth. For the fourth time in five games, the final score was 3-2. After Fingers tossed the ball to first for the final out, the A's swarmed out of their dugout to pound him—bloodlessly—and celebrate being Series winners three years in a row. "This was the sweetest one of all," said Reggie Jackson. "The other times it took us seven to beat the Reds and Mets. Maybe now people will give us credit for being a great team."

While the A's celebrated in their clubhouse amid spraying champagne, fireworks lit up the night sky over the Oakland Coliseum. And the electric message board flashed what turned out to be an optimistic prediction: "Once More in '75."

Catfish Hunter: Same show, new role

During the first game of the '74 Series, Catfish Hunter entered the game in the ninth inning as a relief pitcher. It was only his second relief assignment in five years. Later he described his emotions: *After you have played in one World Series, you have a pretty good idea how it feels, so I didn't feel any great pressure because this was the opening game. But I was more than a little nervous because I was coming onto a mound* [at Dodger Stadium] *that I wasn't used to. I was afraid I'd have trouble with my control, and I didn't have time to get used to the mound with a runner on first in a 3-2 ball game. When I took the ball from Rollie Fingers, he looked at me and I knew he was thinking of what I'd said to him the many times he'd come in to relieve me. He said, 'Get the last out.' When I did get the last out, I was honestly happy, because I don't know what I would have said to Rollie if I hadn't.*

Below: Catfish Hunter, in his farewell game as an Athletic, decks Davey Lopes. Opposite page: Dodgers' Bill Buckner is tagged out at third by Sal Bando in the final game. His team behind, 3-2, Buckner led off the eighth with a single. When the ball bounded by the centerfielder, he ran to second and—not wisely—tried to reach third. His demise was the Dodgers' last gasp.

All photos United Press International

FIRST GAME (Oct. 12, at Los Angeles)
OAKLAND 010 010 010 3 6 2
LOS ANGELES 000 010 001 2 11 1
Holtzman, Fingers (5th), Hunter (9th)
Messersmith, Marshall (9th)

SECOND GAME (Oct. 13, at Los Angeles)
OAKLAND 000 000 002 2 6 0
LOS ANGELES 010 002 00x 3 6 1
Blue, Odom (8th)
Sutton, Marshall (9th)

THIRD GAME (Oct. 15, at Oakland)
LOS ANGELES 000 000 011 2 7 2
OAKLAND 002 100 00x 3 5 2
Downing, Brewer (4th), Hough (5th), Marshall (7th)
Hunter, Fingers (8th)

FOURTH GAME (Oct. 16, at Oakland)
LOS ANGELES 000 200 000 2 7 1
OAKLAND 001 004 00x 5 7 0
Messersmith, Marshall (7th)
Holtzman, Fingers (8th)

FIFTH GAME (Oct. 17, at Oakland)
LOS ANGELES 000 002 000 2 5 1
OAKLAND 110 000 10x 3 6 1
Sutton, Marshall (6th)
Blue, Odom (7th), Fingers (8th)

353

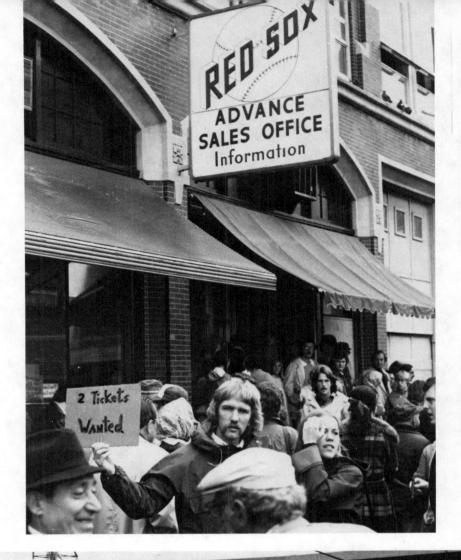

All photos John and Barbara Devaney

CINCINNATI REDS
BOSTON RED SOX
1975

Two on a Seesaw

For the first time since 1968, two of baseball's "originals"—teams that had been doing business at the same old stand since the turn of the century—met in a World Series. Oddly, these two old-timey teams had never before met in a Series game.

Nor had either team been notably successful of late in World Series play. The Boston Red Sox had engaged in seven Series, the most recent in 1967, and had won five; but they had last won a championship flag way back in the World War I days of 1918. Cincinnati had entered six Series and won twice; but Franklin D. Roosevelt was in the White House when they had last won, back in 1940. Twice since 1970 the Big Red Machine, steered by Johnny Bench and Pete Rose, had thundered into a Series and clanked out a loser.

This 1975 clash may not have produced a clear-cut winner or loser. But it gave America some unforgettable days and nights. Five of the games were won by a single run, and two of those came on sudden-death shots in extra innings. Almost every game was a seesawing affair, the score retied or the lead reversed 13 times. In six of the seven games the winning team came from behind. The sixth game was played with near-flawless grace as one team, then the other, surged toward victory only to be beaten back. With the game in extra innings and each pitch followed by mesmerized millions, Cincinnati's Pete Rose came to bat, turned to Red Sox catcher Carlton Fisk, and said, "This is some kind of game, isn't it?" The seventh game—its fate and the fate of the Series decided by a weakly hit liner to centerfield —was watched in more homes than any other single TV program ever. People came away from the Series talking about its heroics and agreeing that baseball indeed is some kind of game, not old-fashioned or dying, but perhaps more akin to the spirit of '76 America than the often brutal battles of football, basketball, or hockey.

For the Cincinnati Reds, these grim Series battles were an abrupt change from their laugher of a season. During one stretch, starting in mid-May, they won 41 of 50 games to shoot far ahead of the Dodgers in the National League West. They came home 20 games ahead, the widest gap ever for a divisional winner. Their 108 victories were the most by a National League team since the 1909 Pirates, who won 110. It was the Reds' fourth divisional title in six years.

Playing in their spacious home park, its artificial surface the color and hardness of a billiard table, the Reds rocketed line drives off the walls and whirled around the bases to win a record 64 of 81 games. "Base-running has been our game plan all season long," said manager George (Sparky) Anderson. "We go from first to third as well as anyone. We'll first-to-third you to death. And with our speed we're hard to double, and

While fans outside (top) plead for tickets, the fortunate 35,000 inside Fenway Park stand with the players under dripping clouds for the National Anthem. Moments later, a mile or so from the site of the first Series opener, game No. 421 began.

355

that keeps big innings alive."

Red base-running traced worry lines onto the foreheads of opposing catchers. In 1975 the Reds stole 168 bases in 204 attempts, a success rate of 82 percent that was another big league record.

"We don't have an easy out in our lineup," bragged Anderson. Only two other National League teams socked more home runs than the Reds. Their sawed-off second baseman, 5-foot-7-inch Joe Morgan, batted .327; and the intense Pete (Charlie Hustle) Rose, shifted from the outfield to third base, hit .317. As a whole the lineup batted a resounding .271.

Only when he looked at his starting pitchers did Sparky Anderson frown. His starters completed only 22 games. During one period the Red starters went 45 straight games without a complete game—a big league record. Sparky pulled his pitchers so often that he got a new nickname: Captain Hook. No Red starter—Don Gullett, Gary Nolan, Fred Norman, Jack Billingham, or Pat Darcy—won more than 15 games. But Gullett, who threw the kind of pitches that knocked bats out of hands, was 15–4 and might have won 20 if he hadn't missed two months with a broken thumb.

In the bullpen were lefthander Will McEnaney and righthander Rawly Eastwick, both in their early 20s, and veterans Pedro Borbon and Clay Carroll. The bullpen won 26 games and saved 50.

In the National League East the Pirates won their fifth division title in six years, their overpowering pitching and lusty hitting making up for an expensive habit of being all thumbs when faced with a batted ball. But with line-drive hitting and speed—the Reds stole 10 bases in 10 tries in the first two games—the Reds swept the Pirates 8–3, 6–1, and 5–3 to win their third pennant in six years.

In the American League East, the Boston Red Sox had been picked to linger well behind Baltimore and New York in 1975. For more than a decade the Red Sox had looked to Carl Yastrzemski to pull them to victory with his home runs, leaping catches, and ropelike throws from leftfield. But Yaz was now 35 and had been moved from the outfield to less strenuous duties at first base. Replacing him in leftfield was a rookie, Jim Rice. In centerfield stood another rookie, Fred Lynn, who had hit only modestly in the minors.

His mask flying, Sox catcher Carlton Fisk bumps into Ed Armbrister as he lunges for the ball in the most disputed play of this—and perhaps any other—Series.

The fervor that this Series aroused is seen in some of the propaganda it produced. Above: A 1940 front page reminds Reds fans of their last championship, while street banners and signs on marquees in downtown Cincinnati exhort and flatter the faithful. Right: Buttons and signs in Boston tell the world what Red Sox fans think of their star and the team.

All photos John and Barbara Devaney

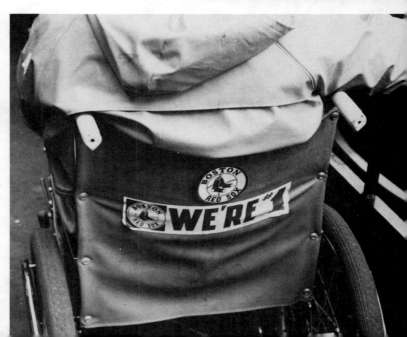

Rightfielder Dwight Evans had been no ball of fire in his two seasons with the Red Sox. Catcher Carlton Fisk was fragile, as was shortstop Rick Burleson; and third baseman Rico Petrocelli, near 32, seemed near the end of his career.

So the Red Sox started the 1975 season with no great expectations in a division that figured to be dominated by the Yankees, who now owned (for a price of more than $3 million) the formidable pitching talents of Jim (Catfish) Hunter, lured from Charles O. Finley and the A's. But early in the going, the Red Sox forged ahead of the Yankees. Their two rookies, Lynn and Rice, were swatting around .330, and Lynn—a stylish fielder with the grace and range of a DiMaggio (Joe or Dominic) and the arm of a Willie Mays—leaped and dived to make miracle catches.

On the mound Rick Wise, back after missing much of 1974 with an aching shoulder, won 19 games. Luis Tiant—with a hand-twitching, body-twisting windup—pretzeled his way to 18. Bill Lee, Reggie Cleveland, and Roger Moret won 44 among them; and Dick Drago, Jim Willoughby, and rookie Jim Burton came in from the bullpen to stamp out trouble. With a combination of the heaviest hitting in the league, marvelous fly-chasing by their young outfielders, and steady pitching, the Red Sox—after keeping New England in a state of alarm through September—held off Baltimore to finish first in the East.

In the West the Oakland A's made up for the loss of Catfish by dipping more often into a well-stocked bullpen. And their best hitters—Reggie Jackson, Sal Bando, and Claudell Washington—still had the knack of dropping in their hits when the rewards were the greatest. Thus Jackson drove in 104 runs with 150 hits and Bando drove in 78 with only 129 hits. The experienced A's won their fifth straight Western title and sought their fourth straight pennant and world championship, an achievement unmatched since the Yankees of 1949 to 1952.

For the playoffs against Oakland, Boston had to make an adjustment. Leftfielder Jim Rice, who had broken a hand, was through for the season. Yaz trotted back to his old pasture in left and Cecil Cooper, a designated hitter much of the season, replaced him at first base.

The move proved to be fortuitous. After the Red Sox won the first game, 7–1, Yaz hit a home run and a double in the second game to lead Boston to a 6–3 victory. And in the third game, with Boston ahead 5–1 in the eighth, he made a diving stop of a line drive to save at least one run and perhaps three. The Red Sox won, 5–3, to wrest the American League flag from the hands of the Oakland team that had held it since 1972. "We missed Catfish," said Reggie Jackson, "but if we had Yaz in left, it would have been us instead of Boston in the Series."

The Series opened on a gray, dreary day in Fenway Park. It was the 421st World Series game (including ties) since that first one in 1903 at the now-vanished Huntington Avenue Grounds, which had stood only a mile or two from Fenway. The dignified, balding Tiant—the newspapers called him El Tiante—walked to the mound in a drizzle that soon ended to throw the first pitch.

Before the Series there had been speculation that the Reds would complain to the umpires that El Tiante's twisting delivery was illegal. "If he isn't balking," said Sparky Anderson, "you might as well throw the rule book out the window."

With a crowd of 35,205 packed in old Fenway and chanting, "Loo-eeee . . . Loo-eeee . . . ," El Tiante seemed to hold the Reds spellbound with his twisting hips and tantalizing pitches. "In the National League," cracked Pete Rose later, "we don't face anyone who throws a spinning curve that takes two minutes to come down." Tiant shut out the Reds, 6–0. His was the first complete game by a Series pitcher since Steve Blass won the seventh game for the Pirates in 1971.

Game No. 2 was played in a piercing rain that came down so harshly in the seventh that the game was stopped for a half hour. The Fenway Park lights glanced off the raindrops to produce a ghostly gray light. The rain moistened the field into mushiness.

Cincinnati's Jack Billingham, a righthander, and Boston's Bill Lee, a lefthander, were the pitchers. The Red Sox dubbed Lee "Spaceman" because of what they considered his way-out views on society. As a pitcher, Spaceman liked to dangle temptation in front of hitters. His Leephus pitch was a direct descendant of the Eephus pitch of the 1940s, a lob that came at the batter like a ball sloping down a hill. The ball looked as big as a beachball, but most times the hitter popped it up.

By the ninth inning the lefthanded Lee had made his way through the rain, fog, gloom, and muck, owned a 2–1 lead, and stood on the mound only three outs away from being able to thumb his nose at the Green Monster. But in 24 of their 108 victories, the Reds had won in their last at-bat. They would do it a 25th time. With Johnny Bench on third and two out, Dave Concepcion smacked a ball up the middle of the mucky infield. Some five hops later the ball arrived in Denny Doyle's glove. The second baseman stared helplessly as Concepcion flew across first and Bench pounced on home plate. The game was tied, 2–2, and the crowd was as sullen as the weather. A minute later the Reds were ahead, 3–2, after Concepcion stole second and scored on a hit by Ken Griffey. In the bottom of the ninth the Reds' Rawlins J. Eastwick III, of Haddonfield, New Jersey, calmly put down the Red Sox. ("I've never been nervous in my life," said the 23-year-old Rawly later.) The Series was tied at one victory apiece.

Game No. 3 was played on a pleasantly cool night in the modern amphitheater that is Cincinnati's spacious Riverfront Stadium. Riverfront's concrete bowl compares architecturally to the boxy, wood-and-iron Fenway about as a Boeing 727 compares aerodynamically to a World War I Spad. "It will be nice," said a Red pitcher, staring at the faraway fences, "not to be pitching in a phone booth." Yet, as if to underscore the perverse way that baseball has of being unpredictable, the two teams that had hit no homers in two games at Fenway would slam six in one game at Riverfront, tying a Series record.

The pitchers were Rick Wise and Gary Nolan. Boston took the early lead when Fisk socked a second-inning homer; but Johnny Bench draped one over the fence with a man on, and the Reds led, 2–1, after four innings. In the fifth Dave Concepcion and Cesar Geronimo clipped homers in succession, and Pete Rose hit a triple to build the Reds' lead to 5–1.

The Red Sox pecked away at that lead with a

The scoreboard at Fenway tells the story: Score tied in the top of the ninth, two out, and Joe Morgan at bat as Jim Burton throws the pitch that would decide the Series. The Red Sox fielders get ready as the ball (under the "R" on the scoreboard) curves toward Morgan, who looped it into centerfield to bring in the winning run of one of the most memorable of all Series.

United Press International

run in the sixth, another in the seventh on a pinch-hit home run by ex-Red Bernie Carbo. By the ninth Captain Hook had his fourth relief pitcher, the nerveless Rawly Eastwick, on the scene, the score 5–3. With one out and a man on base, Rawly threw a fastball that had no muscle on it. Dwight Evans cracked it into the seats to tie the score, 5–5, and the game went into extra innings.

Cesar Geronimo led off the last of the 10th with a single. The elongated Ed Armbrister stepped in to pinch-hit for Eastwick. Everyone expected a sacrifice bunt—and Armbrister bunted. The ball struck the hard AstroTurf in front of the plate and hopped high into the air. Armbrister hesitated, gaping at the ball as though it were a visitor from outer space. The catcher, Carlton Fisk, lunged over Armbrister's shoulder to grab the ball. For a moment their uniforms melded together. Then Armbrister belatedly took off for first, without being tagged by Fisk, who now had the ball and could easily have done so. Instead Fisk lined a throw toward second to force Geron-imo and begin a double play. But Fisk sailed the ball high into centerfield. Geronimo fled to third while Armbrister went to second.

Fisk turned and howled to umpire Larry Barnett that Armbrister had interfered with him. Barnett said nay. There had been a collision, he told Fisk, but Armbrister had not intentionally obstructed Fisk in the performance of his tasks.

When the shouting ceased, the Sox decided, with runners on second and third, to fill the bases and try—with no one out—to get a force at home. A reedlike lefthander, Roger Moret, struck out pinch-hitter Merv Rettenmund. But Joe Morgan then laced a drive over the head of drawn-in centerfielder Fred Lynn. Geronimo trotted in with the sudden-death run that won the game, 6–5, and put the Reds ahead, two games to one.

Luis Tiant won game No. 4 for the Red Sox, 5–4; but Don Gullett, helped by Rawly Eastwick, won the fifth, 6–2. The Reds led, three games to two, as the players flew back to Boston for the sixth game. It would be a contest that one headline writer labelled "A Game for Posterity."

Needing this victory to survive, the Red Sox took an early 3–0 lead off Gary Nolan. The Reds drilled away at Luis Tiant and led by the eighth, 6–3. But pinch-hitter Bernie Carbo cracked his second Series home run off his old teammates, this time against Eastwick, and the game was tied 6–6, turning Fenway Park into a madhouse.

Both teams had opportunities to win. In the bottom of the ninth the Red Sox filled the bases with nobody out. Denny Doyle tried to score from third on a 190-foot fly ball to George Foster in left. Foster threw a strike to Johnny Bench and Doyle was tagged out. In the 11th, with a runner on first, Joe Morgan lashed a liner that seemed certain to crash into the rightfield seats. But Boston rightfielder Dwight Evans plucked the ball out of the seats, then threw to first for another double play. "It was the greatest catch I've ever seen," Sparky Anderson said later.

And so the game turned into the 12th inning, the time now a little past 12:30 in the morning. On the mound for the Reds was Pat Darcy, the 8th Red pitcher and the 12th of the game, the most ever in a World Series. Carlton Fisk was the first hitter. He took a ball. Darcy aimed a sinker that hooked toward Fisk's knees. Fisk undercut the ball and hit a towering fly that arrowed toward the lights in leftfield. The ball vanished into the darkness for a moment, then could be seen—a white dot curving toward the yellow foul pole next to the screen, home run territory.

Foul or fair? At home plate Fisk swayed his body as though he had ropes attached to that ball and could steer it fair. The ball struck the screen, then angled downward onto the grass. In leftfield umpire George Maloney twirled one hand high, signalling home run. A blast of noise erupted out of Fenway into the darkness, a blast that might have rattled windows in houses along Huntington Avenue. The Fenway organist pounded out the "Hallelujah Chorus" of Handel's *Messiah*. The Red Sox mobbed Fisk and roared into their clubhouse 7–6 winners. In the losers' locker room Pete Rose said, "All winter long I'll watch videotapes of this game and get goose bumps every time I see it."

The next night almost 76 million people in 40½ million homes, according to network research, clicked on their TV sets to see if the seventh game would be anything like that sixth.

Don Gullett started against the Spaceman, Bill Lee. The Red Sox jumped out to a 3–0 lead, and Captain Hook and his crew faced the prospect of losing their third Series in six years.

In the sixth Pete Rose cracked a single. With one out Johnny Bench hit a grounder that hopped rabbitlike toward Burleson at shortstop for an almost-certain inning-ending double play. Burleson flipped the ball to Denny Doyle, who stepped on second as Rose thundered toward him. Doyle leaped and threw high to first, the ball landing in the Red Sox dugout, Bench going to second.

Instead of three outs, there were only two outs. The Spaceman lobbed one of his Leephus pitches to Tony Perez, who seemed to guess it was coming. He waited for the pitch to arch down, then swatted it over the wall for his third home run of the Series. The Reds trailed 3–2.

In the seventh Roger Moret replaced Lee for the Red Sox. With two men on base, Rose cracked another single and the score was tied, 3–3. A mood of anxious waiting for the other shoe to drop began to settle over Fenway.

Jim Burton, a 26-year-old rookie lefthander, came in to pitch the ninth for the Red Sox. He got into immediate trouble by walking Ken Griffey. Cesar Geronimo bunted the runner to second. The next hitter poked a grounder to the right side, drawing Griffey to third with two out.

Rose, on a three-and-two count, was walked by the careful Burton. The next hitter was Joe Morgan. The count rose to two balls and a strike. Burton twisted off a slider that veered down and away from Morgan on the outside of the plate. Morgan stretched for the pitch and caught it with the tip of his bat. The ball rose in wobbly flight— "a dying quail," in hitters' parlance—and fluttered over second base as Fred Lynn dashed in from center, glove stretched beseechingly. The ball bounced onto the grass well in front of him and

Griffey crossed the plate in a hushed park with the run that put Cincinnati ahead, 4–3.

In the bottom of the ninth Captain Hook sent Will McEnaney out to guard the lead. He snuffed out the Red Sox one, two, three. The last batter was Yaz, and the veteran watched, his face stricken with disappointment, as Geronimo gloved his soft fly to center for the last out of a Series to be remembered.

Did the better team win? Sparky Anderson probably put it best. "We are the best team in baseball," he said, "but not by much."

John and Barbara Devaney

Rawly Eastwick:
In a fantasy, you are always the hero

Young Red reliefer Rawly Eastwick won two games in the Series and saved another. *When I was a kid, I'd ask my twin brother—he was my catcher in the Little Leagues—how he thought I would do if I pitched in a World Series. I asked him all the time. He used to get sick of me asking. He'd say shut up. Every kid has fantasies of playing in a Series and in them you never fail, you are always the hero. But I have always thought that way. I never think about failing. In that third game Evans hit a home run off me to tie the game, but we won in the tenth and I was the winning pitcher, and it was just like those fantasies as a kid.*

FIRST GAME (Oct. 11, at Boston)
CINCINNATI...............000 000 000 0 5 0
BOSTON.....................000 000 60x 6 12 0
Gullett, C. Carroll (7th), McEnaney (7th)
Tiant

SECOND GAME (Oct. 12, at Boston)
CINCINNATI................000 100 002 3 7 1
BOSTON......................100 001 000 2 7 0
Billingham, Borbon (6th), McEnaney (7th), Eastwick
   (8th)
Lee, Drago (9th)

THIRD GAME (Oct. 14, at Cincinnati)
BOSTON..................010 001 102 0 5 10 2
CINCINNATI.............000 230 000 1 6 7 0
Wise, Burton (5th), Cleveland (5th), Willoughby (7th),
   Moret (10th)
Nolan, Darcy (5th), C. Carroll (7th), McEnaney (7th),
   Eastwick (9th)

FOURTH GAME (Oct. 15, at Cincinnati)
BOSTON.....................000 500 000 5 11 1
CINCINNATI................200 200 000 4 9 1
Tiant
Norman, Borbon (4th), C. Carroll (5th), Eastwick (7th)

FIFTH GAME (Oct. 16, at Cincinnati)
BOSTON.....................100 000 001 2 5 0
CINCINNATI................000 113 01x 6 8 0
Cleveland, Willoughby (6th), Pole (8th), Segui (8th)
Gullett, Eastwick (9th)

SIXTH GAME (Oct. 21, at Boston)
CINCINNATI...........000 030 210 000 6 14 0
BOSTON................300 000 030 001 7 10 1
Nolan, Norman (3d), Billingham (3d), C. Carroll (5th),
   Borbon (6th), Eastwick (8th), McEnaney (9th),
   Darcy (10th)
Tiant, Moret (8th), Drago (9th), Wise (12th)

SEVENTH GAME (Oct. 22, at Boston)
CINCINNATI................000 002 101 4 9 0
BOSTON......................003 000 000 3 5 2
Gullett, Billingham (5th), C. Carroll (7th), McEnaney
   (9th)
Lee, Moret (7th), Willoughby (7th), Burton (9th),
   Cleveland (9th)

363

CINCINNATI REDS

NEW YORK YANKEES 1976

Billy and George
Were Put to Shame

By the end of this abbreviated Series, the first to be wrapped up in four games since 1966, the street-tough Yankee manager, Billy Martin, had been driven to his own wailing wall in the trainer's room at Yankee Stadium, to bawl out his frustration. At every facet of the game—running, fielding, pitching, and hitting—the Big Red Machine of Cincinnati had outperformed Martin's Yankees. While Martin dried his tears, ballplayers on both teams were being asked if this 1976 Cincinnati team was the best baseball team ever.

The Reds led their league in batting with a .280 average. They had scored the most runs, stolen the most bases, and led the league in homers. Up to now the 1927 Yankees of Ruth, Gehrig, and Meusel had been considered the most awesome bunch of hitters ever to come into a Series. According to legend, their booming drives in batting practice had awed the Pirates into dropping the Series in four games. The Yankees of '27 had five regulars batting above .300; this Big Red Machine, as it had dubbed itself, also had five— Pete Rose (.323), Ken Griffey (.336), Joe Morgan (.320), George Foster (.306 and 29 homers), and Cesar Geronimo (.307). Sub-.300 hitters like Tony Perez and Johnny Bench had poled 35 homers between them.

"AstroTurf has changed the game," said former slugger Ralph Kiner after the Series, "and the Reds know how to play it well. They go from first to third, and if they draw the throw, they have a man on second." Their speed opened doors for their hitters. "The first baseman always has to play close to the bag to keep the runner close, because nearly every one of the Reds can steal," pointed out former Yankee shortstop Tony Kubek, now a TV reporter. "And because they know a runner from first may break toward second, the shortstop and the second baseman have to edge closer to the bag. That opens up wide areas to Red hitters."

Only in pitching did the Reds suffer by comparison to the great teams of the past. Their top pitcher, Don Gullett, had won only 11 games, while the entire staff had completed only 33 of 162 games. But Red manager George (Sparky) Anderson, still known as Captain Hook for his quickness in pulling starters, could point to the indisputable fact that in sharing the load the Red pitchers had chalked up 102 wins.

The Reds jumped out to an early lead in the National League West, as did the Philadelphia Phillies in the NL East, the New York Yankees in the American League East, and the Kansas City Royals in the AL West. All led by the first week of June, and only the Phils and Royals suffered September scares before clinching their division titles by comfortable margins.

The Royals had to beat off a late charge by the Oakland A's, that creation of Charles O. Fin-

Billy Martin, his face taut with the tension of losing, walks to the mound to talk to another Yankee pitcher in trouble. This Series, he later said, was the beginning of his feuding with owner George Steinbrenner, which would result in his being fired twice.

United Press International

ley that had won five straight division titles and three straight world championships. Midway through the season Finley had tried to sell outfielder Joe Rudi and relief pitcher Rollie Fingers to the Red Sox for a million dollars each and pitcher Vida Blue to the Yankees for one-and-a-half million. Commissioner Bowie Kuhn cancelled the purchases to "preserve the honor of the game." Finley growled that Kuhn "sounds like the village idiot."

The shrewd Finley had good reason to try to sell away this championship team. The game had entered a new era—the era of the free agent. That summer, after a bitter battle between players and owners, an agreement had been struck: Players with six or more years in the big leagues could declare themselves free agents and sell themselves to the highest bidder. Finley's stars had made it known that they were disgruntled by his despotism and his wariness with a dollar. He knew they

366

The speed of the Reds on the basepaths was, with their bats, the most potent weapon of the Big Red Machine. Left: Cesar Geronimo skids toward home plate with one of the runs that beat New York, 4–3, in the second game. Bobbling the throw is Yankee catcher Thurman Munson.

would jump ship at season's end, leaving him with nothing for their skills except their parting harsh words.

And that was what happened. Minutes after the end of the season, the A's threw a champagne party for themselves in the clubhouse. Celebrating their liberation from Finley, Joe Rudi, Sal Bando, Gene Tenace, Rollie Fingers, Bert Campaneris, and Don Baylor declared themselves free agents and waited with relish for the offers, which soon poured in. The dismemberment of what was without question one of the ten great teams of all time had begun.

The Yankees, under Billy Martin (one of the heroes of the 1952 Series), had become division champions after being out of post-season play since 1964. The club's president, pudgy Gabe Paul, had dipped deeply into the pockets of the wealthy chief stockholder of the team, conglomerate tycoon George M. Steinbrenner III, to buy the best and most expensive talent available. Only two members of the team, catcher Thurman Munson and outfielder Roy White, were products of the Yankee minor league system.

The lineup included first baseman Chris Chambliss (from Cleveland), shortstop Fred Stanley (from San Diego), third baseman Graig Nettles (from Cleveland), centerfielder Mickey Rivers (from California), and pitchers Jim (Catfish) Hunter (the most expensive acquisition, from Oakland), Ed Figueroa (from California), Dock Ellis (from Pittsburgh), and relievers Dick Tidrow (from Cleveland) and Albert (Sparky) Lyle (from Boston).

This group of hired Hessians went into the playoffs against a Kansas City team that was home-grown almost to a man. The Royals were sparked by two robust hitters, third baseman George Brett and outfielder Hal McRae. With averages of .333 and .332, respectively, they had finished one-two in American League batting that season.

The issue was decided in the fifth game, played at Yankee Stadium before 56,821 fans. With the Yankees leading, 6–3, in the eighth, George Brett let loose with a three-run homer that tied the game and turned the roaring arena as quiet as a graveyard ("as though George had switched out a light," someone later said). But in the Yankee half of the ninth, Chambliss caught hold of a fastball and sent it sailing toward the right-center-field wall. Royal outfielder Hal McRae leaped for the ball, but it arched over his glove for the homer that won the game and the Yankees' 30th pennant. It ended the season for a Royal team that was at the beginning of three straight seasons of such bitter disappointments.

In the National League the finish was almost as dramatic. After winning the first two games against a Philly team loaded with sluggers like third baseman Mike Schmidt and leftfielder Greg Luzinski, the Reds were losing the third, 6–4, as they came to bat in the bottom of the ninth at Riverfront Stadium. Pitching for the Phils was Ron Reed, a gangling former pro basketball player. The first batter, George Foster, slammed a homer. The next man up, Johnny Bench, hit another homer to tie the score. Four batters later the bases were filled, only one out. Ken Griffey hit a skipping ground ball toward the right side of the infield. First baseman Bobby Tolan lunged for the ball, but it flew off his glove and trickled into rightfield. By the time the ball was picked up, Dave Concepcion had long since crossed home plate into the waiting arms of his jubilant teammates; and the Big Red Machine had won its second straight pennant.

After such last-inning fireworks in the playoffs, the Series would prove to be something of a fizzle. In the first game, at Riverfront, the Big Red Machine won easily, 5–1. Nevertheless, the Yankees had reason to think positively: The Reds' best pitcher and first-game victor, Don Gullett, had dislocated his ankle in the eighth inning and would not be able to pitch again in the Series.

This Series had its own "first"—the first designated hitter (DH) in National League history. The older league had agreed to use the DH, an American League innovation, in every other Series.

The first NL DH was Dan Driessen, in more normal times a third baseman. Driessen went hitless in the first game; but in the second inning of game No. 2, he doubled off Catfish Hunter to start a Cincinnati merry-go-round that rang up three quick runs.

But for the next six innings, Catfish kept the Reds hitless while the Yankees fought back to tie the score, 3–3. Working with machine-like efficiency, Hunter seemed invulnerable as he mowed down the first two Reds in the ninth. Then Ken Griffey showed the Yankees his specialty—the infield hit, an ace he had used more than 30 times during the season. He knocked a slow roller toward shortstop Fred Stanley, whose off-balance throw to first ended up in the Red dugout. Griffey didn't stop running until he reached second.

Billy Martin, as sunken-cheeked and skinny as he was as a Yankee rookie in 1950, ordered Joe Morgan walked intentionally, which brought up Tony Perez, a long-ball hitter. Hunter threw a high fastball that Perez clipped on a clean line—what the ballplayers call "a frozen rope"—into leftfield, and that was that. The Reds were now two up.

The Series came back to Yankee Stadium for the first time since 1964; the "House That Ruth Built" had been rebuilt (at a cost to taxpayers of over $100 million). The designated hitter, that American League invention called by some NL people the work of the devil, would again engineer the Yankee downfall. Driessen (who hit .357 in the Series) led off the second inning with an infield hit. Once again the Yankees would be bowled over by the speedy Red Machine. Driessen stole second. Foster doubled and Driessen raced home. Bench beat out an infield roller, Foster going to third. Cesar Geronimo hit a roller to short, forcing Bench but scoring Foster, while the speedy Cesar got to first, ruining the double play. He then stole second and scored on a single that barely looped over the infield. Two infield hits, a long double, a short single, and two stolen bases had earned three runs for the Reds in typical Cincinnati style. They went on for a 6–2 triumph, and the Yankees were three down.

The fourth game was played on a frigid night at Yankee Stadium. The Reds came into the ninth ahead by a run, 3–2; but then they blew away starter Ed Figueroa and reliever Dick Tidrow with four runs. The big hit was a three-run homer by Bench, who, with a .533 average, was voted the Series MVP by *Sport* magazine.

Billy Martin, having seen nine Yankees left on base in this contest, was so frustrated that he hurled a baseball from the dugout and was immediately ejected from the game. In tears he sat on the floor of the trainer's room as the Yanks went down meekly in the bottom of the ninth. To make matters worse, Yankee immortal Joe DiMaggio had a box-seat view of the loss.

The Reds had become the first team to win their league pennant and the Series in the minimum seven games. And they had become the first NL team to win back-to-back Series since the Giants of 1921 and 1922. Were they the best Series team ever? Snapped Billy Martin, after drying his tears: "Let them win five Series in a row like we did. That's awesome."

As 1977 would prove, the Reds were not that awesome.

Billy Martin: An awareness of things to come

Speaking to writer Peter Golenbock, with whom he wrote the book *No. 1*, Martin said after the Series: *I was sitting on the floor in the trainer's room when George Steinbrenner came in after that fourth game. I could see daggers coming out of the man's eyes, and he was looking at me as if I'd lost on purpose, and he was saying, 'How could you do this to me?' He was embarrassed, and it was as if he didn't know the rest of us were embarrassed. I knew right then that the guy would try never to let this happen again by becoming much more involved with the team and with how I ran the team.*

The play that was the undoing of Catfish Hunter in the second game: Yankee first baseman Chris Chambliss grimaces as he reaches for a throw from shortstop Fred Stanley that was off the mark. The ball flew into the dugout, and the batter, Ken Griffey, gripping his helmet to make sure it protected him from the ball, went to second. From there he scored the winning run.

FIRST GAME (Oct. 16, at Cincinnati)

NEW YORK.................010 000 000 1 5 1
CINCINNATI...............101 001 20x 5 10 1
Alexander, Lyle (7th)
Gullett, Borbon (8th)

SECOND GAME (Oct. 17, at Cincinnati)

NEW YORK.................000 100 200 3 9 1
CINCINNATI...............030 000 001 4 10 0
Hunter
Norman, Billingham (7th)

THIRD GAME (Oct. 19, at New York)

CINCINNATI...............030 100 020 6 13 2
NEW YORK.................000 100 100 2 8 0
Zachry, McEnaney (7th)
Ellis, Jackson (4th), Tidrow (8th)

FOURTH GAME (Oct. 21, at New York)

CINCINNATI...............000 300 004 7 9 2
NEW YORK.................100 010 000 2 8 0
Nolan, McEnaney (7th)
Figueroa, Tidrow (9th), Lyle (9th)

"Patience, patience, we'll still have a full week!"
In a campaign year, politicians had to wait.

Courtesy Bill Canfield, Newark Star Ledger

United Press International

George Sullivan

REG-GIE

Bob Lowery

NEW YORK YANKEES
LOS ANGELES DODGERS
1977

Mr. October Took Over the Show

Reggie! Or as Yankee fans would chant when Reginald Martinez Jackson strode to the plate, *Reg-gie! Reg-gie!* No player in Series history, Babe Ruth possibly excepted, had overshadowed a Series with his bat as heavily as Reggie Jackson did in 1977.

Jackson had come to the Yankees via the Baltimore Orioles after being traded to Baltimore by Oakland. As a free agent at the end of the 1976 season, he had signed with the Yankees for the largest sum of money ever given to a baseball player up to then: $2.9 million.

Always an annoyance to his teammates (an Oakland player once said, "There isn't enough mustard in the whole world to cover that hot dog"), Jackson immediately began to spar with the Yankees. At spring training in 1977 he told a reporter that it was he, not catcher Thurman Munson, who was the real leader of the Yankees. "Munson," he said in a remark that would dog him for years, "thinks he's the straw that stirs the drink. I'm the straw that stirs the drink." When manager Billy Martin took him out of a game because of his erratic fielding, the two of them, both fiery-tempered, had to be pried apart in the dugout. For much of the season Jackson grumbled loudly that he, not Munson, should bat fourth.

George Steinbrenner had continued to spend and trade for the best talent that his money could buy. What was a Yankee hole in 1976 had been plugged with the acquisition of shortstop Bucky Dent from Chicago. Third baseman Graig Nettles hit 37 homers in the season and had become a

fielder in the image of Brooks Robinson. Munson was a cagey receiver, though sometimes inaccurate or tardy in throwing out base-stealers; but he had driven in a hundred or more runs for the third straight year. Other dependable hitters included outfielders Lou Piniella (.330), Mickey Rivers (.326), and Jackson, who would hit 32 homers and drive in 110 runs.

Pitching had been fortified by the sudden emergence of skinny Ron Guidry, who had languished for a half-dozen years in the Yankee minor league system, as a double-digit winner. Relief pitcher Albert (Sparky) Lyle, a former Bostonian, had provided solid support for the entire staff; his twisting slider won 13 games and saved 26.

On August 10th Martin decided to listen to Reggie. He made Jackson the Yankee cleanup hitter. From that day on the Yankees, who had trailed the Red Sox for much of the season, won 41 of 53 games, taking over first place on August 23rd and never relinquishing it. (A frantic three-game series between the Sox and Yankees in September was decided when Jackson came to bat in the bottom of the ninth of the second game with the score 0–0 and Munson on first, and hit a homer to end the game and Boston's hopes.)

In the American League West, the Kansas City Royals won 26 of 32 games in September to finish comfortably ahead of the Texas Rangers. For the second year in a row this young and obviously improving Royals team of George Brett, Hal McRae, and pitchers Dennis Leonard (20 victories), Paul Splittorff, and Jim Colborn took

The Yankee scoreboard
flashed its salute to
Reg-gie three times in
game No. 6 as he set
Series records that may
never be matched.

on the Yankees. Again, as in 1976, the pennant was won and lost in the last inning of the fifth and final game.

That fifth game began with typical Yankee squabbling. Martin decided to bench Jackson because he had been told that Jackson couldn't hit the starting Royal pitcher, Splittorff, "with a —— paddle." Jackson complained loudly to reporters about being kept on the sidelines in this big game.

As it turned out, Martin sent Jackson in as a pinch-hitter in the eighth. Reggie drove in a run, but the ninth opened before 41,133 screaming Royal fans with Kansas City ahead 3–2. Dennis Leonard was now on the mound, only three outs

Below: The Yanks' Thurman Munson tags out Steve Garvey and holds onto the ball during a collision at home plate. Opposite page: The Dodgers' Dusty Baker slides back to first, eluding a tag by Chris Chambliss after a pickoff throw by Don Gullett appeared to have trapped him between first and second.

away from Kansas City's first pennant. The Yankees put their first two batters on base, and in came a new Royal pitcher, Larry Gura. The Yankee batter, Mickey Rivers, slapped a single for one run, another came in on a sacrifice fly, and a third on an error by Brett. The Yanks led, 5–3. Sparky Lyle put down the Royals in the ninth, and the Yankees had won pennant No. 31.

In the National League, Cincinnati's Big Red Machine clanked to a halt, wheezing, its gears stripped by a lack of strong pitching (the loss of Don Gullett to the Yankees as a free agent had been the crushing blow to an already weak staff). In the NL West race, the Dodgers built an early lead over the Reds and were never seriously challenged.

This Dodger team, managed by the ebullient and portly Tommy Lasorda, boasted a lineup of power hitters. Four Dodgers—Ron Cey, Steve Garvey, Dusty Baker, and Reggie Smith—had hit

United Press International

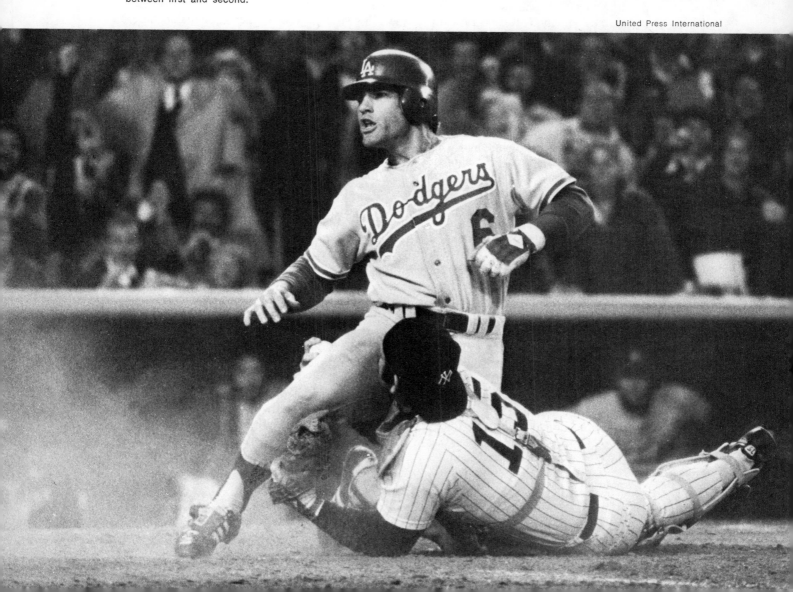

30 or more homers, a big league first. The pitching was anchored by 20-game winner Tommy John, a lefthander, and Don Sutton, a righty, who had won 14 games. Lasorda had dubbed his team the Big Blue Machine.

In the East the Phils parlayed power hitting by outfielder Greg Luzinski (39 homers) and third baseman Mike Schmidt (38 homers) and pitching from Cy Young winner Steve (Lefty) Carlton and Larry Christenson to come from eight and a half games back in June to beat out the Pirates by five games.

In the championship series the Phils won the first game (helped by three errors by the Dodger infield), and the Dodgers won the second. The Phils seemed to have the third game locked up 5–3 in the ninth, with two out and nobody on base. Then the roof fell in as Dodger pinch-hitter Vic Davalillo deftly bunted for a hit, followed by pinch-hitter Manny Mota's single, two straight

Philadelphia errors, and base hits by Davey Lopes and Bill Russell. Suddenly, the Dodgers were 6–5 winners. The next day, during a game played in a steady rain, the Phils bowed, 4–1. The Dodgers had earned their 15th World Series berth.

The first game of the ninth Yankee-Dodger World Series opened in New York with Don Sutton starting against Yankee Don Gullett. At the top of the ninth inning, the Yanks led, 3–2. But even the usually stingy Sparky Lyle—who had relieved Gullett—couldn't stop the Dodgers from tying the game. For two more innings, neither side scored. The game went into the 12th before some 57,000 frantic New York fans. With runners on first and second, Yankee rightfielder Paul Blair, in the game as a defensive replacement for Jackson, tried to bunt and failed. With two strikes on him, he looked to third-base coach Dick Howser, who gave him the order to swing away. And

swing Blair did, striking a single to left that scored the winning run. It was Sparky Lyle's third straight post-season victory.

Billy Martin decided on Jim (Catfish) Hunter for the second game even though Catfish, bothered by arm trouble, hadn't pitched in a month. The Dodgers won 6–1. After the game Reggie needled Martin by telling reporters the manager should have started someone else. Martin shot back, "Reggie has enough trouble playing rightfield without telling me how to manage."

It was in the third game, at Los Angeles, that Reggie began to take over the Series and win for himself a new name: Mr. October. He drove in one run and scored another as the Yankees won, 5–3. Outfielder Lou Piniella was asked if the Yankees, like the A's of 1972–74, played better when they were quarrelling. "We're used to it," he said, "although it does get sickening at times."

The fourth game was attended by the elite of Hollywood—most of them pals of Lasorda. Top personalities like Frank Sinatra, Cary Grant, Walter Matthau, and Shirley MacLaine watched glumly as the Yankees won, 4–2, behind Ron Guidry's four-hit pitching. In the sixth inning, Jackson hit his first homer of the Series, one of four shots that were to explode off his bat.

Down three games to one, the Dodgers rallied in the fifth game to batter Gullett and a succession of relievers for a 10–4 victory. Only Jackson had a reasonably good day—in his last at-bat he hit the first pitch for home run No. 2.

Back in New York for game six, Burt Hooton started for the Dodgers against Mike Torrez. The Dodgers jumped out to a 2–0 lead in the first. In the second inning, Jackson walked on four straight pitches. The next batter, Chris Chambliss, hit a homer to score Jackson and tie the game, 2–2. But the Dodgers regained the lead, 3–2, on a homer in the third by Reggie Smith. It was his third homer of the Series; but within an hour the nation, watching on TV, would be talking of another Reggie.

In the Yankee fourth, Munson singled to left. Up stepped Jackson. On the first pitch from Hooton, he smacked a low, humpbacked liner that sailed into the rightfield seats. The Yanks now led, 4–3.

Jackson came up again in the fifth, again with a man on base. On Elias Sosa's first pitch, Reggie

Opposite page: Yankee hero Joe DiMaggio (top) throws out a first ball for the third game, held in New York. Bottom: Reggie Jackson is congratulated by teammates after his second home run in the final game. At far right is Billy Martin, who had quarreled with Jackson during the season but who would embrace him after the last game.

smacked another low drive that disappeared into the darkness of the rightfield seats. In three successive swings he had hit three homers, two in this game—with more to come.

The Yankees carried their 7–3 lead into the eighth. When Jackson strode to the plate, the crowd gave him a standing ovation in salute to his three homers in three official at-bats. Facing him now was knuckleballer Charlie Hough. Hough's first pitch ducked toward Reggie's shoelaces. Jackson golfed the ball in a high arc toward the distant centerfield wall, where it dropped from sight. Reggie rounded the bases amid a blizzard of paper and a roar that must have been heard a mile from the stadium. Only Babe Ruth before him had ever hit three homers in one Series game —in 1926 and again in 1928. Jackson's five home runs in a Series had set a record, along with his 10 runs scored and 25 total bases. Hitting four successive homers on four swings established a Series first that may never be matched.

The Yankees won the final game 8–4, but even their record 21st Series victory was an anticlimax after those four successive shots. Jackson and Billy Martin embraced after the game, their feuding forgotten for the moment. Although Jackson had talked of quitting after the 1977 season, both he and Martin promised to be back for another Yankee Series. It was a promise only one of them would get to keep.

374

Richard Pilling

Courtesy New York Yankees

FIRST GAME (Oct. 11, at New York)
LOS ANGELES.........200 000 001 000 3 6 0
NEW YORK...........100 001 010 001 4 11 0
Sutton, Rautzhan (8th), Sosa (8th), Garman (9th),
   Rhoden (12th)
Gullett, Lyle (9th)

SECOND GAME (Oct. 12, at New York)
LOS ANGELES.............212 000 001 6 9 0
NEW YORK.................000 100 000 1 5 0
Hooton
Hunter, Tidrow (3rd), Clay (6th), Lyle (9th)

THIRD GAME (Oct. 14, at Los Angeles)
NEW YORK.................300 110 000 5 10 0
LOS ANGELES.............003 000 000 3 7 1
Torrez
John, Hough (7th)

FOURTH GAME (Oct. 15, at Los Angeles)
NEW YORK.................030 001 000 4 7 0
LOS ANGELES.............002 000 000 2 4 0
Guidry
Rau, Rhoden (2nd), Garman (9th)

FIFTH GAME (Oct. 16, at Los Angeles)
NEW YORK.................000 000 220 4 9 2
LOS ANGELES.............100 432 00x 10 13 0
Gullett, Clay (5th), Tidrow (6th), Hunter (7th)
Sutton

SIXTH GAME (Oct. 18, at New York)
LOS ANGELES.............201 000 001 4 9 0
NEW YORK.................020 320 01x 8 8 1
Hooton, Sosa (4th), Rau (5th), Hough (7th)
Torrez

The 1977 Dodgers—Seated on ground: bat boys Dan Ayers, Walt Luchinger.
Front row: Johnny Oates, Glenn Burke, Steve Yeager, Monty Basgall,
Red Adams, Tom Lasorda, Jim Gilliam, Preston Gomez, Steve Garvey,
Manny Mota, John Hale. Second row: Dr. Robert Woods, Bill Buhler,
Reggie Smith, Teddy Martinez, Lee Lacy, Dusty Baker, Bill Russell, Ron
Cey, Davey Lopes, Rick Monday, John Powell, Lee Scott, Jack Homel,
Delfino Galban. Third row: Ed Goodson, Lance Rautzhan, Mike Garman,
Elias Sosa, Don Sutton, Rick Rhoden, Doug Rau, Charlie Hough,
Burt Hooton, Tommy John, Mark Cresse.

376

The 1977 Yankees—Seated on ground: bat boys Joe D'Ambrosio, Felix
Martinez, John Caldarao. Front row: Bucky Dent, Roy White, Art
Fowler, Cloyd Boyer, Dick Howser, Billy Martin, Elston Howard, Bobby
Cox, Yogi Berra, Fred Stanley, Thurman Munson, Fran Healy, Catfish Hunter.
Second row: trainer Gene Monahan, Graig Nettles, Reggie Jackson,
Sparky Lyle, Mickey Klutts, Mike Torrez, Ron Guidry, George Zeber,
Willie Randolph, Lou Piniella, Don Gullett, Ken Clay, Gil Patterson,
Ed Figueroa, Cliff Johnson, Paul Blair, trainer Herman Schneider.
Third row: Carlos May, Ken Holtzman, Dick Tidrow, Chris Chambliss.
Absent from photo: Mickey Rivers, equipment manager Pete Sheehy,
traveling secretary Gerry Murphy.

Reggie Jackson: A trip to dreamland

Reggie Jackson, looking back on that third
homer: *When I was playing in winter ball one
year, about 1970, my manager was Frank Robinson. He told me a lot about how to hit the knuck-
leball. So when I went up there against Hough, I
thought if he threw me anything good, I could hit
another homer. But when I walked up to the plate
and heard all that cheering, I knew I had nothing
to lose. Even if I had struck out against Hough,
they would have cheered me back to the dugout.
But when I hit it and saw it go over the wall, I
thought, 'Hey, man, that's three, and this is the
World Series going all over the country on TV.
This is dreamland.'*

Courtesy Los Angeles Dodgers

Courtesy New York Yankees

NEW YORK YANKEES
LOS ANGELES DODGERS — 1978

Graig's Glove Was Sticky
and Mr. October Knew When to Freeze

The 1978 division races were red-hot by midseason, and all through summer and fall the nation's attention swung from one battle to the other. The Phils and Pirates were at each other's throats in the NL East, while the Dodgers, Reds, and Giants jockeyed for first in the NL West. The Kansas City Royals barely fended off charges by the California Angels and Texas Rangers in the AL West. But it was the American League East race that would hypnotize most fans from its real start, late in the summer, until the last out on a blustery, sunny day at Boston's Fenway Park, when a ball twisted high into the wind off the third-base line and grown men wept.

The Yankees had started the season as co-favorites with the Red Sox. But even though the Yanks got excellent pitching from fastballer Ron Guidry, almost everything else went haywire. The team was plagued by injuries to shortstop Bucky Dent, centerfielder Mickey Rivers, catcher Thurman Munson, pitchers Don Gullett and Jim (Catfish) Hunter. On and off the field, manager Billy Martin smarted under criticism from owner George Steinbrenner.

The Red Sox roared away from the crippled, bickering Yankees. By midseason Boston centerfielder Fred Lynn was hitting .327 and 39-year-old Carl (Yaz) Yastrzemski .322. Four of the Red Sox starting pitchers, Dennis Eckersley, Bill Lee, Mike Torrez, and Luis Tiant, had a com-

United Press International

Opposite page: While Bowie Kuhn,
the commissioner of baseball,
applauds, Mrs. Eleanor Gehrig,
widow of the Yankee first baseman
of the 1930s, throws out a first ball at
a game at Yankee Stadium. Right:
Comedian Bob Hope wets up a
"spitball" before he throws out the
first pitch of game No. 5.

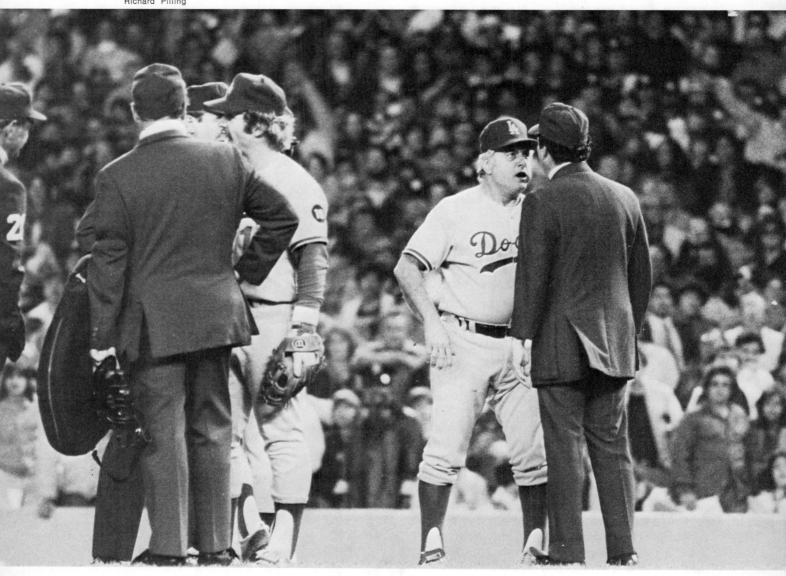

The biggest controversy at this Series (the emblem from its official program is at right) occurred in the fourth game when Reggie Jackson got in the way of a thrown ball, foiling a double-play attempt by the Dodgers. Above: Dodger manager Tommy Lasorda argues with all the persuasiveness in his rotund body that Jackson intentionally got in the way of the ball and should be called out for interference. To his right, shortstop Bill Russell states the same case—with the same result. The umpires ruled no interference.

bined record of 40 wins and only 12 losses.

On July 19th the Red Sox led the Yankees by 14 games. No American League team had ever been that far behind and come on to win. On July 25th, after publicly lambasting Steinbrenner and Reggie Jackson, Martin resigned as manager and Steinbrenner hired Bob Lemon, a former Cleveland pitcher and, most recently, the manager of the Chicago White Sox (he'd been fired at the start of the season). Under the easygoing, unflappable Lemon, the Yankee clubhouse seemed a different place. "Where there was turbulence," wrote New York reporter Phil Pepe in *The Sporting News*, "he brought calm. Where there was anxiety, he brought patience."

The battered New York Yankees suddenly began to heal in more ways than one. Now it was Boston's turn to limp and ache. Lynn, catcher Carlton Fisk, and third baseman Butch Hobson were out of the lineup for long periods. Rightfielder Dwight Evans and the venerable Yaz played in almost constant pain.

While the Yanks won 48 of 68 games, the Red Sox lost 20 of their last 28, including four to the Yanks at Fenway Park in a series that will be forever known in New England as the Boston Massacre. But in the final days of the season Boston steadied, and the two teams finished in a tie. There would be a one-game playoff, the first since the leagues had split into four divisions.

On a windy, sunny day at Fenway Park, Ron Guidry, looking for his 25th victory, started against Mike Torrez. The Red Sox fans, usually boisterous and defiant when the Yanks came to town, were subdued, as though sensing disaster around the corner. The Sox led 2–0 when the Yanks came to bat in the seventh. With two out and two men on base, light-hitting shortstop Bucky Dent, batting ninth, lofted a flyball that hit the netting atop the leftfield wall—Fenway's Green Monster—for a three-run homer. He crossed the plate to shrill yells from the sprinkling of Yankee fans. The Yanks led 3–2. They got another run in the seventh and went ahead 5–2 in the eighth on a Reggie Jackson homer.

The Red Sox closed the gap, 5–4, in their half of the eighth, then put two runners on base in the ninth—the tying and winning runs—with two men out. Rich (Goose) Gossage, another fastballer, was now pitching for the Yanks. Up came

Yaz, who had been Boston's savior in big games for 15 years. (Earlier in this game he had homered and singled.) Gossage threw an inside fastball and Yaz swung feebly. The ball popped high above third base, in foul territory, where Graig Nettles gloved it for the final out. The Red Sox trudged to the clubhouse, where Yaz wept.

The other races had more ordinary conclusions. The Kansas City Royals of Hal McRae and George Brett, managed by Whitey Herzog, won the AL West for the third straight year. And for the third straight year the Royals battled the Yankees for the pennant and for the third straight time bit the dust. In the previous two playoffs the Royals had been beaten in the last inning of the last game; this third consecutive loss was only slightly less jarring.

The teams split the first two games. In the third game, George Brett slammed three straight homers; but the Yankees stayed close enough to win, 6–5, on a two-run homer by Thurman Munson in the eighth. The next day Ron Guidry outdueled Dennis Leonard, 2–1, winning on homers by Graig Nettles and Roy White. The Royals, after stranding the tying run on second in the ninth, watched the Yankees celebrate their 32nd pennant and asked themselves if a time would ever come when Kansas City would own a pennant.

In the National League the Phils won in the East, also for the third straight year. The Phils sought their first pennant since 1950, their first world championship ever. Again they were denied both, for the second time in a row by the Dodgers.

Manager Tom Lasorda had portrayed his Dodgers as a happy family. "We all bleed Dodger blue," he told reporters. This image of fraternal love was shattered when pitcher Don Sutton and first baseman Steve Garvey battled each other in the clubhouse over a remark one made to the other. The fight, however, seemed to spur the Dodgers. Ahead by only a game before the fight, they won 22 of 33 and finished 2½ games ahead of the Reds.

In the playoff the Dodgers won the first two games in front of Philadelphia fans who booed their team. The Phils won the third game, played in Los Angeles, helped immeasurably by Steve Carlton's pitching and hitting (one homer, four runs driven in). In the tenth inning of the fourth game, the score tied 3–3, the Dodgers had a man on first—with two out—when Dusty Baker hit a soft liner to centerfield. The Phils' Garry Maddox loped in, stuck out his glove, grabbed the ball—and dropped it, for reasons neither he nor anyone else could explain. "He catches that ball 999,999 out of a million," third baseman Mike Schmidt said later. The next Dodger tapped a single for the winning run and the pennant. The Phils' record in post-season play, going back to the 1915 Series, was now a not-too-impressive three games won and 17 games lost.

This was the 10th Dodger-Yankee World Series, and the Dodgers had won only twice—in 1955 and 1963. In the first game, at Los Angeles in front of the usual galaxy of stars—Sinatra *et al.*—the Dodgers showed their muscle (they had led the league in homers) by poling three home runs, two by second baseman Davey Lopes. They won, 11–5, behind lefthander Tommy John.

In that first game Reggie Jackson had banged out a homer, his sixth in his last four Series games. So when Jackson came to bat in the ninth inning of the second game, the score 4–3 in favor of the Dodgers and Yankees on first and second, the entire nation wondered if Mr. October would win another game with one jerk of his bat. On the mound stood 21-year-old Bob Welch, a young fastball-throwing righthander who had been pitching for Albuquerque in June.

Welch decided to challenge Jackson with his fastball although Jackson was a fastball hitter. For the next six minutes Dodger Stadium was awash with noise. Jackson swung viciously at each pitch. The count rose to 3 and 2, but Jackson refused to dodge the challenge by trying to slap a hit that would have merely tied the score. Welch threw a high inside fastball. Jackson took another full cut, missed cleanly for the third strike and the final out. While Dodger fans roared, Jackson smashed his bat against the dugout floor and stormed past Bob Lemon. Later he told reporters graciously, "The kid beat me."

Down two games to none but used to comebacks, the Yanks returned to Yankee Stadium. The next three games in New York, as it turned out, decided the Series; and the deciding factor was the infield of both teams. In the third game the Dodgers, trailing 2–1, loaded the bases against Ron Guidry. Earlier in the game third baseman

The Yankees' Lou Piniella winces as he slams into the cushioned wall at Yankee Stadium to pluck down a drive by the Dodgers' Steve Yeager in the fifth game. The stickiness of Yankee gloves stood in sharp contrast to the Dodgers' sloppy fielding.

After the fifth game, in New York, fans celebrate, one game in advance, the Yankee championship and their attainment of the No. 1 place in baseball. Below: After the final game, three of the Yankee infielders, Graig Nettles (l.), Bucky Dent, and Jim Spencer (r.), congratulate reliever Goose Gossage. Moments later, *Sport* magazine named Dent the Series MVP.

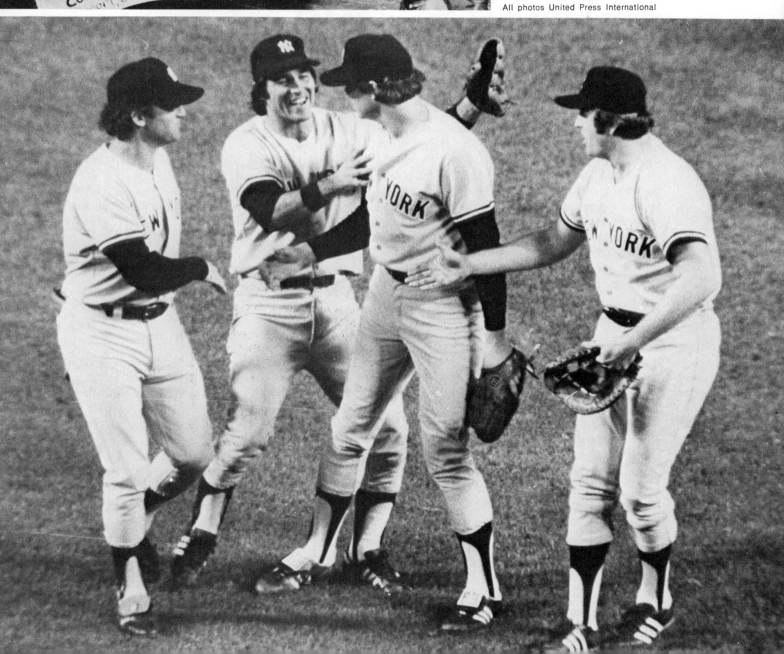

Graig Nettles's flashing glove had taken two hits from the Dodgers. This time Steve Garvey rifled a grass cutter at the third-base bag that seemed sure to streak into leftfield for a double. Nettles lunged to his right, gloved the ball, spun, and in one fluid motion threw unerringly to second base for the force to end the inning. In the next inning he duplicated that play.

"That was one of the greatest exhibitions of playing third base I have ever seen," said Tom Lasorda after the 5–1 Yankee victory. By one calculation, Nettles's glove had stopped the Dodgers from scoring seven runs. In that third game the Dodger infield had failed to execute double plays in the second and seventh innings when the Yanks scored four of their five runs.

In the fourth game, another missed double play would lead to another Dodger defeat. Los Angeles led 3–0 (on a Reggie Smith homer) when Jackson singled in the sixth inning to score Roy White and send Munson to second. Lou Piniella hit a line drive that Bill Russell knocked down near second. Russell stepped on second to force Jackson, then threw toward first for the double play that would have ended the inning. But Jackson, frozen on the basepath a few feet off first, didn't move out of the way of Russell's throw, and the ball ricocheted off his hip. Munson scored on what was later called the Sacrifice Thigh. The Dodgers protested vehemently that Jackson had deliberately jutted out his hip to deflect the throw. They were overruled, and Russell was charged with an error. That run, plus another in the eighth, tied the game 3–3 and put it into extra innings. In the 10th Lou Piniella slashed a single off reliever Welch to score Roy White. The 4–3 Yankee win tied the Series at two games apiece.

The fifth game began with Russell committing his third error. So many ground balls caromed off Russell's knees in the ensuing innings that when he fielded a ball cleanly in the sixth, he got a derisive ovation from the New York fans. The Yanks, meanwhile, peppered the stadium with 16 singles, a Series record, and two doubles during a 12–2 drubbing. Six of the hits came from Brian Doyle, a .192-hitting second baseman during the season, and shortstop Bucky Dent, who hit .243. "In a Series," said Doyle, "the pitchers concentrate on the big guys and not so much when they come down to us."

Down three games to two, the Dodgers sought the refuge of friendly Dodger Stadium. Their fielding improved, but the two "little guys" continued to pester them. With the Dodgers ahead 1–0, Doyle hit a double, his first big league extra-base hit, to tie the score. Dent followed with a single to drive in what turned out to be the winning runs. Dent and Doyle combined for six hits in eight at-bats as the Yankees, behind Catfish Hunter, won the game, 7–2, and the Series, four games to two. (In that sixth game Jackson got his revenge, slamming a long two-run homer off Bob Welch and tipping his hat mockingly to the Dodger fans as he crossed the plate.) The Comeback Team of 1978 was now also the Comeback Team of World Series play, the first club ever to lose the first two games and go on to win the Series in the next four.

"The difference between the teams," said an ever-diplomatic Lemon, and himself a comeback hero, "was Dent and Doyle." Doyle hit .438 in the Series, Dent .417 with seven runs batted in (he was picked as the Series MVP). But perhaps the biggest factors were the glove of Nettles and the hip of Mr. October.

Graig Nettles: What a Series can do for your image

Graig Nettles on the difference between making great plays during a Series and during a season: *I've been making plays like I made in the Series for eight or nine years. But when I was with the Indians in Cleveland, nobody noticed. Nobody in Cleveland draws the attention you get in New York. And when you do this kind of a thing in a Series, then everyone notices. I led the league's third basemen in fielding in 1970, but it wasn't until the Series in 1978 that people started to say, 'Hey, he's a good fielder, isn't he?'*

FIRST GAME (Oct. 10, at Los Angeles)

NEW YORK 000 000 320   5 9 1
LOS ANGELES 030 310 31x 11 15 2
Figueroa, Clay (2nd), Lindblad (5th), Tidrow (7th)
John, Forster (8th)

SECOND GAME (Oct. 11, at Los Angeles)

NEW YORK 002 000 100 3 11 0
LOS ANGELES 000 103 00x 4 7 0
Hunter, Gossage (7th)
Hooton, Forster (7th), Welch (9th)

THIRD GAME (Oct. 13, at New York)

LOS ANGELES 001 000 000 1 8 0
NEW YORK 110 000 30x 5 10 1
Sutton, Rautzhan (7th), Hough (8th)
Guidry

FOURTH GAME (Oct. 14, at New York)

LOS ANGELES 000 030 000 0 3 6 1
NEW YORK 000 002 010 1 4 9 0
John, Forster (8th), Welch (8th)
Figueroa, Tidrow (6th), Gossage (9th)

FIFTH GAME (Oct. 15, at New York)

LOS ANGELES 101 000 000 2 9 3
NEW YORK 004 300 41x 12 18 0
Hooton, Rautzhan (3rd), Hough (4th)
Beattie

SIXTH GAME (Oct. 17, at Los Angeles)

NEW YORK 030 002 200 7 11 0
LOS ANGELES 101 000 000 2 7 1
Hunter, Gossage (8th)
Sutton, Welch (6th), Rau (8th)

PITTSBURGH PIRATES
BALTIMORE ORIOLES
1979

Pops Drove His Fam-a-lee All the Way Home

Way back in 1971, when the Orioles and Pirates battled for the first time in a Series, the Orioles won the first two games and then fluttered helplessly as the Pirates won four of the next five. When this Series ended, the Orioles had reason to think they had relived a bad dream.

Of the 1971 Pirate stars, only one was left as a regular—first baseman Willie Stargell, now 38, who was "Pops" to his younger teammates. More than half the Pirates were black or Hispanic. A visit to the Pirate clubhouse was compared by reporters to a tour of the Spanish Harlem in any American inner city: loud rock and salsa music blaring from tape decks and radios; players shouting back and forth across the room; kids scampering around daddy's locker. The closeness of the team was told best by its theme song, a popular disco song recorded by the Sister Sledge group, "We Are Family." When the Pirates were beating the Reds in the last game of the National League championship series, a bevy of Pirate wives ascended a platform behind home plate as the public address loudspeakers boomed out the pounding rhythms of "We Are Family." Arm in arm, the wives formed an impromptu chorus line and did a high-kicking, shaking dance. Nearly 50,000 fans and some of the Pirate players spurred them on as crowd, wives, and Sister Sledge belted out, "We are fam-a-lee . . ."

The Pirates did not hit as well as they had in previous seasons—only outfielder Dave Parker hit over .300. But the addition of pugnacious Tim (Crazy Horse) Foli at shortstop had tightened the infield and helped to make the defense (the worst in the league the previous season) one of the best. The pitching staff completed only 24 games; lefty John (Candy Man) Candelaria was the biggest winner with only a 14–9 record. But two Pirate relief pitchers, sidearm-throwing Kent Tekulve and left-hander Grant Jackson, won 20 games and saved another 45.

"If ever 25 players won a championship, this club did," said manager Chuck Tanner. Yet of 25 equals, one was more equal than the rest: Pops

Willie Stargell watches his drive disappear out of the stadium at Baltimore in the final game. For such long-distance hammering Stargell was picked by *Sport* magazine as this Series' Most Valuable Player.

United Press International

A freezing rain postponed the first game, but the Oriole mascot (above) came on the field anyway to entertain the few thousand fans who sat in the stands awaiting the official announcement. The following day Commissioner Bowie Kuhn came out early (l.) to inspect gingerly the mucky field. Opposite page: Police dogs check over the seats where President Carter and his party would watch the seventh game.

United Press International

Stargell. In only 424 at-bats, he hit 32 homers. "When we had to win a game," said Tanner, "Pops would hit one out, and we'd be back in the game."

The last third of the NL East race was a nip-and-tuck duel between the Pirates and the Montreal Expos. In the closing week of the season the Pirates jumped into first place ahead of the Expos when Stargell hit two homers in a game against Montreal. The Pirates held onto the lead to win their sixth Eastern title in 11 years.

In the NL West the Houston Astros, a light-hitting bunch with impressive pitching, took an early lead over the incumbent champs, the Dodgers, who had been weakened by the loss of pitcher Tommy John to the Yankees through free agency. A 10-game Astro lead, however, was whittled down by the Cincinnati Reds, even though the Big Red Machine had been dismantled. Gone were the likes of slugger Tony Perez and hustling Pete Rose. Rose had been replaced at third base by Ray Knight, who hit a surprising .318 to co-lead the club. Down the stretch the Reds got 11 straight victories from ex-Met Tom Seaver. They caught the Astros on the last day of

the season for their sixth division title in 11 years.

For Pops Stargell the three-game sweep of the Reds was a hint of even better October days to come. He hit a three-run homer in the 11th to win the first game, 5–2. In the second he walloped a double in the 10th to aid a 3–2 Pirate victory. And in the final game his homer and double drove in two runs as part of the 7–1 win that set the Pirate wives to dancing. For the Pirates the sweep was payment in part for being swept by the Reds twice in these playoffs—in 1970 and 1975. The win brought Pittsburgh its seventh National League flag since 1900.

In the American League the Orioles won in the East with the best record in baseball—102 wins, 57 losses. Manager Earl Weaver had established himself as the league's winningest manager, his Orioles having won four pennants in the past 13 years. This season's team had excellent pitching and a tight infield but base-runners of heavy foot and no .300 hitter among the regulars. The team won with what Weaver called his "instant offense"—two hits and Weaver's favorite weapon, the three-run homer. (The team hit 181 homers, an Oriole record.) And it won close games—32

389

one-run squeakers. It seemed that all Weaver had to do was turn to his bench and wave a magic wand as one reserve after another came up and banged out a game-winning hit.

In the West the California Angels had been built into a championship team through the wallet of ex-movie star Gene Autry. He had plucked out of the free-agent market, for princely sums, such sluggers as Rod Carew (a seven-time league batting champion), Bobby Grich, Don Baylor, and Joe Rudi. After several disappointing seasons for most of them, all came through resoundingly in 1979. Don Baylor, the league's MVP, hit 36 homers, Grich 30 homers, and Carew batted .320. In a race that was close all the way, the Angels beat out the Kansas City Royals to capture their first division title in the team's 18-year history.

Slowed all season by injuries, the Angels entered the playoffs against the Orioles without two big hitters—Joe Rudi and first baseman Willie Mays Aikens. But the Angels were really shot

down in the first game by Earl Weaver's magic wand and his favorite weapon—the three-run homer. With the score tied 3–3 in the 10th, he called on pinch-hitter John Lowenstein with two runners on base. A lefthanded batter, Lowenstein poked a drive to the opposite field that curled over the leftfield wall for a 6–3 triumph.

The Oriole sluggers built up a 9–1 lead in the second game, then fended off a furious challenge by the Angels to win, 9–8. The Angels charged from behind in the third game, winning in the ninth, 4–3. But the Oriole sluggers took charge of the fourth game, winning 8–0 behind the six-hit pitching of Scott McGregor.

The second Pittsburgh-Baltimore World Series of the decade was scheduled to open October 9th in Baltimore, but the weather was more like December in Duluth. A freezing rain caused the first postponement of an opening game in Series history. By the next morning, a light snow was falling. Even though it stopped by game time that evening, the temperature was 41 degrees and dropping. The players' breaths formed clouds of vapor in the near-freezing night air.

In the first inning Pirate second baseman Phil Garner threw to shortstop Tim Foli, trying for a double play—and it was leftfielder Bill Robinson who caught the ball as two runs scored. "My fingers were numb," Garner said later. "It was like throwing a bar of soap." A wild pitch and a homer by Doug DeCinces added three more runs for the Orioles before the inning was over. The Pirates chipped away and closed the gap to 5–4 when Stargell banged a homer in the eighth. In the ninth inning Stargell came to bat again with

the winning run on base. He hit a harmless fly to short left for the final out, the only time he would fail the Pirates in this Series.

The second game began in the same numbing cold. By the seventh inning a drizzle began to fall, turning portions of the field into a thick, slippery ooze. In the ninth, the score 2–2, the Pirates had runners on first and second with two out. Pinch-hitter Manny Sanguillen stood at bat against relief pitcher Don Stanhouse. Sanguillen slapped a single to rightfield. Ken Singleton scooped the ball off the wet grass and threw toward home as the Pirates' Ed Ott, no swifty, rounded third. Singleton's throw toward catcher Rick Dempsey seemed to be right on line and coming in ahead of Ott. But Eddie Murray, the Oriole first baseman, cut off the throw, spun, and threw to Dempsey. The ball arrived a mini-second after Ott, who slid around Dempsey for what turned out to be the winning run. Why had Murray cut off the throw? He explained, "I thought

Nancy Hogue

391

the ball might stick in the infield muck." Whether Murray was right or wrong, the Series was now tied at a game apiece.

The Series moved to Pittsburgh and only slightly warmer weather. There Dame Fortune seemed to jump the Pirate ship. The Pirates led 3–2 after two and a half innings; Scott McGregor's pitches seemed to be easy pickings for the Pirate hitters. Then a torrential rain stopped action for more than an hour. When the game resumed the servings of McGregor were suddenly a mystery to the Pirates while the Orioles blew starter John Candelaria out of the game with a five-run fourth inning and coasted to an 8–4 victory.

The next afternoon the Pirates got a second-inning homer from Stargell and led 6–3 in the eighth. Then the Orioles loaded the bases. Kent Tekulve, scarecrow-skinny, was on the mound in relief for the Pirates. Earl Weaver waved his wand at his "loaded-gun" bench for some instant offense. Pinch-hitter John Lowenstein doubled in two runs, pinch-hitter Billy Smith walked, and pinch-hitter Terry Crowley rocketed another double for two more runs in a six-run inning that won the game, 9–6. The Orioles now led the Series three to one.

Only three other teams had ever come back from such a deficit to win a Series—the 1925 Pirates, the 1958 Yanks, the 1968 Tigers. It was excruciating to the Pirates to know they had whacked 48 hits in the four games—a .329 average—but were not scoring runs. In the fifth game they got more hits, 13 of them, and this time ran up the score, winning 7–1.

Back in Baltimore for game No. 6, the Orioles still needed only one more victory for the world championship. For six innings young John Candelaria and veteran Jim Palmer dueled for a shutout. Then in the seventh the Pirates cracked Pal-mer's armor for two runs and got another two in the eighth. Tekulve had relieved Candelaria in the seventh and continued the goose-egg pitching for a 4–0 victory that evened the Series at three games apiece. Earl Weaver was being snappish about the sudden collapse of his offense. In the last 18 innings the Orioles had mustered only 13 hits. Their big hitter, Eddie Murray, had gone hitless in 17 straight at-bats.

It was the fifth Series in the last nine years to go seven games. The Pirates nominated Jim Bibby as starting pitcher, and Weaver sent Scott McGregor to the mound. The Orioles led 1–0 when Stargell came to bat in the sixth with a runner on base. He timed one of McGregor's off-speed pitches perfectly and slammed a drive that

The Pirates' Phil Garner is caught in a rundown between Orioles Doug DeCinces and Eddie Murray. It was the sudden stoppage in Murray's hitting that hurt Baltimore's offense most in the last three Series games.

Richard Pilling

soared over the upraised glove of rightfielder Ken Singleton for his third homer of the Series. In the ninth the Pirates got two more runs off a parade of five Oriole pitchers, a Series record for one inning, to win the game, 4–1, and capture their fifth world championship.

The Pirates had won with superior hitting, their .323 average the highest ever for a winning team in a seven-game Series. The pitching hero had been Tekulve, who had saved three of the four victories. But *Sport*'s MVP was Pops Stargell, whose three homers and four doubles were a record for extra-base hits in a Series. "The family won," said Pops. "We depended on each of 25 men." In 1979 the Pirate fam-a-lee had become baseball's first family.

Willie Stargell:
After the good, there comes the bad

Willie Stargell, after receiving a car from *Sport* magazine for being the Series Most Valuable Player: *This is good but there are also times for a ballplayer when he messes up everything and nothing seems to go right. I remember a game last season against the Cubs when I threw a ball into leftfield on a throw to third and a man scored with the winning run. I had a chance to make up for the error in the bottom of the ninth by driving in the winning run. I struck out and I could have slit my throat, I was so mad. But you learn in this game that after the bad comes the good and after the good comes the bad.*

FIRST GAME (Oct. 10, at Baltimore)

PITTSBURGH.................000 102 010 4 11 3
BALTIMORE................500 000 00x 5 6 3
Kison, Rooker (1st), Romo (5th), D. Robinson (6th), Jackson (8th)
Flanagan

SECOND GAME (Oct. 11, at Baltimore)

PITTSBURGH.................020 000 001 3 11 2
BALTIMORE.................010 001 000 2 6 1
Blyleven, Robinson (7th), Tekulve (9th)
Palmer, T. Martinez (8th), Stanhouse (9th)

THIRD GAME (Oct. 12, at Pittsburgh)

BALTIMORE.................002 500 100 8 13 0
PITTSBURGH...............120 001 000 4 9 2
McGregor
Candelaria, Romo (4th), Jackson (7th), Tekulve (8th)

FOURTH GAME (Oct. 13, at Pittsburgh)

BALTIMORE................003 000 060 9 12 0
PITTSBURGH................040 011 000 6 17 1
D. Martinez, Stewart (2nd), Stone (5th), Stoddard (7th)
Bibby, Jackson (7th), D. Robinson (8th), Tekulve (8th)

FIFTH GAME (Oct. 14, at Pittsburgh)

BALTIMORE................000 010 000 1 6 2
PITTSBURGH................000 002 23x 7 13 1
Flanagan, Stoddard (7th), T. Martinez (7th), Stanhouse (8th)
Rooker, Blyleven (6th)

SIXTH GAME (Oct. 16, at Baltimore)

PITTSBURGH.................000 000 220 4 10 0
BALTIMORE................000 000 000 0 7 1
Candelaria, Tekulve (7th)
Palmer, Stoddard (9th)

SEVENTH GAME (Oct. 17, at Baltimore)

PITTSBURGH.................000 002 002 4 10 0
BALTIMORE................001 000 000 1 4 2
Bibby, D. Robinson (5th), Jackson (5th), Tekulve (8th)
McGregor, Stoddard (9th), Flanagan (9th), Stanhouse (9th), T. Martinez (9th), D. Martinez (9th)

The 1979 Pirates—Seated on ground: Steve Nicosia, bat boy Steve Hallahan, bat boy Steve Graff, Phil Garner, Ed Ott. Front row: Ed Whitson, trainer Tony Bartirome, coach Al Monchak, coach Harvey Haddix, manager Chuck Tanner, coach Bob Skinner, coach Joe Lonnett, Jim Rooker, Enrique Romo. Second row: Grant Jackson, Rennie Stennett, Matt Alexander, Manny Sanguillen, Tim Foli, John Milner, Mike Easler, Dale Berra, Lee Lacy, Rick Rhoden, traveling secretary Charles Muse. Third row: Bill Robinson, Bert Blyleven, Omar Moreno, Dave Parker, John Candelaria, Jim Bibby, Kent Tekulve, Willie Stargell, Bruce Kison, Don Robinson.

The 1979 Orioles—Seated on ground: Kevin Cashen. Front row: equipment manager Jimmy Tyler, Pat Kelly, Ken Singleton, Elrod Hendricks, Jim Frey, Earl Weaver, Ray Miller, Cal Ripken, Frank Robinson, Al Bumbry, Ralph Salvon. Second row: Tim Stoddard, John Lowenstein, Mark Belanger, Sammy Stewart, Benny Ayala, Tippy Martinez, Eddie Murray, Dave Skaggs, Mike Flanagan, Gary Roenicke, Jim Palmer, Don Stanhouse. Third row: Scott McGregor, Billy Smith, Kiko Garcia, Terry Crowley, Rick Dempsey, Lee May, Rich Dauer, Doug DeCinces, Dennis Martinez, Steve Stone.

Courtesy Baltimore Orioles

PHILADELPHIA PHILLIES
KANSAS CITY ROYALS

1980

Coming from Behind Became the Philadelphia Story

On October 8th, 1915, the Philadelphia Phillies defeated the Boston Red Sox, 3–1, in the first game of the World Series. Grover Cleveland Alexander pitched for the Phils, and the last batter he retired was a Red Sox slugger named Babe Ruth. Sixty-five years would go by before another pitcher, named Tug McGraw, would win the next World Series game for the Phils.

The Phils' futility in postseason play was without equal in baseball. Going back to 1882, when the team was born, it had never won a postseason series. The Phils had been in only two World Series—1915 and 1950—and had compiled a record of eight losses and one victory.

The current Phillies had won the Eastern division title in 1976, 1977, and 1978, and thrice were wiped out, sometimes under humiliating circumstances. (Philadelphia fans still hadn't forgiven centerfielder Garry Maddox for flubbing an easy line drive in the 1978 playoffs.) In 1979 Pete Rose had been imported from Cincinnati as the leader that the bickering Phils seemed to need. With Rose the team sank to fourth place. In 1980 a new manager was brought on board, Dallas Green, a broad-faced ex-pitcher with the bulk of a longshoreman. All season long Green harangued the high-salaried Phils, at times consigning such stars as shortstop Larry Bowa and catcher Bob Boone to his well-populated doghouse.

On paper the team appeared strong, bolstered by sluggers Greg Luzinski and Mike Schmidt, and solidified in the field by such glove artists as shortstop Bowa and second baseman Manny Trillo. Two pitching veterans stabilized the team —35-year-old Steve Carlton, twice a Cy Young winner, and 36-year-old Tug McGraw, the left-handed relief pitcher whose impish humor and loud shout—"You Gotta Believe!"—had buoyed the 1973 Mets to a pennant.

The Phils started slowly and were six games behind Pittsburgh on August 10th. But suddenly all of Dallas Green's head-knocking seemed to make the Phils believers in themselves. With Schmidt, the third baseman, leading the league with 48 homers, the Phils were 36–19 the rest of the way. But most of that way was an uphill slog. The Phils had their fans biting their nails with come-from-behind rallies that would soon be their trademark. They caught Pittsburgh and then Montreal, winning on the next-to-last game of the season with a 6–4 victory in 11 innings over the Expos.

Out West the hitting-rich, pitching-poor Dodgers were locked with the pitching-rich but hitting-poor Houston Astros in a race that also went into the last weekend of the season. The Astros needed only one victory in a three-game series with the Dodgers to win; but the Dodgers swept all three games, forcing a one-game playoff. The Astros captured the victory they needed as knuckleballer Joe Niekro numbed Dodger bats, 7–1. Houston had its first division title.

The Houston-Philadelphia playoff was as close as the two regular-season contests had been. The

Champagne in one hand, Pete Rose is hugged by Phils' manager Dallas Green moments after the sixth and final game. The scoreboard has already flashed the news that the 1980 Phils have won what 96 previous Phils teams had not.

United Press International

The two third basemen were the stars for their teams, George Brett the Most Valuable Player in the AL, Mike Schmidt in the NL. At left: Schmidt slides home with the tying run in the ninth inning of the fifth game as Royals' catcher Darrell Porter waits for a ball that came a moment too late. Below: Brett is upended by a pitch that Phils' manager Dallas Green insisted—to general disbelief—was not a knockdown.

Phils won the first game, 3–1. The second was tied, 3–3, after nine and won in the 10th when Houston scored four runs and smothered a Phil rally for a 7–4 victory. Game No. 3 was won by the Astros in the 11th, 1–0. Down two games to one, the Phils came from behind again, winning the fourth game, 5–3, with two runs in the 10th.

The pennant was decided on a Sunday night under the roof of Houston's Astrodome. The Astros led, 5–2, after seven innings. Once more the Phils struck back, flooding five runs across the plate in the eighth to lead, 7–5. Undaunted, Houston tied the game in their half of the eighth. For the fourth time in this playoff, a game went into extra innings. Refusing to go back to Philadelphia defeated yet again, the Phils pushed across a run in the top of the 10th for an 8–7 triumph and their third pennant. Applauding when the team returned home were some of the surviving Whiz Kids of 1950: manager Eddie Sawyer, pitcher Robin Roberts, and outfielder Richie Ashburn.

The American League finishes were not nearly as dramatic. In the AL West the Royals, who like the Phils had won three division titles in the past four years but no pennant, led by 20 games in August. Most of the attention was fixed on the struggle of Royals third baseman George Brett to stay above .400 in hitting, a mark last attained by Ted Williams in 1941. By October, Brett slipped to .390; but the Royals coasted home, 14 games ahead of Billy Martin's Oakland A's.

The Royals were Kansas City's second big league team. The first had been the A's, who moved there from Philadelphia in 1955. Owner Charles O. Finley shifted the team to Oakland in 1968; and in 1969 Ewing M. Kauffman, a Kansas City businessman, purchased the franchise of the Royals—a new expansion team.

Like the Phils, the Royals had a new manager —stocky, feisty Jim Frey. He inherited much the same team that had been unable to beat the Yankees in three playoffs. The pitching staff had starters Dennis Leonard, who won 20 games, and Larry Gura, who won 18; but a newcomer to the bullpen, Dan Quisenberry, had won 12 and saved another 33, tying him for the most saves in the league. Leadoff man Willie Wilson had stolen 161 bases in the past two years, beating Ty Cobb's two-year league record set in 1915–16. Besides Brett, who had banged 24 homers, the notable hitters included first baseman Willie Mays Aikens (20 homers) and designated hitter Hal McRae (.297 and 14 homers). The team's success hinged on hitting—it led the league with a .286 average —and speed (it ranked first in stolen bases).

The AL East featured the usual Yankee-Oriole pecking duel. The Yankees led by a scant half-game in mid-August. But the two teams didn't meet again for the rest of the season, depriving the American League of the fireworks that had enlivened the last days of the NL pennant race. The Yanks won 18 of 20 games from late August to mid-September and finished three games out front. It was their fourth Eastern title in five years.

This was still a Yankee team made up of the best talent that money could buy. Owner George Steinbrenner had installed a new manager (his fourth, counting two terms by Billy Martin, in five years): Dick Howser. The team still had Reggie Jackson, who hit 41 homers, tops in the league with Milwaukee's Ben Oglivie. Lefthander Tommy John won 22 games, and from the bullpen Rich (Goose) Gossage strode to the mound to throw what the batters call "heat"—a wickedly moving fastball. Steinbrenner had also spent heavily in the free-agent market for lefthander Rudy May, formerly of the Expos, who led the league with a 2.46 ERA.

The Yankee-Royal playoff came down to a climactic moment once the standard fare of Hollywood movies. The Royals won the first two games, 7–2 and 3–2, at Kansas City. In the third game, at Yankee Stadium, the Yanks led 2–1 as the Royals came to bat in the seventh. With two out, Willie Wilson doubled, and Howser replaced Tommy John with Gossage. The next batter, U. L. Washington—a speedster who had a penchant for carrying a toothpick in his mouth even when batting—tapped a bouncing ball over Gossage's head and beat the throw to first by no more than the length of his toothpick.

Up stepped Brett to face Gossage in a classic confrontation—heat versus power, swinging bat against speeding pitch. The battle was over in one blow—Brett lined the first pitch high into the upper rightfield seats. He rounded the bases in a stadium suddenly as silent as a morgue. The Yankees tried to snap back from the 4–2 deficit by loading the bases in the eighth. But a double play quenched that uprising, and Quisenberry's

Microphones are as much a part of the World Series scene as bats and balls. Below: Tug McGraw gives some of his wit and wisdom to TV and radio reporters. Right: Hal McRae (top) tells a Kansas City man how the Series looks to him; Mike Schmidt (middle), cheeks smudged to reduce the sun's glare, tells how he helped win another game; Bob Walk (bottom) relives the first game for a Philadelphia channel.

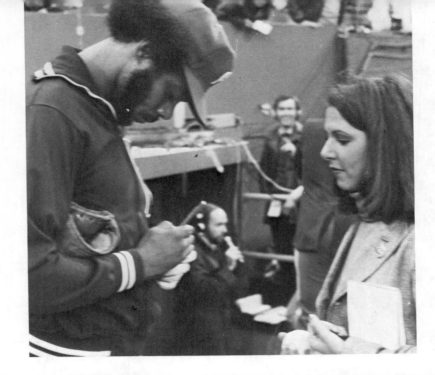

Giving autographs before games and interviews after are among the things ballplayers do to earn their World Series money, which in 1980 was a record. Each Phil got $34,693, each Royal $32,212. Top: The Phils' Garry Maddox pens his name. Above: An obliging Royal (l.) goes to the stands to scribble his name, but the little fan in the KC helmet seems interested in other luminaries; Royal reliever Dan Quisenberry (r.) tells how Manny Trillo's drive popped away from him in game No. 5. Left: His toothpick doesn't get in the way as U. L. Washington readies a reply to a radio reporter's query.

Richard Pilling

off-the-hip, underhand delivery put down the Yanks in quick succession. That night an ecstatic Kansas City team celebrated its first pennant.

This first Philadelphia-Kansas City confrontation set another record—it was the first Series in which all the games were played on a carpet of artificial grass. This year marked the 77th World Series; and the Elias Sports Bureau, looking back at the first 76, told the world that: In 45 instances the winner of the first game went on to clinch the Series; in only three cases had the winner of the first game lost the next four; after winning the first two games, only 6 teams out of 73 lost a best-of-seven Series; there is little or no home-

field advantage in Series play, the home team having won only 53 percent of Series games.

The Series opened in Philadelphia. The Royal ace, Dennis Leonard, started for Kansas City. With the Phils' best, Steve Carlton, exhausted by the Montreal and Houston dogfights, Dallas Green had to use a rookie, Bob Walk, who had an 11–7 record. Walk was the first rookie to start a Series game since Joe Black in 1952.

The scouting report on the Royals said the team didn't have power. The Royals tried to put the lie to that report right from the beginning. Centerfielder Amos Otis socked a homer in the second and first baseman Willie Mays Aikens hit another in the third, both going "downtown," as

402

Opposite page: The Phils' second baseman Manny Trillo
rides high above the shoulders of the Royals' Hal McRae
as he throws to first to complete a double play in the
third game. The Phils completed eight double plays
in the Series, two shy of the record for a six-game Series.
Above: The unsinkable Tug McGraw serves up one of his
fastballs. He and Royal reliever Dan Quisenberry turned
out to be the comedians of the Series, each turning in some
memorable one-liners. Of Yankee reliever Rich Gossage
and himself, Quisenberry quipped, "I don't feel comfortable
being compared to a guy who throws harder than God."
Of his bases-loaded pitching, McGraw said, "With all those
people watching on TV, I like to make the games exciting."

403

In genteel and some-times not-so-genteel ways, Kansas City fans communicated their love for the Royals. Far left: A sign proclaims their esteem for first baseman Willie Mays Aikens, who returns their cheers with a wave of his cap after he hit his second homer in game No. 4. Left, below: Other KC fans express their dislike for No. 14 of Philadelphia. Below: Another banner is carried through the stands in Kansas City during game No. 5, when the Royals had another one of those leads they lost.

the players say, with a man on base. The Royals chalked up a quick 4–0 lead.

The Phils, true to their season and playoff form, came from behind. They roared back with five runs in the bottom of the third, the explosion capped by rightfielder Bake McBride's three-run homer. It was only the second Series homer ever hit by a Philly, the first banged by Fred Luderus 65 years earlier. The Phils led, 7–4, when the Royals came to bat in the eighth. George Brett smacked a double; and Aikens, celebrating his 26th birthday, slugged his second Series homer, singlehandedly tying the all-time Philly total. Dallas Green called for the veteran McGraw to replace the rookie Walk. Tug, who had pitched in all five of the playoff games, still had enough muscle on his fastball to halt the Royals in their tracks, striking out Willie Wilson to end the game. His joyous V for Victory gesture—both arms flung straight up—would soon become a McGraw trademark to millions of TV viewers. The 7–6 victory was the Phils' first Series triumph since 1915, their fourth straight come-from-behind win. More were on the way—and so were more Willie Wilson strikeouts.

Steve Carlton started the second game and struggled through every inning. He could not keep his fastball within the strike zone often enough, and the Royals put men on base in each of the first six innings. But Carlton got outs when he needed them; the Royals managed to score only one run. Meanwhile, the Phils nicked away at Larry Gura to lead, 2–1, as the Royals came to bat in the seventh.

Willie Wilson had struck out swinging three straight times, but now Carlton walked him to lead off the inning. Two more walks filled the bases. Amos Otis cracked a double to score two runs, and a third came home on a flyball. Behind 4–2, the Phils came back again in the eighth. Pinch-hitter Del Unser drove home one run with a double, Bake McBride another with a single to tie the game, 4–4. The raucous Philadelphia crowd, goaded by a flashing scoreboard—"Go . . . Phillies . . . Go"—roared on every pitch. Veterans Stadium crackled with light and sound—"noisiest Series ever," said more than one observer—as Mike Schmidt came to bat and doubled in another run, putting the Phillies ahead, 5–4. Designated hitter Keith Moreland rapped out a single to drive

Schmidt home for a 6–4 lead that reliever Ron Reed preserved. Since that first win back in 1915, Philly fans had waited 65 years for a second Series victory; they had had to wait only 24 hours for the third.

In the seventh inning, George Brett had left the game unexpectedly. The next morning all of America learned why: A painful attack of hemorrhoids had sent him to a hospital. Minor surgery corrected the problem, and the nearly-always-carefree George was on the field for the third game, played at Kansas City's Royals Stadium. As he told reporters cheerfully, "All my troubles are behind me."

He proved it by hitting a home run in his first at-bat. The Phils bounced back to tie the game, 1–1, in the second. The Royals went ahead, 2–1, in the fourth; but Mike Schmidt, who had banged a hit in each game, smashed a homer in the fifth to tie the score again, 2–2. Amos Otis countered for the Royals in the seventh with a homer; but the Phils fought back for the third time, tying the score at 3–3 in the eighth when Pete Rose's single scored Larry Bowa. "Can't we ever hold a lead?" Willie Wilson growled to another Royal.

Kansas City fans, waving blue and white pompoms, were as loud as the Philly rooters—but perhaps more genteel. ("Philly fans wave six-packs," muttered one Phil.) Tug McGraw was pitching for Philadelphia in the 10th, his seventh appearance in these last eight postseason games. With two out and Wilson on first, the fleet Willie showed the Phils his heels by stealing second on a pitchout. George Brett was intentionally walked. Willie Mays Aikens caught a "Cutty Sark fastball"—"It sails," explained Tug—and hit a curving liner that eluded Garry Maddox's outstretched glove. Aikens's shot scored Wilson for a 4–3 Kansas City victory. It was the Royals' first Series triumph, after only an 11-year wait.

The fourth game was marked by the first—and only—bit of nastiness between the two teams. The Royals jumped out to a four-run lead in the first, the big blows a triple by Brett and a homer by Aikens. When Brett came to bat again, a fastball by Dick Noles knocked him down. It was the traditional pitch used to keep a batter's mind on something besides hitting the ball. Royal manager Jim Frey furiously protested what he called a deliberate attempt to hit his player; he got nowhere. The pitch did not very likely intimidate Brett, accustomed as all good hitters are to such hostile fire. But it is a fact that he got only three meaningless singles during the rest of the Series. In this game, the Phils could not come back against Leonard and his successor, Quisenberry. Kansas City's happy fans streamed out of the stadium, rejoicing in a 5–3 triumph that evened the Series at two games apiece.

Game five, played on another sunny and breezy fall day at Royals Stadium, was the scene of the Phils' sixth come-from-behind victory in their last 10 postseason games. As it turned out, this would be the last rally they would need in 1980.

As a hitter during the season Willie Mays Aikens had been outstanding, and he tagged four homers in this Series. But as a first baseman he often waved bye-bye with his mitt at low throws instead of scooping them up. With one out in the third and no one on, he waved at another peg as it flew past him; the batter, Bake McBride, was safe on Aikens's error. The next batter, Mike Schmidt, hit a towering homer, his second of the Series. The Royals retaliated with a run in the fifth and went ahead, 3–2, in the sixth. They still led, 3–2, when the Phils came to bat in the ninth against the sidewheeling Quisenberry, Quiz to his teammates. He had not given up a run in his last six innings of Series pitching.

Schmidt led off and rifled a shot that skipped under Brett's glove at third base for a single (Brett had edged in, looking for a bunt). Pinch-hitter Del Unser hit another twisting one-hopper that shot by Aikens into rightfield for a double, scoring Schmidt and tying the game at 3–3. A sacrifice bunt moved Unser to third, but Quisenberry got the second out on Garry Maddox's grounder to Brett. The next batter was Manny Trillo. He slammed a low liner to Quisenberry's right. Quiz stabbed at the ball with his glove and held it a micro-second before it popped away. Unser flew across the plate with the go-ahead run and Trillo was safe at first with a single. ("I wish it had hit me in the stomach," Quisenberry said later. "Then the ball would have been in front of me, and I could have made a play.")

In the bottom of the ninth, the Royals loaded the bases against McGraw, in action once more. Tug held on and struck out Jose Cardenal to end the game. Ahead three games to two after winning

this pivotal fifth contest, the Phils flew back to a city already planning what would be perhaps its biggest victory celebration ever.

On a cool night in Veterans Stadium, Philly rooters, chanting and shouting, and pleading on almost every pitch, watched a stronger Steve Carlton cut down the Royals inning by inning, seven going down as strikeouts. The Phils, meanwhile, peppered starter Rich Gale and two successors for two runs in the third, another in the fifth, and one more in the sixth. The Royals pushed across a run in the eighth and came to bat in the ninth behind 4–1, facing a Tug McGraw whose energy tank was nearly empty.

Before McGraw could throw his first pitch, the two teams and 65,838 fans—along with millions watching on TV—were astonished to see a line of mounted police trot around the field and take up positions on the warning track, facing the stands. They were backed up by helmeted riot police and their attack dogs, a quiet warning to the sometimes overzealous fans that there would be no postgame tearing up of the field. There wasn't.

The Royals staged their own mini-riot, loading the bases against McGraw with only one out. Then Royal second baseman Frank White hit a towering foul ball; moving quickly, catcher Bob Boone settled under it for a sure out. The ball smacked into his mitt—and popped out, right into the clutching hand of first baseman Pete Rose, who had hustled to Boone's side. The save revived a weary McGraw, and he struck out the next batter, Willie Wilson, Willie's 12th whiff of the Series, a record. The come-from-behind Phillies had won their first World Series.

Horns blared away in the streets that night, and the next day Philadelphia threw a victory celebration that saw at least one million turn out to cheer the team in a wild parade through the streets. After 97 years, Philadelphia had a baseball champion. Larry Bowa spoke for the team when he said, "We stopped the infighting and the bickering. We're the best team in the U. S. of A. and nobody can take anything away from us."

Right: The Phils engulf Tug McGraw, hidden from view, after he struck out Willie Wilson in the last inning of the final game. Watching in the stands were 1950 Phil manager Eddie Sawyer and former Whiz Kids Robin Roberts and Richie Ashburn. Minutes later the Phils sprayed champagne on each other in a jammed, tumultuous clubhouse.

The 1980 Phillies—Front row: bat boy John Bush, ball boy Gary Watts,
bat boy Mark Anderson, assistant clubhouse manager Pete Cera, trainer
Don Seger, assistant trainer Jeff Cooper, clubhouse manager Kenny Bush.
Second row: Lonnie Smith, Ramon Aviles, coach Mike Ryan, coach Billy DeMars,
coach Herm Starrette, manager Dallas Green, coach Lee Elia,
coach Bobby Wine, coach Ruben Amaro, Larry Bowa, Greg Gross.
Third row: traveling secretary Eddie Ferenz, Dick Ruthven, George Vukovich,
Tug McGraw, Manny Trillo, Del Unser, Bob Boone, Garry Maddox,
Keith Moreland, Dan Larson, Pete Rose, Greg Luzinski, Bake McBride,
Vice President and Director of Player Personnel Paul Owens.
Fourth row: batting practice pitcher Hal King, Kevin Saucier, Randy Lerch,
Ron Reed, Bob Walk, Steve Carlton, Lerrin LaGrow, Dick Noles,
Mike Schmidt, John Vukovich, stretch and flexibility instructor Gus Hoefling.

Tug McGraw: No dog

Tug McGraw, after the last game: *I saw all those police dogs coming on the field and I thought, 'That's weird, this doesn't happen in a ball game.' But the dogs reminded me of a guy who dogs it on the field. 'There's no way I'm gonna be a dog out here,' I told myself. And I reached back and got that last strikeout with all I had left. You don't wanna be a dog anytime, but you don't wanna be a dog in a Series, even if you got dogs sittin' all around you.*

FIRST GAME (Oct. 14, at Philadelphia)
KANSAS CITY.............022 000 020 6 9 1
PHILADELPHIA............005 110 00x 7 11 0
Leonard, Martin (4th), Quisenberry (8th)
Walk, McGraw (8th)

SECOND GAME (Oct. 15, at Philadelphia)
KANSAS CITY.............000 001 300 4 11 0
PHILADELPHIA............000 020 04x 6 8 1
Gura, Quisenberry (7th)
Carlton, Reed (9th)

THIRD GAME (Oct. 17, at Kansas City)
PHILADELPHIA..........010 010 010 0 3 14 0
KANSAS CITY...........100 100 100 1 4 11 0
Ruthven, McGraw (10th)
Gale, Martin (5th), Quisenberry (8th)

FOURTH GAME (Oct. 18, at Kansas City)
PHILADELPHIA............010 000 110 3 10 1
KANSAS CITY.............410 000 00x 5 10 2
Christenson, Noles (1st), Saucier (2nd), Brusstar (6th)
Leonard, Quisenberry (8th)

FIFTH GAME (Oct. 19, at Kansas City)
PHILADELPHIA............000 200 002 4 7 0
KANSAS CITY.............000 012 000 3 12 2
Bystrom, Reed (6th), McGraw (7th)
Gura, Quisenberry (7th)

SIXTH GAME (Oct. 20, at Philadelphia)
KANSAS CITY.............000 000 010 1 7 2
PHILADELPHIA............002 011 00x 4 9 0
Gale, Martin (3rd), Splittorff (5th), Pattin (7th), Quisenberry (8th)
Carlton, McGraw (8th)

Index